KW-479-894

CONTENTS

To Irene

PREFACE

It is most fitting that this volume, *Criminal Justice and the Victim,* is being published on the bicentennial of the American Revolution. That historic struggle was against the abuse of government power. Since then the American people have been continually vigilant in checking government excesses. The record is one of considerable success, especially in the closing decades of those two hundred years. The Constitutional rights of citizens have been greatly fortified by court decisions, and the system of government has successfully withstood a severe test. But this success has not been unqualified. The triumph of due process and the rule of law represents only a partial realization of the ideals of our heritage. The goal of ensuring that the government be fair, just, and decent in its treatment of citizens was never intended to be restricted to just the handling of citizens suspected of violating the law. The ideal is to make all government contacts with all citizens fair and decent. A system of government that scrupulously observes the rights of defendants but treats victims of crime with callous indifference does not meet the ideal.

Our treatment of victims is underresearched and poorly understood. What little is known does not reflect favorably upon our system of criminal justice. Although we can take pride in the knowledge that indigent citizens charged with crimes will be provided defense counsel, court transcripts, and adequate opportunities to challenge the government's case against them, we should be outraged when we learn of the frequent plight of victims. They are forced to bear substantial financial burdens in cooperating with the prosecution of cases; witnesses are intimidated and assaulted in the courthouses to the point where public restrooms have had to be closed because of the danger of assault; property taken from victims to be used as evidence is not returned; and victims' privacy is invaded, and their human needs are ignored.

This selection of original articles which William F. McDonald has thoughtfully assembled reveals many of the dimensions of this treatment. The volume represents a landmark effort to begin the systematic study of the role of the victim in the administration of criminal justice. It examines many basic assumptions and practices which have been uncritically allowed to prevail. This volume's focus on the victim in the criminal justice system is a refreshing and valuable new perspective.

The authors of these articles provide a well-documented and critically analytic look at that little-known role that the victim plays. All phases of the criminal process are examined. The important threshold decision of the victim to activate the criminal process by reporting his victimization to the police is examined in four chapters from different perspectives. The victim's needs and perceptions as he cooperates with the prosecution are carefully documented. Also, the victim's influence on the prosecution and outcome of the case is examined. Other chapters report on new programs for improving the treatment which victims receive from the police, prosecutors, and correctional experts as well as from the victim compensation commissions.

The literature in the field of criminal justice has exploded in the last few years. For all the new publications, very little has appeared in the way of genuinely new ideas, insights, and substance. This volume is clearly an exception. The focus is new; the ideas are new; and the data are new. It enlightens and stimulates. I recommend a careful review of the ideas expressed in it and a building on the research it presents.

Dostoevski observed that the degree of civilization in a society can be judged by entering its prisons. A civilization can also be judged by how it treats its victims of crime.

Samuel Dash
Georgetown University
September 1975

FOREWORD

This book is about relations between the victim and the criminal justice system. Initially, the scope was broader. Selections from the entire subject area of victimology were to be included. Two developments, however, narrowed that scope. First there was the gradual realization that this volume is part of a series of "criminal justice system" annuals. Hence selections had to bear some connection to the criminal justice system. This meant that much of the existing work on victimology was not directly relevant to the book. It thus began to appear that finding contributors was going to be more difficult than anticipated. But it was not—a fact which is related to our second point.

The relationship between the victim and the criminal justice system has suddenly become a major point of interest for both researchers and practitioners. Events are happening at a rapid pace. All the chapters in this book are based on original research, which in most cases had not even begun a year and a half ago when the book first got under way. Also during that year and a half, two national and one international conferences on victims were planned and held. In addition, there has been an accelerating commitment of federal and local funds to improving the lot of the victim of crime as he interacts with the criminal justice system. Finally, as recently as the summer of 1975, in his first major address on his anticrime program, President Gerald R. Ford put concern for the victim first.

It is not clear where this concern for the victim will take us. Some of the issues that are being raised are trivial while others are more profound. New programs for improving the handling of crime victims may at best amount to nothing more than mere tinkering with the system, and at worst they may result in new forms of injustice to victims. On the other hand, some of the proposals being considered could eventually lead to major—or, what might be called "radical"—changes in the criminal justice and social welfare systems. Whether the current momentum carries us that far remains to be seen.

The purpose of this volume is not to make predictions about the probable outcome of the new interest in relations between the victim and the criminal justice sysem. That would be crystal ball gazing. Our purpose is to chart some of the issues, present some of the initial findings from current research, provide a benchmark against which future changes may be gauged, and, contribute to the momentum.

In selecting the content of the book, we have included materials from all phases of the victim-criminal process including the victim's relationships with the police, the prosecutor, the judge, the correctional system, and ancillary social service groups, organizations, and commissions, including victim compensation boards. Two assumptions underlie the book. First, although the victim no longer plays the central role in the administration that he once did prior to the centralization of government in England, he continues to play an important, albeit poorly understood, role. Second, a greater understanding of that role may lead to a more humane, just, and effective administration of the criminal law.

William F. McDonald
Washington, D.C.
February 1976

PROLOGUE:
A VICTIM'S VIEW OF CRIMINAL JUSTICE

Victim: I've been a victim. My husband has been a victim.

Interviewer: Is this the first time you've been a victim of an assault?

Victim: Well on the streets it has been, but my place has been burned down before, place of business. It's been burned down and we even knew who did it. And I was told if they didn't catch him pouring the gasoline and striking the match at the same time you could save yourself some trouble. And I've seen a woman get robbed right before me—across the street from my business and all the police would do—before they'd run after the person who did it—they'd ask your name, your age, how old you are, where you live, your phone number, and by that time, everybody is gone. I've seen that happen. That's all they do. They come and ask for your name, address, and age, occupation, and that's it. . . .

. . . Another woman and I were having a dispute over our souvenirs; and because I was selling more than she was, she got mad; and she started calling me names. So I went over to her and asked her what she called me. . . . She ran back and picked up a cane . . . and beat me over the head. . . . So then the officer who was my witness was behind me and he grabbed me from here; and then they locked us both up. I had her charged with assault with a dangerous weapon and they charged me with disorderly conduct for defending myself.

Interviewer: What happened then?

Victim: Well, they took me to the police station. . . . So then I made . . . take me to the hospital to check my head. [Then] they took me to the Woman's Bureau and they wanted to fingerprint me and take pictures . . . and I asked them why they were doing it because I was here because somebody hit me. . . . So it took me from around one in the afternoon to seven at night. . . .

Interviewer: Do you know what was happening to the other lady. . . ?

Victim: I went down a couple of weeks later because I hadn't heard anything about what was going on. I thought maybe they were supposed to call me because I pressed charges against her and I never heard a word.

Interviewer: Were you called in by the district attorney's office the next day?

Victim: No. They never communicated one way. We went down to find out what was going on. . . . This is when he [the assistant District Attorney] told us that if I took her to court they would drop the charges from assault with a dangerous weapon to simple assault. And I told them I wouldn't go for that—that I didn't want that. And so he said he would get in touch and I haven't heard anything yet. I'm still waiting.

. . . See on my charges . . . on disorderly conduct I went down the following day and they dropped it right away.

. . . [That same day the husband of the assailant with the cane] came and delivered a message. . . . He was gonna beat me up when he saw me and he was gonna take and empty his gun into my husband. Well, we went straight up to the District Attorney's office and we filed a complaint. . . . So, they took it all down and I told them I didn't want to be six foot under by the time they got down there and do something about it. They never came down to see if he had a gun. They never came down and checked his wagon. They never did anything. . . . So, he keeps making threats and still nothing's been done.

Interviewer: What do you think should happen to these people?

Victim: I really don't know. . . . The woman that took and beat me up, she's not really that bad, I don't think. I was more surprised than, I think, anything else. . . . Her husband is the type that is the real bully type. . . . He did this in his parole time. In other words, he was on parole. If you violate that parole, they would have picked him up and he would have went back, but see he violated his parole and still nothing happened. So, I don't have too much faith in going down there. I don't have too much faith in corporation counsels [district attorneys] or anything.

. . . It's like everybody else says. The guilty party go unpunished and it's the punished that's punished. . . . The really punished, nothing happens to them in the way of protection. Go down to the courthouse, you can sit all day long. You go from one room to another. It's just like tag . . . and you never know what's been done, or what's gonna be done. So, I don't have no faith in them whatsoever. . . .

A lot of people feel the same way that there's no justice be given.

                    —from the research files of *The Legend of Lenient Justice,* a radio docu-
                    mentary produced by the Evening Star Broadcasting Company, Radio
                    WMAL, Washington, D.C., with the assistance of the Institute of
                    Criminal Law and Procedure, Georgetown University, 1972.

A victim of a criminal can also find he is a victim of the criminal justice system. . . .

Put yourself in the shoes of a crime victim—who finds himself to be that pawn on the criminal justice chessboard, who has to suffer all sorts of indignities, and then sees, as the final straw, the accused offender walking out free.

Donald E. Santarelli, *Administrator*
Law Enforcement Assistance
Administration
February 1974

Chapter 1

CRIMINAL JUSTICE AND THE VICTIM:
AN INTRODUCTION

WILLIAM F. McDONALD

Victims are the forgotten people in the system.

> Tim Murphy, *Judge, Superior Court*
> *District of Columbia, June 1971*

For too long, the law has centered its attention more on the rights of the criminal than on the victim of the crime. It is high time we reversed this trend and put the highest priority on the victims and potential victims.

> Gerald R. Ford
> *Message to Congress, June 1975*

Judges, prosecutors, defendants, defense counsel—they all know how to make their voices heard to some extent. . . . But victims? They're a changing constituency. No one is really listening to them and their particular problems. Railroads for some time have not done much to please the customer. But airlines . . . compete in their services. Look at Dulles Airport. You walk in there and you're taken care of in a very few steps. There is someone to tell you what to do, to take your bags, to be polite. Our system has been behaving like a railroad, because maybe it figures the victim can't just choose another court system. We've got to look at the victim like he's a customer who requires service.

> David Epstein, *Trial Attorney*
> *Washington, D.C., June 1971*

AUTHOR'S NOTE: *Research for this chapter was supported through the Institute of Criminal Law and Procedure and in part by a grant from the William Penn Foundation. However, the views expressed herein are solely those of the author.*

The victim is being hailed as the forgotten man in the administration of justice. The demeaning, neglectful, and unjust treatment which the victim now receives has suddenly caught the attention of researchers, reformers, and public officials. This chapter will review the developments in the field with particular emphasis on formulating some of the questions to which concern for the victim gives rise. The purpose is not only to provide an introduction to this book but an introduction to this field.

THE SCOPE OF THE SUBJECT

The relationship between the victim and the administration of justice encompasses a broad area. Some of the questions included go to the fundamental assumptions of our system of justice. Some involve matters of fact about the way things are, whereas others raise matters of value, questions about policy and about the ways things should be.

There are many questions of fact that need to be answered. What is the current role of the victim in the administration of justice? What functions does he perform? What influences does he have on the decisions which are made? How is he treated? What are the effects of this treatment? Is he satisfied with what he sees done? Will he cooperate again in the future? Will he take justice into his own hands? Will he be more alienated from the society? Is he damaged further by his cooperation with the administration of justice? If so, how does it occur; what does it entail; is it greater than the original injury; and could it be avoided?

What are the needs of the victim of crime—immediately after the victimization, in connection with his assisting in the prosecution of the case, and after conviction? If there are needs which are not now being met, what would be the result of providing services to meet them? Would the victim have a more favorable attitude toward the administration of justice? Would he be more willing to cooperate?

There are still other questions which might be asked by the historian, the student of collective behavior, and the student of comparative legal systems. What is the full history of the decline of the victim's role in the administration of justice? How does the amount of victim participation in the administration of criminal justice differ by type of legal system? What has caused the current increase in the interest in the victim's place in the administration of justice? How and why did the volunteer victim support groups form? How are they doing? What influence are they having on victims and on their current and future role in the administration of justice?

Many of the factual questions about the victim's place in criminal justice are related to policy issues. On the most fundamental level, concern for the victim raises questions about what the goals of the administration of criminal justice should be. Should that system be protecting the interests of individual victims as opposed to the interests of the public in general? When there is a conflict between the two, which should prevail and under what circumstances? What should be the responsibility of criminal justice and social welfare officials and society to the victim of crime? Should new services be provided? Should victim restitution programs be inaugurated? Should the victim be given a larger role in determining the disposition of criminal cases?

These are just a few of the questions which researchers and policy makers face as they begin to move seriously into this area of relationships between the victim and the criminal justice system.

VICTIM AS FORGOTTEN MAN

The political rhetoric of the 1960s was right. The courts have ignored the interests of the victim while they have been busy protecting the interests of the defendant. Not only the courts but the entire criminal justice establishment, including legal scholars and criminologists, have largely ignored the victim. Compare, for example, the attention that has been given the offender with that given the victim. There is an enormous literature on the offender: his rights; the role he plays in criminal process; his perceptions of that process; the influence which that process has and the damage that it can do to his life's prospects by labeling him a criminal; his racial, social, economic, marital, psychological, physical, and behavioral characteristics; and even the effects of his incarceration on his family. Not only is the literature vast but the expenditure of money and concern for the defendant has also been enormous.

The great experiment in correctional reform continues to consume large quantities of human energy. Elaborate and costly physical structures have been built to house criminals and promote their behavioral improvement. The promoters of correctional reform have been revered as pioneers in criminology. Millions of dollars of research have been devoted to determining what happens when the criminal justice system touches the lives of individuals who become defendants. In comparison, virtually nothing has been done on what happens to that other group of citizens touched by the criminal justice system, namely, the victims. There are no schools of victimology and no textbooks on how victims are treated by the criminal justice system and what happens to them, nor are there any architectural monuments constructed on their behalf. The victim has not even been given a room in the courthouse where he can wait comfortably and securely for the hearing to begin. He is left to wait in the halls or some drab room to which the defendant whom he is accusing has free access (Goldman, 1971). He is threatened by the defendant within inches of police, prosecutors, and judges, and nothing happens (Ziegenhagen, 1974; Goldman, 1971). He or she must recount to the prosecutor the sometimes intimate, degrading, and upsetting details of unspeakable crimes while standing in a crowded, noisy hallway with strangers milling around and listening in (see, for example, Columbia Broadcasting System, 1975; also, Subin, 1966).[1] If a criminal viciously kills someone and later is found not guilty by reason of insanity, society will spend thousands of dollars supplying him with psychiatric treatment, special facilities, correctional counseling, job training, and legal aid. But the family of the victim which may have been shattered by the crime (see, for example, Saar, 1975b) will be left to fend for itself.

The few studies of the victim's relation to the criminal justice process that are available are largely buried in and incidental to studies of other related subjects such as the police, the prosecutor, or sentencing. The only exception to this is the literature on victim compensation.

The current wave of interest in relations between the victim and criminal justice stems from several different sources. It is not a unitary interest in "the victim" in general but rather a historical convergence of the interests of scholars, activists, and public officials who are concerned with the plight of different kinds of victims. In some cases the interest has come from people who are not primarily interested in victimology, or even in criminal justice.

Elderly Victims

Gerontology, for example, has become increasingly concerned with victims of crime. (See, for example, Brostoff, 1971; Cunningham, 1973; Forston and Kitchens, 1974.)

Goldsmith and Tomas (1974) have summarized the reasons why the elderly as a class of victims deserve special attention. They tend to have lower incomes, which means that they tend to live in higher crime neighborhoods, that they cannot afford to move to better areas, that they are forced to rely on public transportation, and that any economic loss they incur has a greater relative impact. Also, older people are more likely to be victimized repeatedly—often by the same offender. They live alone and are physically less able to defend themselves or recover from injuries inflicted. Many have their monthly pension or benefit checks stolen from their mailboxes or are robbed on the way back from cashing their checks (Saar, 1975a). They are particularly susceptible to fraud and confidence games. And they appear to be less likely to process complaints through the criminal justice bureaucracy or draw upon available community resources for protection and redress.

The White House Conference on Aging dealt specifically with victim-criminal-justice relations in its recommendations summarized in *Towards a New Attitude on Aging* (U.S. Congress. Senate, 1973):

> These recommendations dealt with assisting the elderly to participate in the criminal justice system and with the prevention of both white collar crimes such as fraud and crimes of violence such as assault. These recommendations included: making physical protection and crime prevention an element of the planning of facilities for the elderly; expanding police protection of minority neighborhoods; establishing formal liaison between social service agencies and police departments so that elderly who are victims of crime can obtain all necessary assistance; providing better street lighting; making training grants available to police officers and others to acquaint them with the special situation of the elderly and their special susceptibility to particular types of crime; and granting Federal funds to State and local prosecuting officers to expand or establish trained fraud units which are well acquainted with schemes used to deceive the elderly.

> Police protection of the elderly should become a top priority. A portion of Federal funds for the prevention of crime allocated to the States or local communities should be earmarked for this purpose.

Child Victims

The legal apparatus's handling of child victims of crime, especially the battered child and child victims of sex offenses, has also received special attention.[2] Child victims pose several dilemmas for the criminal justice system. First there is the question of whether or not to proceed with the prosecution. On the one hand, dangerous criminals should be stopped. But at what price? Research suggests that in both sexual offenses against children (Karpman, 1954) and child beating cases,[3] the prosecution may do more harm to the child than the original offense. If so, then why should Peter be further damaged to prevent harm from happening to Paul?

The Israel Law of Evidence (Protection of Children) of 1955 has been advanced as a model for resolving the problem of revictimizing the child victim by forcing him or her to go through the ordeal of a prosecution (Reifen, 1958). The law provides for a trained "youth examiner" appointed by the court whose duty it is to take a statement from any alleged child victim of a sexual assault. If the child is under 14, he has the right to decide whether the child is fit to give evidence in court. If he decides that this would be harmful, the examiner may be cross-examined in court instead of the child. He may be asked to return to the child and ask it further questions, but he may refuse to do this if he believes it undesirable. A conviction is not possible on the evidence of the youth examiner unless it is supported by some other evidence.

Such a proposal violates the fundamental Anglo-American rule against admitting hearsay evidence. It also deprives the defendant of his right to cross-examine the accuser. Thus, in this conflict between protecting the interests of the defendant and protecting those of the victim[4] Anglo-American law reformers in England have suggested that the *administration* of the law might be changed. Four modifications have been recommended (Gibbens and Prince, 1963:19): (1) reduce the number of cases involving child victims which have to appear in a higher court; (2) speed the trial process so that the waiting period, which is regarded as the main source of stress, is reduced as much as possible; (3) arrange so that the child has to give evidence only once; (4) make procedure in court less formal and frightening. It was also pointed out that there is a great need for aftercare of victims. Gibbens and Prince (1963) suggest the creation of a special criminal justice officer trained in social work and appointed as a police and probation officer. This officer would visit child victims in their homes and take from them statements about the crime. Once this police role had been fulfilled, the officer's duty would be to work with the family to mitigate the consequences, accompanying and advising them on all subsequent medical and legal examinations.

In the United States, the Michigan Governor's Study Commission on the Deviated Criminal Sex Offender (1951:9) concluded that "the inept handling which victims often receive following a sex crime is at the root of much of the reluctance of parents to file complaints; the experience at this stage can be worse than the experience of the crime itself." The commission recommended that "more consideration and study should be given to improving the handling of the victims of sex crimes, particularly children, by the police, prosecuting attorneys, defense counsel and courts, in order to reduce the often traumatizing effect of the total experience." It also endorsed some reforms which had already been initiated in Detroit. Chief among the reforms were (1) a reduction in the number of times a victim is questioned about the details of the incident and (2) the setting of priority for the hearing of sex crimes.

However, it does not appear that the Detroit reforms were ever institutionalized nationally, nor are they currently being pushed by victim assistance programs.[5] Also, the commission's recommendation for more study of the criminal justice system's handling of sex crime victims has been largely ignored until very recently.

Victims of Sex Offenses

An area of victim-criminal-justice relations which has recently been receiving intense concern is the legal system's treatment of female victims of sex offenses—regardless of their age. The complaints are many and sometimes bitterly voiced, and once again they generally add up to the conclusion that as far as the victim is concerned justice is as bad as the crime, if not worse (see, for example, Stumbo, 1972).

It is a common complaint of all victims that they are treated like defendants, that they are only used for the information they can supply, and that their human needs are completely ignored by criminal justice officials (see Ziegenhagen, Chapter 12 in this volume; Lynch, 1975). But sex crime victims resent this dehumanized and accusatory treatment more than others (Barker, 1972; Washington Post, 1973; National Organization for Women, 1973; Wood, 1973), and they have better reason for feeling that way. For one thing, their injury is a far more personal matter involving a taboo subject surrounded by highly charged emotions. If any class of victims needs tactful and sensitive responses, it is they. Compared to the aloof and unsympathetic treatment accorded other victims, that experienced by the sex crime victim is a greater relative deprivation.[6] But ironically the victims who are in need of the most tactful and sensitive treatment are accorded the least. Sexist police, prosecutors, and judges degrade and humiliate the victim with leering derision.[7] The police often will not believe the victim's report that a sex crime has been committed (University of Pennsylvania Law Review, 1968); and prosecutors even go so far as to require that she submit to a lie detector test before they will charge a suspect with a crime (Miller, 1974:36). Judges apply sparingly the law relating to the asking of "insulting questions" on cross-examinations and thus permit defense counsel wide latitude in probing the private life of the victim and asking humiliating questions. The audience in the public courtroom is titillated; and the victim's responses to the questions become a permanent part of the public record (Columbia Broadcasting System, 1975; see also, Ash, 1972:401; Hibey, 1973).

The law itself is biased against the rape victim (Washington Post, 1973:C1). More evidence is needed to convict a rapist than a murderer, robber, or any other criminal. The victim of robbery, for example, usually only has to report her victimization to be believed. If later she can correctly identify the defendant, a conviction can be obtained. In contrast, the victim of sexual assault must also support her complaint with corroborating evidence (Columbia Law Review, 1967; New York University Law Review, 1969; University of Pennsylvania Law Review, 1970).

There is also the matter of consent. The presence of consent changes the crime of rape into a lawful occurrence. While that may sound reasonable on its face, in practice it places a heavy burden on the victim. Even if the attacker is a stranger, the victim's lack of consent is not taken for granted by the law. The victim must show that she resisted. What is more, if the defense chooses to raise the consent issue, then the law allows the victim's character to, in effect, be attacked on the theory that a reputation for unchastity is relevant to determining whether consent was given (Hibey, 1973:325).

A further opportunity to invade the victim's personal life is presented by the matter of testimonial competence. The possible use of psychological and psychiatric testing of the competence of witnesses in general has long been recognized (Hutchins and Slesinger, 1928). Proposals for such testing have usually been linked to the presence of "mental illness" in the witness—as poorly as that concept may be defined.[8] But, when the crime is a sex offense the courts, legal commentators, and the medical profession virtually presume that the *victim* must be psychiatrically examined despite the absence of any indications of mental illness.[9]

Reformers of the criminal justice system's handling of sex offense victims have advocated a variety of changes both in the law (National Organization for Women, 1974; Ludwig, 1970; Yale Law Journal, 1972) and in its administration (District of Columbia, 1973; Prince George's County, 1973; Seyfret, 1974; Noble, 1975). One noteworthy development has been the founding of numerous "rape crisis centers"; between 1972 and 1974 approximately 100 such programs have been established across the country. These "centers" are groups of individuals—usually all females and usually some of them victims—who make themselves available through a telephone "hot line" or a staffed office to other female victims of sex offenses for purposes of assisting and counseling them. Several centers have sprung up independently. Others have been sponsored or encouraged by the National Organization for Women. They differ in terms of the kind of person or persons who found them; the kind of persons who participate in their activities; and the style of their organization, philosophy, and outlook. What they share in common is a concern for the sex crime victim (Center for Women Policy Studies, 1975). Some of them have established a cooperative and amicable relationship with the police and other criminal justice officials (Rape Crisis Center, 1972). But others have taken a negative or even antagonistic attitude toward the criminal justice system (Center for Women Policy Studies, 1975).

The latter group represents a special challenge and an interesting case study for students of social change and group conflict. These "antagonistic" centers tend to share certain views about the relationship between criminal justice and the victim. Not all the centers state these views with equal force, nor do all centers subscribe to all views. But a composite portrait of the views of an ideal antagonistic-type center can be drawn. They are as follows: (1) The sex victim does not benefit from and only stands to suffer further degradations by reporting her victimization to the police and cooperating with the prosecution of the case. (2) Nothing is lost by not reporting the victimization to the police because the criminal justice system is grossly ineffective in apprehending, successfully prosecuting, and successfully rehabilitating or even incarcerating dangerous sex criminals. (3) Psychiatry, the behavioral and social sciences, and the "helping" professions have nothing to offer the female victim of sex crimes. They do not know how to protect her by rehabilitating sex offenders, and they do not know how to treat her as a victim. (4) The best therapist for the female sex victim is another victim.

Particularly striking about this set of views is their contrast to the views of citizen reformers of a short three decades ago. They too were concerned about sex crimes, but in their response they did not reject the criminal justice system and psychiatry. They endorsed them. They believed that the criminal justice system could handle the problems and that psychiatry could transform desperate "sex fiends" into reasonably safe individuals. They supported the passage of sexual psychopath laws which turned much of the matter over to psychiatry (Sutherland, 1950). Their concern for the individual victim was mixed.[10] The Michigan Governor's Study Commission, for example, believed that the individual victim should cooperate with the criminal process even though that would cause additional trauma for the victim.[11] But, it softened its position by also arguing that "the community must recognize its duty to deal with the side effects of such crimes on society and the individual, as reflected in venereal diseases, illegitimate pregnancies, traumatic consequences of contacts with courts and official agencies, and other personally disturbing experiences to the victim" (1951:75; see also California State Assembly, 1949; Tappan, 1950; California, Department of Mental Hygiene, 1954; New York Citizen's Committee on the Control of Crime, 1939).[12]

Consumer Victims

Another recent source of interest in victim-criminal-justice relations has come from the consumer movement. The consumer has many problems. He is deceived and defrauded into parting with his money; he receives defective goods and services; he is given worthless guarantees and warrantees; he is subjected to high-pressure sales tactics; and he is largely unprotected by the law. To a great extent, he does not realize he has been the victim of a crime; or, if he does, he does not believe that the criminal justice system will help.[13] When he correctly suspects that he has been criminally victimized and he takes his complaint to the criminal justice officials, he is told that courts are not "collection agencies"; there is nothing they can do; he should "get an attorney" and file a civil suit against the perpetrator. This advice is no real remedy. Losses are often too small for a lawyer to accept on a contingency fee basis and too large for small claims court.[14]

Class action suits alleging fraud or misrepresentation have been available in both the federal and state courts. But they too have been found to be an inadequate remedy for the victim. A private attorney handling such a case seldom knows of the other victims nor does he have the capital to seek them out (Bowley, 1974).

Consequently, reformers are trying to make the criminal justice system more responsive. Since the early 1960s several states have passed civil remedial legislation enforceable by the state attorney general through a "consumer fraud bureau" (Eovaldi and Gestrin, 1971). The legislation enables attorneys general to bring injunction proceedings against merchants engaging in certain fraudulent practices. However, most state consumer fraud bureaus have not utilized their power to seek injunctions. Instead they have concentrated their efforts on informal mediation activities. These bureaus have had some successes in mediating between consumers and merchants. In a few states where they are authorized to seek restitution, they have recovered impressive amounts of money. More recently, consumer fraud divisions have been established in local district attorneys offices, and imaginative use has been made of existing injunctive powers (Lorenz, 1970).

Despite these successes, however, the individual consumer who has been victimized should not be too quick to believe that there is a light at the end of the tunnel. One perennial policy issue that continues to dim his prospects is described by Eovaldi and Gestrin (1971:301) as follows:

> Are consumer fraud bureaus to give primary emphasis to preventing harm to consumers as a group by vigorously seeking to enjoin fraudulent practices with incidental compensation to injured individuals, or does top priority go to obtaining restitution for individuals, with only secondary concern for whether the merchant's operations pose a significant threat to other consumers? Restitution should be available once conduct has been litigated and an injunction issued, but some initial decision must be made as to which cases are to be litigated. Given limited resources, an effective preventive program cannot be implemented if the agency does not select for attack those practices which are most likely to result in future injury to the public. Such a process of selection leaves the individual [victim] . . . at the mercy of the agency. . . . The alternative—to litigate for the sake of obtaining restitution—would result in the sacrifice of the interests of consumers as a class.

Future policy choices of the enforcement agencies will be of interest to the victimized consumer as well as the victim researcher. The consumer may be told that he is being sacrificed to a larger interest or that he could recover his loss only if he happened to fit into a category of victims whom the law enforcement agency has chosen to vindicate. The researcher will want to know how this affects the attitudes, behavior, and life circumstances of the "low priority" victims; how the law enforcement priorities are set; whether they are consistently followed; and why exceptions are made when they are.[15]

The potential conflict referred to earlier between the interest of the individual victim and that of society is also an important area for research in connection with victims of consumer and other white collar crimes. For example, what has the impact of the nolo contendere plea been on individual victims, and whose interests does it really serve? It is not the street criminal but the rich and powerful white collar offender who pleads "nolo." A nolo plea is the same as a total admission of guilt except that it cannot be used as prima facie evidence against the defendant in any subsequent civil suit. This means that the victims of his criminal activity will not easily be able to recover any of their losses. Most fraud cases and other white collar crimes require time-consuming and expensive investigations. It may take the government several man-years to successfully litigate a fraud case. If, in the end, the defendant is permitted to plead nolo contendere, that enormous investment of resources cannot be put to direct use. The victim cannot go into civil court, point to the criminal conviction, and win recovery. He must start over again from the beginning presenting whatever evidence he is able to secure.

There is no data on the impact of the nolo plea on victims, nor have researchers studied how the prosecutor decides whether to accept a nolo plea and what weight he gives to the victim's interests. Also, there has been no analysis of what interest groups stand to lose by modification or elimination of the nolo plea or what resistance they have put up to prevent such changes.

A related issue equally in need of study is the handling of victims' interests in bankruptcy proceedings following criminal frauds. It appears that the extent of the effort on behalf of these victims depends solely upon the personal skills and inclinations of the referee appointed by the court to oversee the proceeding (see, for example, Nunes, 1975a, 1975b). But little is known about this or other aspects of how well the victim fares in similar settlements involving large sums of money following criminal activities. What is known suggests that he does not fare well (see, for example, Kotz, 1971; but also, Meyer, 1973a, 1973b).

DATA ON VICTIMS

Victim Surveys

Since the President's Commission on Law Enforcement and Administration of Justice (1967a) pioneered the victim surveys, there have been many such surveys, and now a national victim survey is being routinely conducted by the

Law Enforcement Assistance Administration. The victimization survey was originally conceived of as a more reliable measure of the true amount of crime in society than official crime statistics. But now it appears they will be used more to study victim-criminal-justice relations.

At a national conference on victimization surveys held in Washington, D.C., in June 1975, it was agreed that the "honeymoon" with victim surveys was over and "phase two" was about to begin. The conferees noted that the victim surveys have their own methodological limitations as measures of the real amount of crime. They are better—methodologically sounder—as sources of information about victim-criminal-justice relations. While this was not the original purpose of the surveys, the conferees felt that it was an important subject matter in its own right and should be studied more in the future.[16]

Prosecutorial Data on Victims

A turn of events similar to what is happening with the victim surveys is happening with another source of new data. Within the last 5 years district attorneys offices have begun to computerize their operations. This has resulted in the collection and storage of large volumes of data. The primary purpose of the computerization is to assist prosecutors with their management tasks (Hamilton and Work, 1973). Incidental to that purpose, a substantial amount of data about victims is being accumulated. Analyses of that data have already begun. The victim surveys were able to get at the question of why victims failed to report their victimization to the police. The new prosecutor data have made it possible to study the next set of questions. Once the crime has been reported, how many cases have dropped out of the system because victims or witnesses would not cooperate with the prosecution (McDonald, 1973) and for what reasons (Cannavale et al., 1975)? Also, what influences do victim characteristics have on the decision making of prosecutors, judges, and juries (see Williams, Chapter 8 in this volume)?

NEW PROGRAMS FOR VICTIMS

For decades reformers have urged that victims—in their roles as witnesses—be accorded better treatment. The National Commission on Law Observance and Enforcement (1931:418-419) concluded that the economic losses due to service as witnesses in criminal cases have a special significance. "They come definitely home to the individual citizen, and may affect in some cases his whole attitude toward the administration of public justice. Effective administration of criminal law requires . . . willing witnesses. If . . . [testifying] in court [imposes] unreasonable burdens on the citizen, the administration of justice is bound to suffer."

A decade later things had not changed. The American Bar Association (1938:8-11) reported that witness fees were deplorably low; courthouse accommodations were inadequate and uncomfortable; witnesses were being intimidated; and frequently witnesses were summoned to court numerous times only to wait around all day and eventually be informed that the case was continued again or dismissed. The ABA argued that "the state owes it to the witness to make the circumstances of his sacrifice as comfortable as possible." Similar findings and recommendations have continued to be made by others (Graham, 1948; Cutler, 1952; President's Commission on Law Enforcement and Administration of Justice, 1967a:156-157; Ash, 1972; National Advisory Commission on Criminal Justice Standards and Goals, 1973:208-214).

Reformers in the 1930s and 1940s knew intuitively that the administration of justice was "bound to suffer" if victims and witnesses were dissatisfied with the treatment they received. By the 1970s, studies made possible by advances in computer technology and social research methods had begun to show in hard quantitative terms the extent to which the administration of justice was in fact suffering because of victim-witness-related actions. The pioneering victim surveys of the mid-1960s showed for the first time the extent to which victims did not even report their victimizations to the police—and it was substantial.

The early reformers were aware of studies of criminal courts which showed that cases were frequently lost because witnesses failed to appear. This problem was usually seen in terms of faulty administrative practices by courts that scheduled more cases than they could dispose of in a day; or failure to properly notify witnesses of a court appearance; or ethically questionable practices of defense attorneys who would seek continuances until the witnesses would tire of coming to court and who would then obtain dismissals. But, in 1972, this old problem was seen in a new light. The new computerization of a prosecutor's office[17] had just become operational, and one of the first studies based on the new data focused on a phenomenon which had never been systematically studied before. It showed that, after the victim had decided to report the crime but before the problem of continuances and delay had begun to operate, many crime cases were lost because witnesses did not want to cooperate. Of 4,188 cases of murder, rape, robbery, burglary, and serious assault between strangers, 47% were dropped at the prosecutor's initial screening because witnesses were "uncooperative" (Evening Star Broadcasting Company, WMAL, 1972; McDonald, 1973).[18]

The results of these studies became the foundation for a Law Enforcement Assistance Administration program to sponsor projects to improve the criminal justice system's handling of victims and witnesses. Donald Santarelli, Administrator of LEAA, highlighted the poor treatment of victims in public speeches.[19] He stated (1974:8) that "the odds are better than even that any citizen who comes into contact with the system will come out of that experience with a sour taste in his mouth, with his or her confidence eroded." And he announced that "everything we do—everything that is done with LEAA funds—must include a component for treating citizens better and making the system more responsive to them."

Between fiscal years 1970 and 1975 LEAA spent $22,440,000 for "victim-witness" projects.[20] Part of that effort included the holding of a national competition for grants to help victims and witnesses. Over 200 proposals were submitted, and 18 were funded. Meanwhile, during the same time, many other programs to help victims began to appear independently of LEAA funding. Among these were the rape crisis centers; the urban vigilantees and citizen protective associations (see, Baluss, 1975; Russell, 1975); projects to improve police handling of victims (Fremont, California, Police Department, 1974; Sacramento, California, Police Department, 1974); programs to assist victims of child abuse (Baluss, 1975); and programs to handle domestic and neighborhood disputes through arbitration rather than criminal prosecution (National Center for Dispute Settlement, 1970; Irwin, 1975; Hoff, 1974; Anno and Hoff, 1975).

The various LEAA and non-LEAA sponsored programs for victims differ in many ways, including: the services they perform; their location and affiliation; the size, training, and experience of their staffs; their philosophies, operations, and goals; their potential for institutionalization; and their potential for substantially improving or even altering victim-criminal-justice relations. The services include one or more of the following: referring victims to social services; assisting victims in obtaining benefits; supplying other information of various sorts, such as advice about residential security measures, the status or disposition of the criminal case in which the victim is involved, and the rights of victims to insurance, restitution, compensation, or other benefits; comforting or counseling the victim immediately after the crime or later; advising the victim as to what he or she can expect as a witness; assisting in obtaining witness fees; providing transportation or baby-sitting services for witnesses; providing a special witness notification system designed to prevent unnecessary trips to the courthouse; ensuring that witnesses have their property returned once it has been used as evidence; providing witness lounges in courthouses; and arranging for victim-offender confrontations designed to allay victim fears and improve the offender's chances for rehabilitation. In some programs victim "advocates" attempt to influence the decisions of criminal justice officials in the direction favored by the victim.

Some victim programs are located in police agencies, others in DAs' offices; others are found in probation and correctional departments; and still others are not affiliated with any governmental agency. The staffs vary from all-volunteer, nonprofessional, lay people to paid, professional staffs of social workers.

The groundswell of interest in the victim is gratifying at this initial stage; but hard questions remain to be asked. One fundamental concern is whether these programs are diverting attention from the uninviting but necessary task of effecting fundamental changes in the American way of administering justice.[21] Another question is about the potential of these new programs for producing real change in existing practices. One indirect indicator of this potential of any new program is the reception it receives from agencies handling existing programs. Thus, the fact that many of the new victim programs have been not only warmly received but hotly competed for by criminal justice agencies does not augur well for their prospects as staging areas for radical reformations of the administration of justice.[22] This is not to say that they may not be worthwhile. Victims should be paid their witness fees; have their property returned; and be treated decently by the public officials who, after all, are supposed to be their servants. But whether those changes would be best thought of as long-overdue improvements or radical reforms is certainly arguable. Of course, the evidence is not in yet. The programs have just gotten under way. While they accumulate experience, policy makers and researchers are pondering the possibilities and watching the issues as they arise.

FUTURE POSSIBILITIES

Arbitration. One possibility that has already occurred to more than one legal thinker is the potential for increasing the application of the arbitration model to the criminal justice system. Arbitration programs in which victims and offenders are brought together to discuss their dispute and reach a settlement without resorting to the criminal process have been successfully tried on a limited basis in several cities. It is now being advocated that this approach be tried on a broader range (Gracen, 1975; Morris, 1975). To the extent that this model is adopted, the hands of time will be turned back toward that period in history when the victim's interest was not subrogated to that of the state. It may even be possible to strive for a system of justice like that of the Zapotec Indians, whose goal of justice is not to declare one party to a conflict the winner and the other the loser. Instead the idea is to restore the balance, to have both parties leave feeling satisfied and able to live in harmony again in the same community (Nader, 1969).

Extortion of victims. While these happy thoughts are being entertained, however, new problems are arising. Experience has already shown that one problem that needs to be examined carefully is whether or not to place victim assistance programs (which have benefits to dispense) in the hands of criminal justice agencies. There are obvious advantages to their being so located; they thereby command greater cooperation from government officials than might otherwise occur. On the other hand, agents of programs may not be so aggressive in their advocacy of victim interests if they are organizationally tied to the very system that they have to fight. Even more ominous is the possibility that the programs will serve only one master—and with a potent tool for extortion. Agents of programs with benefits to give may predicate their delivery of services on a victim's willingness to cooperate with the arrest and prosecution of a case.

Undeserving victims. Another problem is that of the "undeserving" victim. Ultimately the problem here is twofold. One involves resource allocation; the other, the social valuation of "sympathetic" or "unsympathetic" victims.

Existing social welfare and volunteer resources in any community are not unlimited and cannot be continually expanded to provide for new claims. Programs that are designed to help victims to take advantage of community services are, in effect, asking for a reallocation of existing services. Some programs have tried to get services on an expedited schedule for victims. The program staff have accompanied victims to the welfare agencies and tried to have their cases brought to the front of the line. But the experience has been that the welfare agencies are unwilling to have priorities imposed upon them. When other applicants with equally legitimate claims are standing in line, why should someone be advanced just because he is the victim of a crime? Actually, welfare agency personnel appear to develop their own informal system of setting priorities. When it comes to victims, distinctions seem to be made between "deserving" and "undeserving" victims.[23] The man who was shot in the foot during a drunken brawl in a bar is not likely to move the welfare administrator to give him special attention. Whether these initial impressions are in fact correct and whether the problem involved is a general one that affects not just the welfare administrator but also the administrator of the victim assistance program as well are matters for future research to resolve.

Assistance, Advocacy, or Control

Some programs for victims have been indiscriminately called "victim advocate" programs. This is misleading. The term "advocate" automatically brings to mind the image of the lawyer fighting to maximize his client's rights, benefits, and advantages. But it is not clear that many of the victim programs plan to do this or would want to if they could. For instance, the idea of "advocacy" is opposed to the spirit and method of the new victim-offender arbitration programs.[24] Their goal is not to vindicate the rights of any particular individual but to restore harmony and help the disputants live together again in peace.[25] Both parties may have to compromise their demands. This is no place for advocacy. In fact, lawyers are not involved in these arbitration programs. The parties represent themselves. Thus, to regard them as "victim advocate" programs is misleading both as to their spirit and as to their actual operation. However, it is certainly not incorrect to bill them as victim assistance programs. They do provide some victims with a remedy for dealing with the nuisances and harrassment that go with living in a crowded society.[26]

Aside from the arbitration programs, it is questionable whether other victim programs should be referred to as "advocate" programs. Of course, there is no harm in calling someone doing good things for victims an "advocate." But it is a different matter—and something more than just picking at words—to use that term to describe programs operating in conjunction with the legal system in which the word "advocate" is a term of art and has a rather definite meaning and connotation (Pound, 1953; DuBow and Becker, Chapter 6 in this volume). In that context the term raises the obvious comparison. Is the victim's advocate like the other two advocates in the system, namely, the defendant's and the state's? This raises further questions. Is he a lawyer? Does he have standing? Can one advocate represent all victims, or will conflicts of interest arise? Will the state ever have to provide indigent victims with advocates if they cannot afford their own?

Some "victim advocate" programs like the Kenwood program in Chicago (see DuBow and Becker, Chapter 6 in this volume) are clear attempts to fashion their advocates in the mold of the lawyer fighting for his client's cause. Other programs, such as the Jacksonville, Florida, Sheriff's Department's Victim Advocate Program (Baluss, 1975),[27] are better thought of as ombudsmen or social-welfare type programs designed to assist victims but not represent their interest in the prosecution of their case. A third kind might be referred to as controlling the victim.

The ombudsman and control kinds of programs present fewer challenges and greater rewards to the criminal justice agency sponsoring them than does the true advocate type program. Thus, it is probably no coincidence that the ombudsman and control types are being replicated more often than true advocate programs.

Some of the aspects of the true advocate program that are considered undesirable (from the point of view of the criminal justice system) are outlined in DuBow and Becker's study (see Chapter 6 in this volume). When a true advocate is involved, the low-visibility decisions of the system—especially those of the prosecutor—are no longer hidden. Prosecutors are not used to having their discretionary decisions about plea bargaining or other matters challenged except on rare occasions (see, for example, Dash, 1975; Miller, 1974). The Hyde Park victim advocate not only challenged prosecutors but took his criticisms to the newspapers when he was dissatisfied with responses to his challenges. Of course, newspapers have always had courthouse reporters acting as a form of community watchdog. But the creation of the victim advocate concerned with the interests of individual victims has greatly intensified the potential threat to the system and to the political careers of public officials.

The threat to the system lies in the fact that the criminal courts rely on the practice of plea bargaining to dispose of the vast majority of their cases. That is, the government gives the defendant some concessions—such as a reduced charge—in exchange for a plea of guilty (Newman, 1956). Chief Justice Warren Burger (1970) has indicated the disastrous consequences of significant changes in the rate of guilty pleas. If there were a 10% drop in the rate, the courts and the prosecutors would have to double their resources to handle the additional work. True advocate programs that successfully prevent plea bargaining will be pushing the justice system toward that disaster. What is more, the true advocate may represent a threat that cannot be easily blunted. Defense attorneys who practice regularly in the courts are co-opted into an unspoken agreement not to force the system to break down by refusing to plead their clients guilty (Blumberg, 1967; Grossman, 1969; Cole, 1970). The co-optation is possible because the defense attorney relies on the courts for his livelihood. Earning that living can be made more difficult if court officials so choose. There is also the fact that the defense attorney becomes a part of the courthouse social system and identifies more strongly with judges and prosecutors than with his clientele. In contrast, the victim advocate may have much less reliance on the court for his living and may be less fully integrated into the social world of the courthouse. Thus, the system may find it more difficult to "control" him.[28]

Private Prosecutors

A remote but intriguing possibility in the future of victim advocacy is that private prosecutor statutes may be rediscovered and used.[29] These laws provide that a victim may hire his own lawyer to either assist the government's prosecutor or conduct the prosecution himself if the government chooses not to prosecute. These private prosecutors are known as "solicitors" or "DAs." They are advocates in the truest legal sense. They have the legal powers of the government prosecutor. They sit with him in court as co-counsel, examine witnesses, and make opening and closing statements to the jury. If they make legal errors in their conduct of the case, the case can be reversed (North Carolina Law Review, 1972).

So far, the new victim advocate programs have not tried to use existing or resurrect old private prosecutor statutes.[30] But if this began to happen to any significant extent, it could have serious consequences, and it would raise fundamental policy questions about priorities among victims' interests (again, the individual victim against the larger society) and about what the basic goals and purposes of the administration of justice should be. Projections about the impact of the use of private prosecutor laws can be extrapolated on an unscientific basis from some observations on how the system works in North Carolina—one of the few states where it continues to be used regularly. It is believed by some that the existence of the private prosecutor system is one of the reasons for the comparatively large number of convicts on death row.[31] However, David Kendall, an attorney[32] directly familiar with 34 North Carolina death row cases, reports that private prosecutors were involved in only about 10 cases and their participation was not critical to the imposition of the death penalty. As a general rule, private prosecutors engage in "grandstanding" techniques during the trial, which Kendall believes do not alter the result that would otherwise have occurred. The real impact of the private prosecutors is on plea bargaining. He believes that cases in which private prosecutors have been retained are virtually never plea-bargained.[33]

If Kendall is right and if the experience of private prosecutors operating in rural, Southern jurisdictions with small criminal caseloads can be generalized to what might happen in large urban jurisdictions, then the implications are ominous. The private prosecutor style of victim advocacy would bring the courts to their knees.

Controlling the Victim

Some projects that are billed as "assisting victims" are more accurately described as assisting the criminal justice system and extending government control over victims. Whether the victims so controlled would regard the project as "assisting" them is problematic.

One project, for example, is devoted largely to helping victim-witnesses get to court to testify when needed. It provides transportation services for elderly and injured victims; it operates a computerized witness notification system; and it employs a bilingual staff to interview witnesses in the complaint room and *verify* their addresses and phone numbers.

No doubt the project's services will be beneficial to many victims. But a significant number of victims may not appreciate having their addresses and phone numbers verified—as if they were defendants seeking bail. Not all victims are interested in becoming involved with the authorities. Even those who do cooperate to the extent of reporting their victimizations to the police are not to be regarded as thereby committing themselves to full cooperation. Many of them give fictitious names and addresses (Cannavale, 1975; McDonald, 1973; Ziegenhagen, Chapter 12 in this volume).[34]

Bringing the Victim In

Some of the proposals for restoring the victim's influence over the administration of justice are less ominous than the private prosecutor possibility but nonetheless do represent various degrees of threat to the existing system. The least threatening of all is the proposal to provide victims with information about the final disposition of their case. This is something which the ombudsman-type victim assistance programs are already doing. The potential threat here is that victims might not like what they hear and may cause trouble—in the form of either demanding explanations or taking political actions. But so far these possibilities have not developed.

Greater problems are raised by proposals that victims be allowed to participate in the decision process. Here the problems are several. There is the logistical problem of getting all the relevant parties together at the same time and place. This kind of problem is certainly not new for the courts, but the addition of yet another party to the hearings could contribute to court delay. Also, depending upon how radical the proposal is, there could be additional problems. A moderate version is to simply allow the victim to allocute his views so that they might be taken into account by the relevant criminal justice official—either the prosecutor, if the victim is commenting on a proposed plea bargain, or the judge, if the issue is the sentence.[35] A more radical proposal is to give the victim veto power over the decision. Such power transfers are not likely to be accepted quietly by the officials. Giving the victim that power again creates the possibility of fewer plea bargains being accepted. What is more, it may be a step away from the goal of increasing the rationality and uniformity of the sentencing process. Also, it could personalize and solidify an emnity between the victim and the defendant that did not exist before. And, finally, it could place the victim under great personal strain. Again, these are all matters which await future research.

VICTIM SERVICES: PERCEIVED NEEDS AND ACTUAL USE

Ziegenhagen (1974) has found that victims do not perceive themselves in need of social services. But people interested in assisting victims are unwilling to accept these results at face value. They believe that the victims are unable either to recognize or to articulate their needs.[36] Where victim assistance programs have operated, the requests for services have varied. In Philadelphia, victims have asked the district attorney's victim-witness project to help them learn the status or dispositions of cases and to assist them, through such services as transportation or baby-sitting, in making court appearances. The most frequent request has been for help in obtaining witness fees.

In Jacksonville, Florida, the most frequent service provided by the Sheriff's Victim Advocate Program is largely referring victims to existing government welfare programs for short-term crisis assistance—i.e., food, clothing, rent money—especially when the victim is the family breadwinner.

In Tucson, Arizona, the victim-witness program of the Pima County District Attorney's Office has referred victims to welfare agencies; arranged for volunteers to stay with victims until they were over their fears; and provided information about the statuses or dispositions of criminal cases.

In West Philadelphia a volunteer citizens' group has sought out victims at the local hospital and police precinct and provided them with "friends," i.e., volunteer residents in the community who visit the victim and "debrief" him in an effort to break the cycle of social isolation, withdrawal, and depression that the volunteers believe accompany victimization.[37] Also the friends are encouraged to participate in crime-preventing activities such as greater sociability on the streets and looking out for one's neighbors.[38]

In some cities citizens have begun acting as watchmen supplementing the work of the police. In some places the volunteers carry whistles (Griffin, 1974); in others, compressed air horns. The idea is to sound alarms when danger appears (Flanagan, 1974). In other places the groups are closer to the old-fashioned vigilante committees (Russell, 1975; Marx and Archer, 1973; Severo and Campbell, 1969; Claiborne, 1973).

COMPENSATION AND RESTITUTION

Another source of interest in victim-criminal-justice relations, one which long predates the advent of the victim assistance programs, is the movement for victim compensation programs. It is not necessary to recapitulate all the issues involved in compensation since they are extensively treated elsewhere (see, for example, Edelhertz and Geis, 1974). But a brief sketch on the subject with special emphasis on its linkage to the separate but related matter of victim restitution is in order.

At one time in history the aim of the criminal law was to repair the damage done to the victim or his family. The offender or his family was required to make the victim whole again. He had to pay restitution to the victim. However, with the centralization of government power in England, this arrangement was gradually transformed to the point where the victim no longer received any reparation for the harm done (Schafer, 1968).

The full history of this transformation has yet to be written, but pieces of it are available. In America the end of victim restitution coincided with the American Revolution and the discovery of the asylum.[39] During the colonial period the victim exercised considerable control over the administration of criminal justice (Nelson, 1967). It was his interests that were at stake not the community's or the government's. In theft cases, for example, the defendant had to pay treble damages to the victim. If the defendant could not pay, he had to sell himself into servitude to the victim for a period equal to the value of the damages. The government had no stake in the outcome of the case. The victim could waive his right to the damages and thereby preclude prosecution of the case.

Shortly after the Revolution this changed. The institution of servitude to victims was replaced by new institutions, the work-house and the correctional asylum, which theoretically were not forms of servitude but instruments for human reformation. As a practical matter, the correctional movement severed the link between the victim and the offender. The payment of restitution decreased over the years until 1805, when the last instance of treble damages was imposed in Middlesex County, Massachusetts (Nelson, 1967).

Since then the issue of restitution has occasionally been discussed by correctional reformers (see Schafer, Chapter 10 in this volume), but not until 1972 has there been a major effort to reintroduce restitution as a correctional device.

Meanwhile, in 1951, social reformer Margery Fry published an influential book, *Arms of the Law*, in which she argued that victims of crime should be compensated by the state. The underlying rationale for such a program is as follows: the government has an obligation to protect the well-being of its citizens. If the government fails in that task, it should be required to make good the harm it failed to prevent.

Fry's proposal provoked a flurry of activity on behalf of victims. In America, 13 states have passed victim compensation legislation (Edelhertz and Geis, 1974), and President Ford has made federal victim compensation legislation a top priority in his anticrime efforts (Ford, 1975). Much of what has been written about the subject has been concerned with the desirability and propriety of these programs, as well as their limitations, use, and pitfalls (see, for example, Geis, Chapter 11 in this volume).

The distinction between compensation and restitution must be kept in mind here. Both are intended to provide some victims with some reparation for damages done. But with restitution the offender is required to make the reparation, whereas with compensation there is no link between the offender and the victim. Rather, the state pays the compensation much like an insurance company paying a damage claim. The recent interest in restitution programs as correctional measures has been concerned with restoring the linkage between the offender and the victim. The correctional movement has come full circle.[40]

In what is being billed as the "progressive" reform of the Illinois correctional system, compensation and restitution are tied together. A portion of the proceeds from inmate labor will be paid into the account from which the state victim compensation program draws its funds.

Other programs have made the linkage between victim and offender considerably more direct. The leading example of this is the work in Minnesota. In 1972 the Department of Corrections began operation of its Minnesota Restitution Center. This is a program for selected property offenders sentenced to prison. The offenders are placed on parole status during the fourth month following admission to prison. A restitution contract is worked out between the offender and the victim for full restitution for the damages done and for the costs of assisting in the prosecution of the case. Negotiations are completed on a face-to-face basis, and continued contact between the victim and the offender is encouraged.

As of January 1975 (Minnesota Restitution Center, 1975) 62 offenders had been admitted to the center. They were responsible for victimizing 79 individuals and 216 organizations. The total financial obligations of the restitution contracts that they signed was $18,374. Of that amount, $5,627 had already been paid; $3,505 was not going to be paid because offenders had been returned to prison; and the remaining amount was expected to be paid on schedule as the monthly payments fell due.

The results of the Minnesota experiment have been encouraging.[41] In addition to it, other projects are linking the victim back to the offender. In Tucson, Arizona, the Pima County District Attorney's Office has operated a unique pretrial diversion program since October 1974.[42] The diversion program itself is not unusual. The prosecutor screens the cases. Eligible defendants are placed on voluntary probation programs for 6 months to a year. If they satisfy the conditions of probation, the charges are dropped. If not, they are reinstated.

The unique aspect of the Tucson program is the requirement that the victim consent to the diversion. In many cases this is done by bringing the victim and the offender together to negotiate the terms of the diversion. Restitution may be part of the diversion plan,[43] but it does not seem to be the only benefit of the confrontation. The evidence is sketchy but some anecdotes suggest additional benefits. One woman who had been burglarized was able to get her fears under control when she saw the burglar was not the diabolical monster whom she had imagined but a scrawny teenager who told her he meant her no harm. In another case the victim ultimately provided the offender with a $10,000 scholarship to attend medical school. The other side of the coin is that offenders who have seen the consequences of their actions in human, personal terms have shown real evidence of contrition for their behavior and concern for their fellow human beings. In one case, a young man who had stolen a color television set found that his victim was an invalid old woman whose only pleasure in life was the TV. In the end he not only returned the TV but agreed to paint her house, mow her lawn, and drive her to the doctor for her weekly appointments. The final twist to the story is that neighbors began hiring him to do similar work, and he now has a growing business.

A project in Suffolk County, Massachusetts—modeled in part after the Tucson experiment[44] —is going to have victims in selected offenses participate in sentencing councils which will advise judges. The face-to-face confrontation and discussion between the victim and the offender that has been successfully used in the Tucson experiment is a key element in the Suffolk project.

The underlying rationale of all three projects—in Minnesota, Tucson, and Suffolk—is basically the same. All three recognize the creative uses that can be made of victim-offender encounters. Restitution is only part of what can be achieved. There are other possible benefits for the victim, the offender, and society. The victim may gain psychological benefits by an encounter with the offender. The possibility of rehabilitation may be enhanced, and, hence, ultimately the safety of the community may be enhanced. The offender may be less able to deny the responsibility for his actions and turn the tables to the point that he can "reject the rejectors" (McCorkle and Korn, 1954) and believe that he is the innocent victim of a corrupt and oppressive system of laws. Perhaps Norval Morris (1975:56-57) is right. He recommends victim participation in plea negotiations[45] because "self-reform presupposes self-forgiveness. Mercifully time allows most of us this privilege, no matter what happens, but self-forgiveness is very much more swift and practicable when the person we have injured forgives us. . . . A pretrial settlement in which the victim agrees does give the convicted criminal, in prison or not, an opportunity to begin again if he wants to—and immediately."

Perhaps the correctional reformers' mistake of two hundred years ago lay in not realizing that human sentiment is moved far less by abstract discussions of morality and just desert than by the graphic and personalized portrayal of human suffering and misery. Perhaps the reason why one never hears a convicted defendant say that he is sorry[46] is that the criminal justice process so successfully submerges the victim and his suffering that the defendant's ability to deny his act is facilitated and even encouraged. Perhaps a reentry of the victim into the criminal process will change this in some important ways. All the answers here await future research.

SOCIAL PSYCHOLOGY AND THE VICTIM

One final source of interest in the victim that has special relevance for victim-criminal-justice relations comes from the experimental, social psychological research on observers' reactions to victims—research such as done by Lerner (Lerner and Simmons, 1966; Lerner and Matthews, 1967; Lerner, 1971a, 1971b) and others (Aderman et al., 1974; Chaikin and Darley, 1973; Glass, 1964; Jones and Davis, 1960; Miller et al., 1975; Stokols and Schapler, 1973). Some of the work has used simulated jurors to determine the effect of personal characteristics of the victim on the jurors' tendency to punish the convicted defendant. Landy and Aronson (1969), for example, found that jurors gave longer sentences when the character description of the victim was favorable than when it was neutral or unfavorable.

Lerner (1971b) began his research in an attempt to explain why innocent victims of injustice are not helped by their fellow man and, for that matter, are even condemned. The Kitty Genovesse murder—in which an attacker stabbed the woman to death over the course of a half hour while 38 witnesses ignored her screams for help (see Rosenthal, 1964)—prompted much soul searching and some scientific research on bystander apathy. Latane and Darley (1968) showed that bystanders are not as apathetic as they have been portrayed. When they do fail to take action, it is often because an emergency situation catches them unprepared on how to cope or because, if more than one witness is present, each waits for another to act.

Lerner pursued the matter further, starting with the belief that most people find it quite painful to know that innocent victims are suffering and, furthermore, that their pain is increased when they believe that they are in any way responsible for the suffering. Lerner postulated his "just-world theory" and tested it experimentally. According to his theory, people need to believe that there is justice in the world—not only in the legal sense but in a more basic sense. Good things happen to good people and bad things happen to those who deserve it, including, among the latter, people who are unwilling to avoid suffering or who are in some way blameworthy. This need to believe in a just world influences the perceptions that people have of victims. If an "innocent" victim is suffering, and an observer cannot do anything to alleviate the suffering, then the observer will make himself more comfortable by deciding that the victim is not innocent after all. In this way the observer is able to maintain his view that justice prevails in the world; he simply condemns the victim as undesirable, bad, or deserving of his fate. Of course, this imaginary transformation of the victim is not necessary if the observer is able to help the victim and thereby reestablish justice in the world.

Lerner's experiments (Lerner and Simmons, 1966) bore out his hypotheses. He (Lerner and Matthews, 1967) and others (Glass, 1964; Jones and Davis, 1960; Chaikin and Darley, 1973; Miller et al., 1975) also found that derogation of the victim is less likely to occur if the observer identifies with the victim and that it is more likely to occur if the observer regards himself as being responsible for the harm done a victim either directly or by identifying with the agency causing the harm. Ryan's observations (1971) of instances of observers blaming victims have shown that in real life observers are not neutral. In all the cases that he observed the observer was linked to or identified with the social institutions that oppressed victims.

The implications of these studies for research on relationships between victims and the criminal justice system should be obvious. The perception of the victim undoubtedly influences many criminal justice decisions.[47] The mere appearance of a victim as honest, clean-cut, and sincere or as arrogant, pushy, and stupid may have important influences on the kind of treatment that he receives. Courthouse folklore already places great stress on the importance of appearance as an influence on decision makers. Defense attorneys will plead their clients early rather than have a trial judge see sympathy-inducing victims. On the other hand, prosecutors talk about the ideal victim whom whey would like to have in every case so that conviction would be assured. That victim would be a clean-cut, polite war veteran with a Purple Heart for losing an arm while saving a buddy. Many years ago the legal realists suggested that the state of a judge's digestion may determine the kind of justice that was dispensed on a given day. They called this "gastronomical jurisprudence" (Schur, 1968:146). Today, victimologists should be aware that the appearance, social class, character, and other attributes of the victim are part of that vast body of extralegal factors which determine the quality of justice that is dispensed both to the offender and to the victim. Perhaps this will be called "victimological jurisprudence."

NOTES

1. Subin's description has been outdated by recent innovations in the District of Columbia, but his description of the victim's interaction with the prosecutor is still illustrative of what occurs in other places.

2. This is not a recent development (see, Great Britain Parliamentary Commission, 1925, 1926; Shield, 1932; Association of Moral and Social Hygiene, 1935; California, State Assembly, 1949; Tappan, 1950; Michigan, Governor's Commission, 1951; California, Department of Mental Hygiene, 1954; Karpman, 1954; Gibbens and Waler, 1956; Reifen, 1958; Schutz, 1959). In the last decade and a half it has received increased attention (see, for example, Van Krevelen, 1960; Gibbens and Prince, 1963; Boecherer, 1965; Barton, 1968; De Francis, 1969, 1970, 1971; Libai, 1969; White House Conference on Youth, 1970; Solomon et al., 1970; Smith, 1970; Flammang, 1970).

3. Gibbens and Walker (1956:8) concluded that "children are surprisingly tolerant of physical cruelty provided it is only occasional and their parents are at other times affectionate, as they may well be; they know no better. But the sight of their father being sent to prison for the first time is an adult view of his behavior."

4. The conflict is actually between three interests: the defendant's, the individual victim's, and society's. In practice it is not merely a matter of deciding that since the child may be damaged and since the law favors the defendant—and for good reason cannot be changed—the whole matter should be dropped. Prosecutors do not want it dropped even if they are sympathetic to the victim's well-being. They want to prosecute on behalf of future victims who might be saved. This is a terrible dilemma for both the prosecutor and the child's parents. Unfortunately research is of little help. It does not clearly inform us as to the probability of the child's being further damaged or the defendant's being prevented from recidivating.

Illustrative of the legal establishment's neglect of the interests of the individual victim is the American Bar Association's position on how the prosecutor should resolve the dilemma. The ABA (1971:95) approves the dropping of cases in which the victim refuses to testify—recognizing the fact that sometimes prosecution would damage the victim. But then the ABA goes on to say: "In serious cases, however, the interests of the community *require* that the prosecutor try to obtain the victim's cooperation and in some instances it may be his duty to use the subpoena power to compel his attendance as a witness." (Emphasis added.)

The Michigan Governor's Study Commission on the Deviated Criminal Sex Offender (1951:75) took a similar position regarding subrogating the interests of the individual victim to that of society. Knowing full well that "many parents and even social workers refuse to report cases [of sex crimes] because it is believed that the best interests of the victim lie in her being allowed to forget what has happened," the Commission nonetheless took the position that "inasmuch as [this] leaves the offender free to commit another crime . . . those victimized have an obligation to the public to cooperate by reporting."

5. For example, they are not listed in *16 Ideas to Help District Attorneys Help the Victims and Witnesses of Crime* (National District Attorneys Association Commission on Victim Witness Assistance, n.d.).

6. The point here is that the police do not discriminate. They treat all victims "like defendants," but for the sex crime victim that treatment is experienced as a greater insensitivity than for other victims—who are usually able to rationalize that the police task is merely to get information (Ziegenhagen, Chapter 12 of this volume). (Of course, reformers are asking whether the unsympathetic information-gathering role is the appropriate role for the police. Given the low probability that any crime will result in an arrest, conviction, and sentence to prison, perhaps it makes greater sense for the police to be victim counselors and sympathizers than crime investigators. Since they can do very little about the crime problem, they could at least not alienate the victims.)

A simple experiment will illustrate how easy it is to appear to become accusatory when one is seeking information from another. Try writing a letter for a friend—one you are willing to lose—who wants to clear up a complaint he has about some service or product he has purchased. You quickly find yourself trying to exercise the utmost diplomacy in finding tactful ways to ask for information which your friend may have innocently neglected to supply.

7. "You are tried by a kangaroo court of every male" is a sex crime victim's description of her treatment by the police (Taylor, 1971:C52).

8. Some commentators have advocated that psychiatric evaluation be made compulsory for any witness who "may be suffering from a 'mental illness' likely to affect his credibility" (Yale Law Journal, 1950:1340; but see, Ash, 1972:402).

9. In Wilson v. United States, 271 F.2d 492 (D.C. Cir. 1959), the court in dictum quoted Professor Wigmore: " 'No judge should ever let a sex offense charge go to the jury unless the female complainant's social history and mental makeup have been examined and testified to by a qualified physician.' 3 J. Wigmore, Evidence, § 924(a) (3d ed. 1940)."

The 1937-1938 Report of the ABA Committee on the Improvement of the Law of Evidence stated: "Today it is unanimously held (and we say 'unanimously' advised) by experienced psychiatrists that the complainant woman in a sex offense should *always* be examined by competent experts to ascertain whether she suffers from some mental or moral delusion or tendency, frequently found especially in young girls, causing distortion of the imagination in sex cases." (Emphasis in the original.)

The latter recommendation that the victim *always* be psychiatrically examined is in striking contrast to the law's position regarding the defendant whose mental health and character are not questioned unless he chooses to raise the issues—Michelson v. United States, 335 U.S. 469 (1948). "The rule, then, firmly and universally established in policy and tradition, is that the prosecution may not initially attack the defendant's character" 1 J. Wigmore, Evidence §57 at 456 (3d ed. 1940).

10. In those days sex victims from "respectable society" kept their victimizations to themselves. It seems that sex victims were not a part of the citizen reform groups of the 1940s. The only victims studied by the commissions which were formed were the official, reported victims, who were powerless and unsympathetic types.

11. See note 4 above.

12. The change in attitudes from the 1940s may be the result of a combination of several factors including: two decades of disappointing and disillusioning experience with the sexual psychopath laws; more general disillusionment with psychiatry, rehabilitation, and the prospects for changing people through existing therapeutic strategies; a recognition of the difficulty of predicting dangerousness; an increased understanding that the criminal justice system arrests few criminals and convicts fewer compared to all other crimes that occur; the belief that the criminal law revolution of the sixties, together with the crime explosion, has made the criminal justice system even less effective; the fact that victims themselves are openly participating in the current reforms and are actively protecting their special interests as a group; and the possibility that nonprofessionals assisting sex victims and feminist groups who see the potential for using sex victim assistance programs to advance their cause may have staked out a claim to the sex victim. Whatever its causes, the new attitude represents a healthy cynicism and a fruitful source of soul-searching thought. What is more, this pessimism is not limited only to outsiders. The criminal justice establishment itself is beginning to publicly express doubts that it can do anything to reduce crime. Two successive Attorneys General, William Saxbe and Edward Levi, have described the country's efforts to reduce crime as "failures." Boston Police Commissioner Robert di Grazia has said, "We cannot eliminate or reduce crime. That's something that's beyond our capabilities and I wish that politicians would recognize it" (Meyer, 1975).

13. Some 90% of the victims of consumer fraud surveyed for the President's Commission on Law Enforcement and Administration of Justice did not report their victimizations to the police (1967a:22). This was by far the highest rate of nonreporting of all the types of crimes included. Of the nonreporters, 50% said they felt it was a private matter or they did not want to harm the offender; 40% believed that the police could not be

effective or would not want to be bothered; and 10% said they were too confused or did not know how to report.

14. In fact, some professional defrauders deliberately arrange to have their transactions slightly above the limit of the small claims courts (Bowley, 1974:556).

15. In addition to worrying that his victimization may not be one which the district attorney is presently interested in, the victim of fraud has recently been given even more cause to lose hope. A recent Supreme Court ruling has made it more difficult for victims of stock fraud to recover their losses.

16. But, as was noted, the current surveys will have to be modified if this new purpose is to be fully pursued. The current surveys ask victims if they reported their victimizations to the police. If not, then a series of questions as to the reasons why not are asked. But if the victim did make a report, his reasons for doing so are not questioned. This bias reflects the original interests of the creators of the victim surveys in better understanding the meaning of official crime statistics by determining the reasons for failure to report. However, if the focus of interest shifts to victim-criminal-justice relations, then the victim would be asked his reasons for reporting as well as not reporting his victimization. One survey has already begun asking this question (see Smith and Maness, Chapter 3 in this volume).

17. At the Superior Court Division of the U.S. Attorney's Office for the District of Columbia, the PROMIS computer program (see Hamilton and Work, 1973) was pioneered and had just accumulated enough data (one year's worth) to allow research to begin.

18. The unique professional relationship between the assistant U.S. attorney in charge of the Superior Court Division and the top leadership of the Law Enforcement Assistance Administration hastened the communication of this startling finding to LEAA. That assistant U.S. attorney subsequently became one of the three top administrators of LEAA.

A follow-up study was later funded by LEAA to determine the reasons for the noncooperation. But it came up with a baffling finding. Some 90% of the witnesses who had been listed by assistant prosecutors as "uncooperative" thought that they had been cooperative (Cannavale, 1975:39). However, that study was not completed until spring 1975. In the meantime, LEAA had already committed itself to improving the lot of the victim-witness.

19. Criticism of the criminal justice system even from an "insider" is never popular when it is strong, accurate, and public. For example, Francis Looney, Deputy Commissioner of the New York City Police Department and President of the International Association of Chiefs of Police publicly responded to Santarelli's speech to the National Conference of State Criminal Justice Planning Administrators (January 14, 1974). To Santarelli's statement that "when people go to report crimes, they sometimes can find no one to talk to . . . even worse, they find that they are being badgered by the police," Looney retorted, "This indictment, with no specifics offered, rejects the sincere efforts of again thousands of outstanding police officers" (International Association of Chiefs of Police, 1974).

20. Memo from H. Paul Haynes, Acting Assistant Administrator, Office of National Priority Programs, to Richard W. Velde, Administrator, Law Enforcement Assistance Administration, U.S. Department of Justice, June 10, 1975, regarding "The Origins of the Citizens' Initiative Program."

21. For example, should New York City really be trying to assist victims and witnesses participate in a system of criminal justice which is on the verge of total collapse (see Claiborne, 1975)? Or would the efforts be better spent on decriminalization or finding alternative ways of processing criminal complaints?

22. Programs for victims offer public officials and government agencies a great

opportunity for favorable press and public relations. With so much being done for the criminal, it is the happy elected official who can announce he is doing something for the people who "really deserve" help, the victims. In Philadelphia, for example, a "victim-witness assistance week" was declared by the mayor. He and the district attorney made several public appearances, and a strong publicity campaign was operated as part of the federally funded project. In New York, Mayor Beame campaigned on the promise that he would do something for victims.

Also, the state and local criminal justice planning agencies which disburse LEAA funds seem to be relieved to have a new idea to sponsor. There seems to be a nascent feeling among some of them that the police have been given about as much equipment as they can use and that the police and other justice agencies are running out of things to ask for. Furthermore, for all the money that has been spent, crime does not seem to have been affected so why not do something for the victim.

23. This observation was reported to the author in a personal communication from Mary Baluss.

24. The arbitration programs are new in a limited sense. Domestic disturbances and neighborhood quarrels have been handled by criminal justice systems in the past through the use of peace bonds. The defendant would not be prosecuted if he agreed to cease and desist in whatever he had been doing. If he violated the agreement, he would either lose a money bond or be found in contempt of court, or both. The arbitration programs have changed the peace bonds to agreements to submit to arbitration. Once both parties agree, then they must abide by the terms of the arbitration, or the cases will be referred back to the district attorney's office for processing as criminal complaints. The arbitration appraoch brings both parties together and proceeds only if both parties agree. Also, given that these disputes frequently involve victims who precipitate or at least add to the dispute, the arbitrated agreement is written so that either party might be a violator of it. (This information based on the author's interview with a representative of the National Center for Dispute Settlement, Philadelphia, July 1, 1975.)

An additional aside that is relevant in connection with these programs concerns the implications that the experience of these programs have for victimization surveys. As noted above, the victimization surveys do not satisfactorily portray the kinds of ongoing quarrels seen by these programs. The surveys probably also do not reliably measure domestic violence. It is not uncommon for citizen complaint centers to have middle-aged women come in asking for help in preventing their husbands from beating them. Under the circumstances, the staff is able to learn that the woman has been seriously injured by her husband many times over their 10 or 20 years of marriage; but the woman is willing to do something about it only now because she is getting so old that she feels she cannot take the beatings anymore. It is unlikely that a survey researcher would have elicited information about the violence when the woman was younger and more stoical.

25. For that matter, they frequently cannot even decide who is the victim. In many cases both parties are guilty of some criminal behavior. The "victim" is merely the party who "wins the race to the prosecutor's office." In this respect, the experience of these arbitration projects parallels that of the police, only the latter are in a much more difficult situation. They are on the scene with far less control over their environment. When they arrive they frequently cannot determine who is guilty or who should be designated victim or defendant. Both parties will have conflicting, confusing, or incomplete versions of what happened; and both will want the police to act on their behalf. While trying to avoid being used or forced into one or the other side of the dispute, the police will try to learn as much

as they can about what happened in order to make their own independent judgment as to who, if anyone, should be charged with a crime. A by-product of this is that the victim begins to feel he is being treated "like a defendant." Sometimes that feeling will be very accurate because the police will charge both parties with a crime as a way of gaining control over the situation. (This appears to be what happened to the victim whose story is reported in the prologue to this book. One would expect that this tactic is used only on victims who in the policeman's judgment are powerless to "cause trouble"—i.e., in civil suits or complaints to review boards.)

26. Programs for arbitrating community disputes are especially valuable to the poor, who cannot pack up and move to a new neighborhood, put up a fence, or pay an attorney to send a threatening letter when bad feelings with troublesome neighbors develop. But it remains to be seen whether the poor will use these programs or whether something similar to what happened with the small claims courts will occur; i.e., their original purpose was altered in actual practice (Carlin et al., 1967).

Biderman (1975) argues that it is really the cumulative effect of continuing harassment, petty neighborhood disputes, minor extortions of school-boy or street-corner bullies, and unabated nuisances rather than the instances of serious crime that shape the citizen's view of the quality of his social well-being. These, he notes, are continuing conditions as opposed to discreet incidents. He raises the point to illustrate one of the difficult methodological problems for victimization surveys which are designed to count incidents. But his observation has a more general applicability. Not only victim surveys but the legal system is not well adapted to dealing with these problems efficiently. In Philadelphia, for example, a neighborhood dispute that resulted in 20 stitches for one party to an assault was regarded as "mere harassment." The complainant was turned away from the district attorney's office. (Personal communication to the author from a representative of the National Center for Dispute Settlement in Philadelphia.)

This case was not untypical of the kinds of disputes—frequently involving assaults with weapons other than guns or, at least, threats of assault between people who may live in the same neighborhood but are not relatives—that are ignored by the criminal justice system. It appears that neither the police nor the prosecutors want to get involved unless someone is killed or almost killed. The individual who may have been completely innocent at the outset of one of these quarrels loses any chance of having his rights vindicated by the criminal justice system as soon as that system determines it is a "neighborhood quarrel." Once that label is attached, the individual's claim to victim status is denied by the officials, and he may be ignored. The new arbitration programs are an alternative to this. They do supply victims—totally innocent or partially blameworthy—with a solution short of engaging in the high level of violence necessary to activate official interest and earn cognizable victim status.

27. This information comes also via personal communication to the author from Rufus Smith, Deputy Director of the Jacksonville program.

28. On the other hand, depending on how victim advocate programs develop, their advocates could become susceptible to co-optation. If, for example, they have to appear to "produce results" as defense attorneys do, then the system may arrange to give them what appear to be real concessions but are in fact bogus concessions. There might develop something similar to the practice of "overcharging" so that extra charges can be dropped during plea bargaining in a display of apparent leniency.

A third possibility—which already began to appear in the Hyde Park experience—is that the advocate will begin to see fighting for individual victims as inefficient and unrewarding and may turn to larger, more exciting interests such as working on legislation for victims or filing class action suits. If this happens, victims as a class may benefit, but individual victims will continue to be ignored.

29. The author wishes to thank Stuart S. Nagel for bringing these laws to his attention.

30. It does not appear that they have even used the less exotic measures of quitam suits or mandamus proceedings.

31. The other two reasons are believed to be race prejudice and the unusual law of evidence which allows the jury to determine the degree of murder. The author wishes to thank John Stein for bringing these possible reasons to his attention.

32. Kendall is an attorney with the Legal Defense and Education Fund of the National Association for the Advancement of Colored People. His observations are based on his personal experience and were reported in a personal communication with the author.

33. In the Joanne Little case—which received national attention—the relatives of the murdered deputy sheriff proposed to hire a private prosecutor to assist in the case. However, the attorney they wanted to hire had formerly been defense counsel for Little in two unrelated cases—a possible conflict of interest situation which Kendall believes is not uncommon. The trial judge ruled on an objection and allowed the attorney to appear in court (Watson, 1975).

34. Also, in South Bronx, New York, 20% of the witness names and addresses are inaccurate. (Personal communication from David Friedman, Victim Consultation Project.)

35. An experiment is being tried in Suffolk County, Massachusetts, wherein victims will participate in sentencing boards which will make sentence recommendations to judges. The victim will not have any veto power (Justice Resource Institute, 1974).

36. This information was drawn from discussions at the Conference on Crime Against the Elderly, Washington, D.C., June 1975.

37. These descriptions of the Philadelphia, Jacksonville, Tucson, and West Philadelphia projects are based on the author's personal communications with project representatives. (See also in this volume DuBow and Becker, Chapter 6; Ziegenhagen, Chapter 12; Lynch, Chapter 7.)

38. The West Philadelphia group believes that a properly organized community could greatly reduce the need for police because of the reduced crime that would occur. The group has already broken a burglary modus operandi by keeping track of "ghost" calls which the police had told them were probably just pranksters. The group found that the "pranksters" were burglars who had a reverse telephone directory and would call each floor of an apartment building successively to determine who was home. Then they would burglarize the empty apartments.

39. For an account of the course of the penological movement in America see Rothman, 1971.

40. It is not entirely accurate to suggest that restitution was rediscovered as a correctional practice in the 1970s. Restitution has been extensively used as a condition of probation for a long time. It is not uncommon for large probation departments to collect millions of dollars in restitution for crime victims each year (President's Commission on Law Enforcement and Administration of Justice, 1967b:35).

41. Those who would like to see the victim restored to an influential role in criminal justice decision making as well as to have his financial losses replaced will regard the Minnesota experiment as a mixed blessing. It is clear from the center's literature (undated) that the victim's decision-making role has been narrowly restricted. He may negotiate the terms of resitution, and his approval of the final terms, as well as the convict's approval, is required. But the victim is not allowed to decide whether the offender will be permitted to

participate at all. The center has eliminated the victim veto: "Victims, for any number of reasons, may not wish to participate in a restitution agreement with the offender. If such a stance on the part of the victim eliminates a particular offender from consideration for a restitution plan, the victim, in fact, holds a 'veto.' In order to remove the victim from this powerful position, it may be necessary to adopt a 'symbolic' victim with whom negotiations are undertaken and restitution made" (Minnesota Restitution Center, n.d.:3).

42. The information derives from personal communication to the author from David A. Lowenberg, Adult Diversion Division, Office of the Pima county District Attorney. See also Greacen, 1975.

43. There are philosophical difficulties with diversion programs that have restitution components. Theoretically, early diversion operates on the rationale that the charges will be dropped and the defendant will not be brought to trial and hence not found guilty of anything—providing, of course, that he successfully completes the pretrial probationary program. Making him pay restitution is punishing him without a trial and forcing him to make an implied admission of guilt. This kind of program of punishment without trial is yet another step in the already substantial transformation of the American criminal justice system from a judicial to an administrative system. (The author wishes to thank Christopher Erlewine, Deputy Counsel, Senate Subcommittee on National Penitentiaries, for pointing out the philosophical problems on pretrial restitution.)

44. The information derives from a personal communication to the author from John A. Calhoun, Justice Resource Institute. (See also Justice Resource Institute, 1975.)

45. However he opposes giving the victim veto power.

46. This is an observation of Judge Tim Murphy, Superior Court of the District of Columbia, personally communicated to the author.

47. See Williams, Chapter 8 in this volume, for an application of just-world theory to prosecutorial data.

REFERENCES

ADERMAN, D.; BREHM, S.S.; and KATZ, L.B. (1974). "Empathic observation of an innocent victim: The just world revisited." Journal of Personality and Social Psychology, 29:342-347.

American Bar Association (1938). Recommendations of the Committee on Improvements in the Administration of Justice of the Section of Judicial Administration (as approved by the Assembly and House of Delegates, July 27). Chicago: Author.

——— (1971). Standards relating to the prosecution function and the defense function (approved draft). Chicago: Author.

ANNO, B.J., and HOFF, B.H. (1975). Refunding evaluation report on the Philadelphia 4-A (Arbitration-As-An-Alternative) Project. Unpublished report to the Philadelphia Region Governor's Justice Commission. Washington, D.C.: Blackstones' Associates.

AREEN, J. (1975). "A reappraisal of the state's role in child neglect and abuse cases." Georgetown Law Journal, 63(4):887-937.

ASH, M. (1972). "On witnesses: A radical critique of criminal court procedures." Notre Dame Lawyer, 48(December):386-425.

Association for Moral and Social Hygiene (1935). "Sexual offenses against young children." Health and Empire, 10.

BALUSS, M.E. (1975). Integrated services for victims of crime: A county based approach. Washington, D.C.: National Association of Counties.

BARKER, B. (1972). "She felt like a defendant." Washington Post, December 2, p. 1.

BARTON, L. (1968). Vulnerable children. New York: Schocken.

BIDERMAN, A. (1975). Remarks at the Conference on Victimization Surveys, Washington, D.C., June 24.

BLUMBERG, A.S. (1967). "The practice of law as confidence game: Organizational cooptation of a profession." Law and Society Review, 1(June):15-39.

BOECHERER, C. (1965). "The accent on protecting children." Law and Order, 131(3):22.

BOWLEY, G.F. (1974). "Law enforcement's role in consumer protection." Santa Clara Lawyer, 14:555-574.

BROSTOFF, P.M. (1971). District of Columbia Report to the 1971 White House Conference on Aging. Appendix II: Metropolitan police contracts with the elderly. Washington, D.C.: Washington School of Psychiatry.

BURGER, W.E. (1970). "The state of the judiciary." Address to the annual meeting of the American Bar Association, Washington, D.C.

California, Department of Mental Hygiene (1954). Final report on California sexual deviation research (20, 1). Sacramento: Assembly of the State of California.

California, State Assembly, Subcommittee on Sex Crimes (1949). Preliminary Report. Sacramento: Author.

CANNAVALE, F.J., and Institute for Law and Social Research (1975). Witness cooperation with a handbook of witness management. Lexington, Mass.: D.C. Heath.

CARLIN, J.; HOWARD, E.; and MESSINGER, S. (1967). Civil justice and the poor: Issues for sociological research. New York: Russell Sage.

Center for Women Policy Studies (1975). Rape and its victims: A report for citizens, health facilities and criminal justice agencies. Washington, D.C.: Law Enforcement Assistance Administration.

CHAIKIN, A.L., and DARLEY, J.M. (1973). "Victim or perpetrator? Defensive attribution of responsibility and the need for order and justice." Journal of Personality and Social Psychology, 25:268-275.

CLAIBORNE, W. (1973). "Vigilantism increasing in New York." Washington Post, September 16, pp. A1, A11.

——— (1975). "Time works in favor of N.Y. felons." Washington Post, August 10, pp. A1, A18.

COLE, G. (1970). "The decision to prosecute." Law and Society Review, 7:331.

Columbia Broadcasting System (1975). "Justice in America: The district attorney." Telecast, May 26.

Columbia Law Review (1967). "Corroborating charges of rape." 67:1137-1148.

Commission on Victim Witness Assistance (1975). Philadelphia Field Office Survey Research Report. Unpublished paper (February). Washington, D.C.: Author.

——— (n.d.). 16 ideas to help district attorneys help the victims and witnesses of crime. Pamphlet. Washington, D.C.: Author.

CUNNINGHAM, C.L. (1973). "Crime and the aging victim." Midwest Research Institute Quarterly (spring).

CUTLER, A.S. (1952). "Why the good citizen avoids testifying: Symposium on judicial administration and the common man." The Annals, 287:103-109.

DASH, L. (1975). "12 NW victims criticize easing of teen gang's pleas." Washington Post, April 19, pp. B1-B6.

DE FRANCIS, V. (1969). Protecting the child victim of sex crimes committed by adults: Final report. Denver: American Humane Association Children's Division.

––– (1970). Child abuse legislation in the 1970's. Denver: American Humane Association.

DE FRANCIS, V., and BOYD, O. (1971). The status of child protection–A national dilemma. Denver: American Humane Association.

District of Columbia, Public Safety Task Force on Rape (1973). Report. Unpublished paper. Washington, D.C.: City Council.

EDELHERTZ, H., and GEIS, G. (1974). Public compensation to victims of crime. New York: Praeger.

EOVALDI, T.L., and GESTRIN, J.E. (1971). "Justice for consumers: The mechanics of redress." Northwestern University Law Review, 66(3):281-325.

Evening Star Broadcasting Company, WMAL (1972). The legend of lenient justice. Nine-part radio documentary broadcast, Washington, D.C., May 29-31, June 1-9.

FENDEL, I. (1958). "Corroboration in the New York criminal law." Brooklyn Law Review, 24:324-343.

FLAMMANG, C.J. (1970). The police and the underprotected child. Springfield, Ill.: Charles C Thomas.

FLANAGAN, R. (1974). "Community crime prevention." Pretrial Justice Quarterly, 3(2):11, 23-24.

FORD, G.R. (1975). "Crime message to Congress." LEAA Newsletter, 5(1).

FORSTON, R., and KITCHENS, J. (1974). Criminal victimization of the aged. Denton, Texas: School of Community Service, North Texas State University.

Fremont, California, Police Department (1974). A proposal to conduct a program to improve and standardize police treatment of victims and witnesses. Washington, D.C.: Police Foundation.

FRY, M. (1951). Arms of the Law. London.

GIBBENS, T.C.N., and WALKER, A. (1956). Cruel parents. London: Institute for the Study of Treatment of Delinquency.

GIBBENS, T.C.N., and PRINCE, J. (1963). Child victims of sex offenses. London: Institute for the Study and Treatment of Delinquency.

GLASS, D.C. (1964). "Changes in liking as a means of reducing cognitive discrepancies between self-esteem and aggression. Journal of Personality, 32:531-549.

GOLDMAN, I.G. (1971). "Crime is just the start of victim's difficulties." Washington Post, June 6, pp. D1, D12.

GOLDSMITH, J., and TOMAS, N.E. (1974). "Crimes against the elderly: A continuing national crisis." Aging (June-July).

GRAHAM, P.L. (1948). "Treatment of witnesses: Laymen's suggestions for better handling." American Bar Association Journal, 34:23-25.

GREACEN, J.M. (1975). "Arbitration: A tool for criminal cases?" Barrister Magazine, 2(winter):10-14.

Great Britain Parliamentary Commission (1925). Report of Departmental Committee on Sexual Offenses Against Young Persons (Cmnd. 2561). London: Her Majesty's Stationery Office.

––– (1926). Report of the Departmental Committee on Sex Offenses Against Children and Young Persons in Scotland (Cmnd. 2592). London: Her Majesty's Stationery Office.

GRIFFIN, W. (1974). "Side whistle campaign cuts crime." Chicago Tribune, May 16.

GROSSMAN, B.A. (1969). The prosecutor: An inquiry into the exercise of discretion. Toronto: University of Toronto Press.

HAMILTON, W.A., and WORK, C.R. (1973). "The prosecutor's role in the urban court system: The case for management consciousness." Journal of Criminal Law and Criminology, 64:183-189.

HIBEY, R.A. (1973). "The trial of a rape case: An advocate's analysis of corroboration, consent, and character." American Criminal Law Review, 11(2):309-334.

HOFF, B.H. (1974). Final evaluation report: Philadelphia 4A Project. Unpublished report to the Philadelphia Region Governor's Justice Commission. Washington, D.C.: Blackstones' Associates.

HUTCHINS, R.M., and SLESINGER, D. (1928). "Some observations on the law of evidence—The competency of witnesses." Yale Law Journal, 37:1017-1028.

International Association of Chiefs of Police (1974). "News release" (February 4). Gaithersburg, Md.: Author.

IRWIN, T. (1975). "Talking things over—It beats jail." Parade, July 6, pp. 6-9.

JONES, E.E., and DAVIS, K.E. (1960). "Changes in interpersonal perception as a means of reducing cognitive dissonance." Journal of Abnormal and Social Psychology, 61:402-410.

Justice Resource Institute (1974). "The urban court program." Unpublished manuscript. Boston: Author.

KARPMAN, B. (1954). The sex offender and his offenses. New York: Julian.

KOTZ, N. (1971). "Plumbing suits profit lawyers: Settlement ignores victims." Washington Post, June 6, pp. A1, A12.

LANDY, D., and ARONSON, E. (1969). "The influence of the character of the criminal and his victim on the decisions of simulated jurors." Journal of Experimental Social Psychology, 5(2):141-152.

LATANE, B., and DARLEY, J.M. (1968). The unresponsive bystander. New York: Appleton-Century-Crofts.

LERNER, M.J. (1971a). "Observers' evaluation of a victim: Justice, guilt and veridical perception." Journal of Personality and Social Psychology, 20:127-135.

——— (1971b). "All the world loathes a loser." Psychology Today, (June):51-54, 66.

LERNER, M.J., and SIMMONS, C.H. (1966). "Observers' reactions to the 'innocent victim': Compassion or rejection?" Journal of Personality and Social Psychology, 4:203-210.

LERNER, M.J., and MATTHEWS, G. (1967). "Reactions to suffering of others under conditions of indirect responsibility." Journal of Personality and Social Psychology, 5:319-325.

LIBAI, D. (1969). "The protection of the child victim of a sexual offense in the criminal justice system." Wayne Law Review, 15:977-1032.

LORENZ, M.J. (1970). "Consumer fraud and the San Diego District Attorney's Office." San Diego Law Review, 8:47-61.

LUDWIG, K. (1970). "The case for repeal of the sex corroboration requirement in New York." Brooklyn Law Review, 36:378-386.

LYNCH, M.C. (1975). "Tough luck if you're ripped off." Wall Street Journal, August 7, p. 10.

MARX, G.T., and ARCHER, D. (1973). "The urban vigilante." Psychology Today, (January):45-50.

McCORKLE, L.W. (1954). "Resocialization within the walls." The Annals, 293(May):88-98.

McDONALD, W.F. (1973). "Prosecutorial decisions and case mortality at the initial screening." Unpublished paper delivered at the annual meeting of the American Criminological Society.

MEYER, L. (1973a). "78 swing for relief on notes: Home fraud victims ask return of cash." Washington Post, July 24, pp. C1, C3.

——— (1973b). "Judge voids home repair fraud debts." Washington Post, July 25, pp. B1, B5.

——— (1975). "Experts doubtful on crime control." Washington Post, August 3, pp. A1, A8.

Michigan, Governor's Study Commission on the Deviated Criminal Sex Offender (1951). Report. Lansing: State of Michigan.

MILLER, F. (1974). Prosecution: The decision to charge a suspect with a crime. Boston: Little, Brown.

MILLER, F.D. et al. (1975). "Innocence, culpability, and identification with the victim: A balance theory interpretation of the just world." Unpublished manuscript. Cambridge, Mass.: Harvard University.

Minnesota Restitution Center (1975). Interim research report. Unpublished paper (January 15). Minneapolis: Author.

——— (n.d.). "The Minnesota Restitution Center." Unpublished paper. Minneapolis: Author.

MORRIS, N. (1975). The future of imprisonment. Chicago: University of Chicago Press.

NADER, L. (1969). "Styles of court procedure: To make the balance." Pp. 69-91 in L. Nader (ed.), Law in culture and society. Chicago: Aldine.

National Advisory Commission on Criminal Justice Standards and Goals (1973). Courts. Washington, D.C.: U.S. Government Printing Office.

National Center for Dispute Settlement (1970). "Community dispute settlement rules." Unpublished paper. Washington, D.C.: American Arbitration Association.

National Commission on Law Observance and Enforcement (1931). Report on the cost of crime, No. 12. Washington, D.C.: U.S. Government Printing Office.

National Organization for Women (1973). "A report on rape in the suburbs. Chicago: Author.

——— (1974). Rape task force newsletter (March).

NELSON, W.E. (1967). "Emerging notions of modern criminal law in the Revolutionary era: An historical perspective." New York University Law Review, 42(May):450-482.

New York Citizen's Committee on the Control of Crime in New York (1939). The problem of sex offenses in New York City. New York.

New York University Law Review (1969). "Corroboration held necessary to prove sexual abuse in the third degree where underlying act is rape." 44:1025-1033.

NEWMAN, D.J. (1956). "Pleading guilty for considerations: A study of bargain justice." Journal of Criminal Law, Criminology and Police Science, 46(March-April):780-790.

NOBLE, J. (1975). "Women as the victims of crime." Unpublished manuscript. Canberra: Australian Institute of Criminology.

North Carolina Law Review (1972). "Private prosecution: The entrenched anomaly." 50(special issue, August):1171.

NUNES, D. (1975a). "After 2 years savers still await funds in Norfolk S&L collapse." Washington Post, May 10, pp. C1, C6.

——— (1975b). "Receiver aids S&L victims." Washington Post, May 11, pp. A1, A22.

POUND, R. (1953). The lawyer from antiquity to modern times. St. Paul, Minn.

President's Commission on Law Enforcement and Administration of Justice (1967a). The challenge of crime in a free society. Washington, D.C.: U.S. Government Printing Office.

——— (1967b). Task Force Report: Corrections. Washington, D.C.: U.S. Government Printing Office.

Prince George's County, Report of the Task Force to Study the Treatment of Victims of Sexual Assault (1973). Report. Maryland: Author.

Rape Crisis Center (1972). How to start a rape crisis center. Washington, D.C.: Author.

REIFER, D. (1958). "Protection of children involved in sexual offenses: A new method of investigation in Israel." Journal of Criminal Law, Criminology and Police Science, 49(3):222-229.

ROSENTHAL, A.M. (1964). Thirty-eight witnesses. New York: McGraw-Hill.

ROTHMAN, D.J. (1971). The discovery of the asylum. Boston: Little, Brown.

RUSSELL, D. (1975). "What citizens are doing to fight crime: Police aides—yes! vigilantes—no!" Parade, June 22, pp. 8-10.

RYAN, W. (1971). Blaming the victim. New York: Vintage.

SAAR, J. (1975a). "Check thieves prey on sick and aged." Washington Post, March 2, pp. A1, A15.

——— (1975b). "Traumatized family suffers after murder of a daughter." Washington Post, March 30, pp. A1, A14.

Sacramento, California, Police Department (1974). A seven-part program to improve the manner in which crime victims are handled by police and other agencies of the criminal justice and health care communities. Washington, D.C.: Police Foundation.

SANTARELLI, D.E. (1974). Address to the National Conference of State Criminal Justice Planning Administrators. Washington, D.C.: Department of Justice.

SCHAFER, S. (1968). The victim and his criminal. New York: Random House.

SCHULTZ, L.G. (1959). "Interviewing the sex offender's victims." Journal of Criminal Law, Criminology and Police Science, 50:448-452.

SCHUR, E. (1968). Law and society. New York: Random House.

SEVERO, R., and CAMPBELL, B. (1969). "Addicts' victims turn vigilante." New York Times, September 23, pp. 1, 34.

SEYFRET, S. (1974). "Help for the rape victim." Parade, May 26, p. 19.

SHIELD, C. (1932). "Offenses against young children." Editorial. London.

SMITH, H.A. (1970). "The legal aspects of child abuse." Southern Medical Bulletin, 58(3):19-21.

SMITH, R. (1972). "The rape victim's dilemma: How to react?" Washington Post, December 2, p. E1.

SOLOMON, T.; BERGER, D.; and PESSIRILO, G. (1970). The Mayor's Task Force on Child Abuse and Neglect. New York: Center for Community Research.

STOKOLS, D., and SCHAPLER, J. (1973). "Reactions to victims under conditions of situational detachment: The effects of responsibility, severity and expected future interaction." Journal of Personality and Social Psychology, 25:199-209.

STUMBO, L. (1972). "Rape: Does justice turn its head?" Los Angeles Times, March 12, p. E1.

SUBIN, H.I. (1966). Criminal justice in a metropolitan court. Washington, D.C.: Office of Criminal Justice, U.S. Department of Justice.

SUTHERLAND, E. (1950). "The diffusion of sexual psychopath laws." American Journal of Sociology, (September):142-148.

TAPPAN, P.W. (1950). The habitual sex offender: New Jersey report and recommendations of the Commission of the Habitual Sex Offender. Trenton: State of New Jersey.

TAYLOR, A. (1971). "The rape victim: Is she also the unintended victim of the law?" New York Times, June 15, p. C52.

U.S. Congress, Senate (1973). Post-White House Conference on Aging reports. Joint Committee Print, 93rd Congress, 1st session (September).

University of Pennsylvania Law Review (1968). "Police discretion and the judgement that a crime has been committed—Rape in Philadelphia." 117:277-322.

——— (1970). "The corroboration rule and crimes accompanying rape." 118:458-472.

VAN KREVELEN, D.A. (1960). "The child as victim." Fourth International Criminological Congress Papers. The Hague, 2(2).

Washington Post (1973). "D.C. law on rape scored." September 21, p. C1.

WATSON, D. (1975). "Trial of Joanne Little opens." Washington Post, July 15, p. A3.

WOOD, P.L. (1973). "The victim in a forcible rape case: A feminist view." American Criminal Law Review, 11:335-354.

White House Conference on Youth (1970). "Children in trouble." In White House Conference on Youth. Washington, D.C.: U.S. Government Printing Office.

Yale Law Journal (1950). "Psychiatric evaluation of the mentally abnormal witness." 59:1324-1341.

——— (1972). "The rape corroboration requirement: Repeal not reform." 81:1365-1391.

ZIEGENHAGEN, E. (1974). "Victims of violent crime in New York City: An exploratory survey of perceived needs." Unpublished report to the Crime Victim's Consultation Project, New York.

Chapter 2

THE VICTIM'S DECISION NOT TO INVOKE
THE CRIMINAL JUSTICE PROCESS

MICHAEL J. HINDELANG and
MICHAEL GOTTFREDSON

In recent years attention has been focused increasingly on the victims of criminal behavior. This attention is reflected in a rapidly growing body of literature concerning victims of crime (e.g., Drapkin and Viano, 1974; Schafer, 1968) and in recent legislation, particularly in the area of victim compensation (see for example, Edelhertz and Geis, 1974). At the same time, considerable interest has developed in viewing the criminal justice process in terms of key decision-points which arise throughout the process. One advantage of this conceptualization of the criminal justice system is that by focusing on decisions (e.g., the police decision to arrest or the prosecutor decision to charge), the interrelation of the various stages of the process becomes clear. That is, police decisions regarding arrests have profound impact on later stages of the criminal process and, hence, on later decisions. Because many decision makers can "filter" cases out of the system, decisions made at the earliest stages may have the greatest effect on the entire process; to a large degree prosecutorial decisions are constrained by the police decisions, and so forth.

Under this rationale, the victim, while not typically viewed in this fashion, is an important and influential criminal-justice decision maker. To a large extent, the victim, by reporting the victimization to the police, is the initiator of the criminal justice process. Thus, the victim's decision whether or not to report the victimization to the police is an important control on the input to the system. For most traditional crimes, the victim serves as the "gatekeeper" of the criminal justice system.

While the impact of victim reporting behavior on the criminal justice system is clear, the criminal justice system, in turn, may have considerable impact on both victims and the public at large. Thus, in order to understand more fully the impact that the victims of crime have as key decision makers in the criminal justice system, it may be important to examine these decisions in light of public attitudes toward the criminal justice system. The relationship between public attitudes about the system and public involvement with the system may give a clearer picture of the role played by victims in the process.

An expanding body of data exists concerning the public's attitudes toward, and involvement with, various aspects of the criminal justice system. Recently, a large number of national public opinion polls of relevance to criminal justice have been undertaken in the United States. Presidential commissions—e.g., on law enforcement and criminal justice (Ennis, 1967), marijuana and drug abuse (National Commission on Marijuana and Drug Abuse, 1972), violence (Mulvihill et al., 1969), and obscenity and pornography (President's Commission on Obscenity and Pornography, 1971)—have sponsored surveys which often serve as the basis for recommendations regarding critical policy issues. In addition to these governmental commissions, national polling organizations—in particular, the American Institute of Public Opinion (Gallup) and Louis Harris and Associates—often incorporate crime and criminal justice questions into their more general public opinion polls. Finally, recent victimization surveys, undertaken jointly by the Law Enforcement Assistance Administration (LEAA) and the Bureau of the Census, have generated extensive data regarding the involvement of victims with the criminal justice system. The aim of this chapter will be to review briefly some findings from these surveys in order to explore the impact of the criminal justice system on the public and, in turn, the impact of victims, by virtue of their crucial "gatekeeper" function, on the criminal justice system.

ATTITUDE SURVEYS

Fear of Crime and Victimization

The problem of crime in any society must be gauged not only by the actual extent and nature of criminal activity but also by public concern regarding crime. That is, regardless of actual levels of crime, public perceptions of crime may shape individual behavior and affect the quality of life; persons *perceiving* high levels of criminal activity may curtail their activities outside the home and may even feel unsafe within the home.[1]

A Gallup poll undertaken in 1948 asked respondents in large cities what they regarded as their city's "worst problem." In that poll, 4% listed crime as the worst problem. In 1972, 21% regarded crime as the worst problem.[2] Another question frequently asked in public opinion polls is, "Is there any area right around here—that is within a mile—where you would be afraid to walk alone at night?" In a 1965 survey (American Institute of Public Opinion, 1965), 17% of the men and 48% of the women responded affirmatively to this question. In 1972 (see Table 1), 20% of the males and 58% of the females responded affirmatively.

Table 1 shows that community size is strongly related to this fear; that is, a substantially greater percentage of those living in cities of more than one million in population, relative to those living in rural areas, report this fear (53% versus 24%). This table also shows that twice the percentage of those 50 years of age and older, as compared with those 18 to 20 years of age, answered this question affirmatively (49% versus 24%). Finally, the table shows that education and income are inversely related to this fear: those with less education and lower incomes are substantially more fearful than are those with more education and higher incomes.

Respondents in 1972 were also asked how safe and secure they felt in their homes at night.[3] Of all respondents, 17% reported that they did not feel safe and secure at night, even in their own home. More females than males (21% versus 12%), more persons with grade school educations than persons with college educations (23% versus 10%), and more persons with incomes under $3,000 than persons with incomes of $15,000 or more (25% versus 12%) did not feel safe and secure in their own homes at night. In summary, these and other data indicate that fear about one's own safety and security is related not only to characteristics associated with high crime areas (low income, low education, and large cities) but also to what seem to be "victim vulnerability" factors (for example, age and sex).

Respondents have also been asked whether the crime rate in their own neighborhoods increased in the past year. Surveys conducted in 1964 and 1973 revealed that 73% and 48% of the respondents, respectively, believed that in the past year the crime rate in their own neighborhood has been increasing.[4] For every year (1964, 1967, 1969, 1970, 1973) in which this question was asked, a substantial proportion of the respondents believed that the crime rate in the current year was greater than it has been in the previous year; in no year did more than 7% of the respondents believe that the crime rate was lower than it had been in the previous year. In sum, not only does a substantial proportion of the public have fear of crime, but each year a substantial proportion of the public perceive the crime problem to be increasing.

Table 1. FEAR OF WALKING ALONE AT NIGHT, BY DEMOGRAPHIC
CHARACTERISTICS, 1972 (in percentages)

Question: *"Is there any area right around here—that is, within a mile—where you would be afraid to walk home at night?"*

	Yes	No
National	41	59
Sex		
Male	20	80
Female	58	42
Race		
White	39	61
Nonwhite	49	51
Education		
College	30	70
High school	41	59
Grade school	52	48
Occupation		
Professional and business	30	70
White collar	46	54
Farmers	18	82
Manual	39	61
Age		
18-20 years	24	76
21-29 years	36	64
30-49 years	37	63
50 and over	49	51
Religion		
Protestant	41	59
Catholic	40	60
Jewish	_a	_a
Politics		
Republican	37	63
Democrat	45	55
Independent	35	65
Region		
East	41	59
Midwest	36	64
South	43	57
West	42	58
Income		
$15,000 and over	28	72
$10,000-$14,000	38	62
$ 7,000-$ 9,999	36	64
$ 5,000-$ 6,999	46	54
$ 3,000-$ 4,999	46	54
Under $3,000	58	42

Table 1 (continued)

	Yes	No
Community Size		
1,000,000 and over	53	47
500,000-999,999	43	57
50,000-499,999	49	51
2,500-49,999	42	58
Under 2,500, Rural	24	76

a. Percentages not reported because there were too few respondents in this category.

SOURCE: American Institute of Public Opinion, Study No. 861.

Public Attitudes Toward Criminal Justice Processing

A Harris survey conducted in 1970 asked respondents whether they believed that the American "system of law enforcement works to really discourage people from committing crime" (Louis Harris and Associates, 1970). More than half the nonwhite respondents and 7 out of 10 of the white respondents reported that they believed that our system does *not* discourage people from committing crime. In light of these views, it is not surprising that a later (1972) survey showed an overwhelming majority of Americans in favor of tougher responses to "crime and lawlessness." Table 2 shows that more than 4 out of 5 respondents believed that police and other law enforcement agencies "should be tougher than they are now in dealing with crime and lawlessness." Persons 18 to 20 years of age, nonwhites, and persons with incomes under $3,000 were less likely to support a "tougher" approach, but even among these respondents, about 7 out of 10 endorsed tougher law enforcement.

Not only are Americans strongly in favor of tougher law enforcement by the police, but they are also in favor of tougher judicial responses. In a 1969 survey respondents were asked, "In general, do you think the courts in this area deal too harshly or not harshly enough with criminals?" Although 2% of the respondents believed that the courts were too harsh, 75% believed that they were *not* harsh enough.[5]

In a 1972 poll, respondents were asked whether they were more likely or less likely to vote for a political candidate who advocated tougher sentences for law breakers. Among the respondents, 79% reported that they would be more likely to vote for such a candidate; more of those with grade school educations than those with high school educations (88% versus 71%) and more of those 50 years of age or older than those 18 to 24 years of age (88% versus 60%) were likely to endorse such a candidate. These data are unequivocal in demonstrating that the vast majority of the American public supports a tougher response on the part of the police and the courts to crime and criminals.

Table 2. BELIEF THAT POLICE SHOULD BE TOUGHER IN DEALING WITH CRIME
          AND LAWLESSNESS, BY DEMOGRAPHIC CHARACTERISTICS, 1972
          (in percentages)

Question: *"Which of the two statements, A or B, would you vote for?"*
A. I think the police and other law enforcement agencies in the U.S. *should* be
   tougher than they are now in dealing with crime and lawlessness.
B. I think the police and other law enforcement agencies in the U.S. *should not*
   be tougher than they are now in dealing with crime and lawlessness.

	A	B	Don't Know
National	83	14	3
Sex			
Male	81	16	3
Female	84	12	4
Race			
White	84	13	3
Nonwhite	72	23	5
Education			
College	78	17	5
High school	86	12	2
Grade school	79	16	5
Occupation			
Professional and business	80	15	5
White collar	81	15	4
Farmers	93	7	—
Manual	84	14	2
Age			
18-20 years	66	29	5
21-29 years	76	22	2
30-49 years	87	11	2
50 and over	85	10	5
Religion			
Protestant	86	11	3
Catholic	82	16	2
Jewish	—[a]	—[a]	—[a]
Politics			
Republican	90	7	3
Democrat	79	17	4
Independent	83	14	3
Region			
East	82	15	3
Midwest	85	13	2
South	84	10	6
West	78	19	3
Income			
$15,000 and over	88	8	4
$10,000-$14,999	86	11	3

Table 2 (continued)

	A	B	Don't Know
Income			
$7,000-$9,999	82	17	1
$5,000-$6,999	80	16	4
$3,000-$4,999	80	19	1
Under $3,000	73	17	10
Community Size			
1,000,000 and over	79	17	4
500,000-999,999	83	15	2
50,000-499,999	82	14	4
2,500-49,999	86	12	2
Under 2,500, Rural	84	12	4

a. Percentages not reported because there were too few respondents in this category.

SOURCE: American Institute of Public Opinion, Study No. 861.

The public opinion data reviewed here may have important implications for the criminal justice system especially when viewed in conjunction with victimization survey results. Several such surveys are reviewed below.

VICTIMIZATION SURVEYS

The President's Commission Survey

In 1966, the President's Commission on Law Enforcement and the Administration of Justice sponsored the first nationwide survey of criminal victimization. This survey of 10,000 households was undertaken by the National Opinion Research Center (NORC) of the University of Chicago. The NORC survey found that many victimizations were not reported to the police. For example, 35% of the robberies and aggravated assaults, 42% of the burglaries, 40% of the larcenies (over $50), and 11% of the vehicle thefts were not reported to the police (Ennis, 1967).

Table 3 shows the reasons given by respondents for not having reported the victimization to the police. The most common reasons given were that the "police couldn't do anything about the matter" (58%), the matter "was private, not criminal, affair" (41%), the victim was "not sure if the real offenders would be caught" (31%), and the "police wouldn't want to be bothered" (28%).[6] We will return to these results after a detailed examination of some more recent victimization results.

The LEAA-Census Bureau Surveys

The National Crime Panel (NCP) victimization surveys are a joint effort of the LEAA and the Bureau of the Census. There are two distinct parts to the

Table 3. REASONS FOR NOT NOTIFYING POLICE AMONG THOSE
          NOT REPORTING INCIDENT[a] (in percentages)

Reasons For Not Notifying Police	Mentioned At All
1. Did not want to take time	13
2. Did not want to harm offender	12
3. Afraid of reprisal	5
4. Was private, not criminal, affair	41
5. Police couldn't do anything about matter	58
6. Police wouldn't want to be bothered	28
7. Didn't know how or if they should notify police	6
8. Too confused or upset to notify police	6
9. Not sure if real offenders would be caught	31
10. Fear of insurance cancellation	1
N = 1,017	

a. Because respondents could have given more than one reason, the percentages sum to
more than 100%.

SOURCE: P.H. Ennis, *Criminal Victimization in the United States,* Field Survey II (1967),
Table 24.

NCP—the national sample and the city samples. The NCP national sample
involves interviews with national probability samples of approximately 10,000
households (about 25,000 individuals) and 1,500 businesses each month. In a
period of 6 months, then, about 60,000 households and 9,000 businesses are
surveyed. Every 6 months respondents are reinterviewed; thus, members of
60,000 households (about 150,000 persons) and 9,000 businesses are interviewed twice in one calendar year.

In the NCP city samples the design is less complex. Interviews with household
members and businesses have been conducted in 26 cities in the U.S. In each of
these cities, 10,000 households (about 25,000 individuals) and 2,000 businesses
have been surveyed. In the NCP city samples, respondents are interviewed only
once, rather than on a continuing basis.

In both the national and the city samples all household members 12 years of
age and older are included in the sample. Each of the eligible household
respondents is personally interviewed[7] about victimizations that he or she
may have suffered during the reference period.[8] In addition, the household
respondent, a person knowledgeable about the affairs of the household, reports
on victimizations suffered by the household. In the business portion of the
survey a respondent who is knowledgeable about the affairs of the business
reports on business victimizations. For each victimization that is reported to the
survey interviewer, a series of detailed questions is asked. The analysis that
follows is focused on those questions relating to whether or not the
victimization was reported to the police.

The personal crimes that fall within the scope of the survey are rape, robbery, aggravated assault, and larceny from the person; specifically excluded is homicide. Household crimes include burglary, larceny from the household, and vehicle theft. Business crimes include robbery and burglary; excluded are thefts of business vehicles and business larcenies, such as shoplifting and employee theft.

The NCP survey results discussed here are *estimates* of population parameters that are based on the sample results; hence, these estimates include a certain amount of sampling error. However, because of the large number of sample cases, the sampling errors for most of the estimates presented here are small. Results from both the national sample and the city samples will be presented and discussed below.

EXTENT AND NATURE OF NONREPORTING TO THE POLICE

The NCP National Results

As noted above, all respondents who reported to the interviewer that they had been a victim of one of the survey crimes during the reference period were asked: "Were the police informed of this incident in any way?" The validity of the responses to this question—and to all other questions in the survey—depends upon the victim's willingness and ability to give accurate responses. In connection with this particular question, respondents may have been reluctant to tell interviewers that they did not report the victimization to the police, or they may have believed erroneously that someone else had reported the victimization to the police, etc. Hence, it should be noted that the rates of nonreporting discussed below are subject to these kinds of measurement difficulties.

Table 4 shows that the rate of nonreporting of victimizations to the police varies tremendously according to the type of crime. For example, completed vehicle theft and business robbery have very low rates of nonreporting (13% and 14%, respectively), while household larceny of items worth less than $50 and attempted purse snatching have extremely high rates of nonreporting (85% and 83%, respectively). In general, business victimizations have a lower rate of nonreporting than either personal or household victimizations. For example, business robbery has a nonreporting rate of 14% compared to a rate of 47% for personal robbery; similarly, the rate of nonreporting for business burglary is 21%, compared to 53% for household burglary. An examination of Table 4 makes it clear that completed victimizations had lower rates of nonreporting than attempted victimizations and victimizations that did not involve force. The elements of the victimization and the characteristics of the victim that are associated with nonreporting will be considered in more detail below.

Table 4. Estimated Number of Personal, Household, and Business Victimizations, by Reporting to Police, United States, 1973[a]

Type of victimization	Total Number	Total Percent	Reported to police Number	Reported to police Percent	Not reported to police Number	Not reported to police Percent	Don't know whether reported to police Number	Don't know whether reported to police Percent
Personal victimizations:								
Rape and attempted rape	159,670	100	69,920	44	89,740	56	10	0
Robbery	1,120,110	100	576,500	51	528,600	47	15,010	1
Robbery and attempted robbery with injury	385,940	100	289,720	62	189,020	36	7,200	2
Serious assault	210,330	100	148,990	71	57,640	27	3,700	2
Minor assault	175,610	100	90,730	52	81,380	46	3,500	2
Robbery without injury	416,060	100	234,430	56	179,570	43	2,060	0
Attempted robbery without injury	318,110	100	102,350	32	210,010	66	5,750	2
Assault	4,213,840	100	1,817,870	43	2,347,140	56	48,830	1
Aggravated assault	1,681,190	100	868,550	52	790,010	47	22,630	1
With injury	545,340	100	323,860	59	213,750	39	7,740	1
Attempted assault with weapon	1,135,850	100	544,700	48	576,260	51	14,890	1
Simple assault	2,532,650	100	949,320	37	1,557,130	61	26,200	1
With injury	625,570	100	294,100	47	326,530	52	4,940	1
Attempted assault without weapon	1,907,080	100	665,220	34	1,230,600	65	21,260	1
Personal larceny with contact	512,350	100	165,550	32	342,140	67	4,660	1
Purse snatching	106,170	100	51,820	49	53,140	50	1,210	1
Attempted purse snatching	72,850	100	12,060	17	60,800	83	0	0
Pocket picking	333,330	100	101,670	31	228,200	68	3,460	1
Personal larceny without contact	14,275,650	100	3,038,000	21	11,032,030	77	205,620	1
Household victimizations:								
Burglary	6,433,030	100	2,946,490	46	3,429,190	53	57,350	1
Forcible entry	2,043,670	100	1,437,990	70	583,380	29	22,300	1
Unlawful entry without force	2,955,390	100	1,071,580	36	1,860,980	63	22,830	1
Attempted forcible entry	1,433,970	100	436,910	30	984,830	69	12,230	1
Larceny	7,590,750	100	1,872,530	25	5,663,620	75	54,590	1
Under $50	4,887,190	100	729,550	15	4,131,540	85	26,100	1
$50 or more	1,887,010	100	976,960	52	891,210	47	18,850	1
Amount not ascertained	271,480	100	54,700	20	208,360	77	8,410	3
Attempted	545,070	100	111,380	20	432,610	79	1,230	0
Vehicle theft	1,330,470	100	893,940	67	427,570	32	8,970	1
Completed	865,260	100	747,030	86	114,780	13	3,450	0
Attempted	465,220	100	146,910	32	312,780	67	5,520	1
Business victimizations:								
Robbery	264,113	100	225,446	85	37,133	14	1,534	1
Burglary	1,384,998	100	1,093,306	79	288,638	21	3,054	0

a. Subcategories may not sum to total because of rounding.

SOURCE: M.J. Hindelang, C.S. Dunn, L.P. Sutton, and A.L. Aumick *Sourcebook of Criminal Justice Statistics, 1974* (Washington, D.C.: U.S. Government Printing Office, 1975).

The reasons given by respondents for not reporting personal and household victimizations to the police can be examined in Table 5. The categories of reasons given for not reporting victimizations to the police are rather broad and somewhat ambiguous. For example, "nothing could be done" has several possible interpretations. In an assault, for instance, this reason may reflect the victim's belief that the physical harm done cannot be rectified or, alternatively, his or her belief that an unknown assailant—whom the victim may not be able to identify—could not be apprehended. The response "police wouldn't want to be bothered" may mean that the victimization was so minor that the victim was reluctant to request police involvement; on the other hand, it could mean that the victim believed that the police would simply be uninterested in his or her victimization, even if it is relatively serious. Also, "victimization was reported to someone else" may mean that it was reported to a different official agency, a private security guard, a teacher, a friend or relative who will take matters into his or her own hands, etc. Finally, the "other" category contains a large proportion of the reasons given, indicating that more refinement of the response categories is required. Although these and other difficulties in the reasons given for not reporting do exist, the data are still quite informative.

Table 5 shows that although the reasons given for not reporting victimizations to the police vary considerably by type of crime, in general the most common reasons are "nothing could be done" and "victimization not important enough." For rape and attempted rape, the belief that the victimization "was a private matter" (37%) and the "fear of reprisal" (21%) were noted quite frequently, while "victimization not important enough" (7%) was rarely stated. For assaults, the belief that the event was a "private matter" (23%) was cited quite frequently. These reasons given for not reporting rapes and assaults reflect, in part, the fact that one-quarter of the rapes and two-fifths of the assaults were committed by persons who were known to the victim.[9]

In general, the reason most often given for not reporting crimes against the household and crimes of personal larceny was that "nothing could be done." In this regard, it is interesting to note that this reasoning is probably quite realistic. These are the very offenses for which the *Uniform Crime Reports* show the lowest clearance rates—less than 20% (Kelley, 1973).

It may be of further interest to examine characteristics of the incident and the victim that are associated with failure to report victimizations to the police. Data bearing on these relationships are available for some of the NCP city samples—in particular, for Atlanta, Baltimore, Cleveland, Dallas, Denver, Newark, Portland (Oregon), and St. Louis.

Table 5. Reasons Given for Not Reporting Personal and Household Victimizations to the Police, United States, 1973[a]

Type of victimization	Total victimizations not reported	Nothing could be done Number	Per-cent[b]	Victimization not important enough Number	Per-cent[b]	Police wouldn't want to be bothered Number	Per-cent[b]	Did not want to take time Number	Per-cent[b]	It was a private matter Number	Per-cent[b]	Fear of reprisal Number	Per-cent[b]	Victimization was reported to someone else Number	Per-cent[b]	Other Number	Per-cent[b]	Not ascertained Number	Per-cent[b]
Personal victimization:																			
Rape and attempted rape	89,740	20,170	22	6,710	7	9,070	10	5,670	6	33,310	37	19,080	21	8,510	9	34,380	38	0	0
Robbery	528,600	216,750	41	121,590	21	59,290	11	21,810	5	63,550	12	33,020	6	59,340	11	118,040	22	3,300	1
Robbery and attempted robbery with injury	139,020	52,530	38	20,960	15	13,760	10	8,910	6	32,250	23	10,750	8	13,600	10	32,690	24	1,030	1
Serious assault	57,640	19,520	34	8,960	16	6,950	12	6,840	12	13,470	23	3,450	6	3,120	5	21,970	38	0	0
Minor assault	81,380	33,010	41	12,000	15	6,810	8	2,070	3	18,790	23	7,300	9	10,480	13	10,720	13	1,030	1
Robbery without injury	179,570	82,200	46	39,320	22	16,900	9	8,830	5	17,520	10	11,640	6	24,420	14	39,310	22	950	1
Attempted robbery without injury	210,010	82,020	39	64,310	31	28,630	14	7,070	3	13,770	7	10,630	5	21,320	10	46,040	22	1,320	1
Assault	2,347,140	446,720	19	848,370	36	166,230	7	83,670	4	543,110	23	104,010	4	354,510	15	500,150	21	24,700	1
Aggravated assault	790,010	180,500	23	217,300	28	63,850	8	24,750	3	207,390	26	44,840	6	93,360	12	191,120	24	8,590	1
With injury	213,750	48,720	23	43,030	20	16,050	8	3,530	2	72,210	34	16,050	8	27,980	13	57,900	27	0	0
Attempted assault with weapon	576,260	131,780	23	174,270	30	47,800	8	21,220	4	135,180	23	28,790	5	65,380	11	133,220	23	8,590	1
Simple assault	1,557,130	266,220	17	631,070	41	102,380	7	58,920	4	335,780	22	59,170	4	261,150	17	309,030	20	16,110	1
With injury	326,530	46,870	14	78,420	24	17,590	5	9,070	3	102,480	31	24,020	7	73,820	23	66,110	20	2,080	1
Attempted assault without weapon	1,230,600	219,350	18	552,650	45	84,790	7	49,850	4	233,240	19	35,150	3	187,330	15	242,920	20	14,030	1
Personal larceny with contact	342,140	185,350	54	60,820	18	16,310	5	19,760	6	20,890	6	11,090	3	48,670	14	67,500	20	2,370	1
Purse snatching	53,140	23,950	45	9,110	17	2,470	5	5,710	11	2,230	4	3,420	6	14,270	27	10,140	19	0	0
Attempted purse snatching	60,600	24,310	40	19,790	33	2,080	3	3,510	6	990	2	4,430	7	3,220	5	20,230	33	0	0
Pocket picking	228,200	137,090	60	31,920	14	11,760	5	10,560	5	17,670	8	3,240	1	31,180	14	37,130	16	2,370	1
Personal larceny without contact	11,032,030	4,562,790	41	4,005,520	36	790,710	7	455,380	4	338,540	3	37,240	0	2,924,230	27	1,265,800	11	118,470	1
Household victimization:																			
Burglary	3,429,190	1,636,780	48	1,116,550	33	343,690	10	109,000	3	243,980	7	48,490	1	285,000	8	716,100	21	28,400	1
Forcible entry	583,380	240,090	41	162,290	28	76,040	13	25,120	4	66,610	11	11,990	2	51,980	9	148,710	25	6,800	1
Unlawful entry without force	1,860,980	932,770	50	569,110	31	138,750	7	54,190	3	156,940	8	21,600	1	145,680	8	375,660	20	11,160	1
Attempted forcible entry	984,820	463,920	47	385,150	39	108,910	11	29,690	3	20,430	2	14,900	2	87,350	9	191,720	19	10,440	1
Larceny	5,663,620	2,740,890	48	2,565,020	45	626,490	11	167,790	3	385,160	7	33,000	1	202,190	4	805,580	14	40,910	1
Under $50	4,131,540	1,916,330	46	2,179,030	53	458,250	11	121,710	3	249,760	6	24,540	1	122,720	3	467,250	11	26,290	1
$50 or more	891,210	522,670	59	129,670	15	103,080	12	31,310	4	100,950	11	8,450	1	47,650	5	218,700	25	6,250	1
Amount not ascertained	208,360	96,950	47	80,640	39	23,750	11	6,350	3	10,380	5	0	0	12,840	6	26,090	13	6,320	3
Vehicle theft	432,510	204,930	47	175,880	41	41,400	10	8,430	2	24,070	6	0	0	18,990	4	93,530	22	2,060	0
Completed	427,570	214,220	50	132,790	31	37,830	9	23,830	6	40,570	9	0	0	16,770	4	105,530	25	2,160	1
Attempted	114,780	28,370	25	14,880	13	4,160	4	3,240	3	37,450	33	0	0	3,280	3	47,690	42	2,170	1

a. Subcategories may not sum to total because of rounding. Because respondents may have given more than one reason for not reporting the victimization to the police, the row sum of the reasons for not reporting may exceed 100.

b. Less than 0.5 percent.

SOURCE: M.J. Hindelang, C.S. Dunn, L.P. Sutton, and A.L. Aumick *Sourcebook of Criminal Justice Statistics, 1974* (Washington, D.C.: U.S. Government Printing Office, 1975).

NCP City Samples

In general, factors bearing on the seriousness of the victimization are strongly related to reporting behavior. It is clear from Table 6 that in these eight cities the decision not to report victimizations to the police is closely associated with whether the victimization was completed or was only attempted. For each category of personal, household, and business victimization, completed victimizations were more often reported to the police than were attempted victimizations. This difference is especially notable for vehicle theft (6% versus 64%) as well as for business robbery (3% versus 29%) and business burglary (17% versus 43%). It is also of interest that—with the exception of business victimizations—the majority of *attempted* victimizations were not reported to the police; in fact, for crimes of personal and household larceny, only a small minority of the attempted victimizations were reported to the police.

Another indicator of the seriousness of the victimization that is associated with the decision not to report the victimization to the police is whether a weapon was used or not.

Table 6. ESTIMATED PERCENTAGE OF NONREPORTED PERSONAL, HOUSEHOLD, AND BUSINESS VICTIMIZATION, BY COMPLETED VERSUS ATTEMPTED, EIGHT CITIES AGGREGATE

	Completed	Attempted
Personal		
Rape	34%	54%
	(570)	(2,760)
Aggravated Assault	40%	53%
	(6,800)	(17,010)
Simple Assault	55%	70%
	(7,490)	(29,780)
Robbery	38%	67%
	(18,140)	(12,620)
Larceny With Contact	55%	80%
	(25,740)	(4,340)
Household		
Burglary	37%	68%
	(60,721)	(36,842)
Larceny	69%	79%
	(416,470)	(41,320)
Vehicle Theft	6%	64%
	(46,450)	(19,240)
Business		
Burglary	17%	43%
	(13,049)	(13,012)
Robbery	3%	29%
	(14,400)	(4,585)

Table 7 shows that if a weapon was used, the victim was more likely to report to the police than if the offender(s) did not have a weapon. In rapes, for example, one-third of the "weapon-present" but more than one-half of the "no weapon present" victimizations were not reported. Similarly, for assaults, less than half of the "weapon-present" but two-thirds of the "no weapon present" victimizations were not reported to the police. It is noteworthy that the presence of a weapon in business robberies appears to have made more of a difference in reporting than did the presence of a weapon in personal robberies. This may well be due to the fact that when a weapon was used in a business robbery it was a gun 9 out of 10 times, while for those personal robberies in which a weapon was used it was a gun about half the time.

In addition to the factors of completed-attempted and weapon-no weapon, the consequences of the crime to the victim—especially physical injury and monetary loss—are also associated with failure to report the victimization to the police. For each category of personal victimization, those that involved injury to the victim had lower rates of nonreporting than those that did not involve injury to the victim. For instance, in aggravated assaults that involved injury, 37% were not reported to the police, while in those that did not involve injury 51% were not reported to the police.[10] For rape, the comparable figures were 42% and 54%.

In general, as the amount of monetary loss resulting from the victimization increased, the rate of nonreporting to the police decreased. In business burglaries, for example, the overall rate of nonreporting to the police was 24%. However, for losses of less than $50 the nonreporting rate was 39%; for losses of $50-$249 the rate was 19%; and for losses of $250 or more the rate was 5%. A similar trend is apparent for business robbery, in which the respective rates of nonreporting for the three categories of loss are 18%, 2%, and 1%.

Table 7. ESTIMATED PERCENTAGE OF NONREPORTED PERSONAL AND BUSINESS
VICTIMIZATIONS BY PRESENCE OF A WEAPON, EIGHT CITIES AGGREGATE[a]

	With Weapon	No Weapon	Total
Personal			
Robbery	40%	54%	47%
	(34,910)	(31,280)	(66,190)
Assault	49%	66%	58%
	(47,680)	(57,800)	(105,560)
Rape	33%	55%	49%
	(1,811)	(5,018)	(6,829)
Business			
Robbery	5%	22%	8%
	(14,630)	(2,571)	(17,201)

a. Subcategories may not sum to total due to rounding.

So far, our analysis of completed-attempted, weapon-no weapon, injury, and loss has shown that these characteristics are associated with failure to report victimizations to the police. It should be noted that these characteristics are not independent. That is, although some completed victimizations may involve no financial loss, attempted victimizations cannot involve financial loss. Likewise, attempted victimizations cannot involve injury. When an injury or an actual theft occurs, by definition, the victimization has been completed. In addition, the presence of a weapon is correlated with the completion of the crime. Although these factors are interrelated, in general the separate factors do have independent effects on the failure to report victimizations to the police.

While an examination of the simultaneous effects of all possible combinations of these factors is beyond the scope of this chapter, some indication of the joint effects of these variables can be seen in the tree diagram presented in Figure 1. In this figure, the estimated percentages of nonreported victimizations for all personal victimizations combined (e.g., rape, robbery, assault, and personal larceny) are shown under various conditions. For all attempted personal victimizations, 65% were not reported, whereas the corresponding figure for completed personal crimes was 46%. Among attempted victimizations, 55% of those in which a weapon was present were not reported, while 72% in which a weapon was not present were not reported. Similarly, there are important differences in nonreporting rates for completed victimizations according to whether a weapon was used: 36% of the completed victimizations in which a weapon was used, as opposed to 52% in which no weapon was used, were not reported to the police. This figure indicates (and much more detailed analyses not presented here substantiate) that, in general, the factors discussed in this section have independent effects on nonreporting.

Victim Characteristics and Failure to Report

It may be that characteristics not only of the victimization but also of the victim are associated with nonreporting. Of those characteristics of the victim available for analysis (age, race, sex, family income, marital status, employment, and educational level), age in general was most strongly related to failure to report victimizations to the police. Typically, those victims under 35 years of age had higher rates of nonreporting than did those victims over 35.

Because the type of victimization is so closely associated with the rate of nonreporting, the type of victimization must be controlled in examining victim characteristics associated with nonreporting. As an illustration, Table 8 shows rates of nonreporting for personal robbery by the age and race of the victim. For both whites and black/others[11] there is a monotonic decrease in the rate of nonreporting as age increases. For whites, the rate drops from 68% in the 12-19

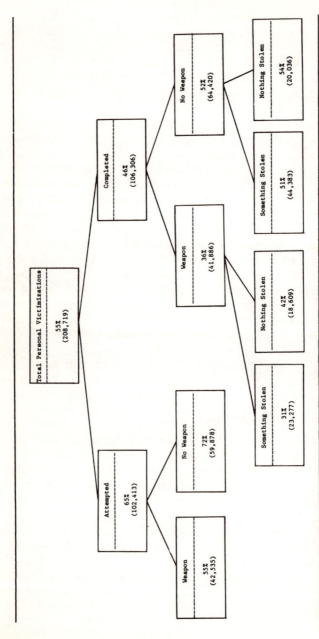

Figure 1. ESTIMATED PERCENTAGES OF NONREPORTED PERSONAL VICTIMIZATIONS FOR SELECTED CHARACTERISTICS OF VICTIMIZATIONS, EIGHT CITIES AGGREGATE

Table 8. ESTIMATED PERCENTAGE OF NONREPORTED PERSONAL ROBBERIES BY AGE AND RACE, EIGHT CITIES AGGREGATE[a]

Race	12-19	20-34	35 or Older	Total
White	68%	43%	36%	47%
	(11,630)	(9,890)	(16,130)	(37,650)
Black/Other	58%	44%	34%	44%
	(8,740)	(8,840)	(12,280)	(29,860)
Total	64%	43%	35%	46%
	(20,370)	(18,730)	(28,410)	(67,510)

a. Subtotals may not sum to totals due to rounding.

age group to 36% in the 35 or older age group, and for black/others the respective decrease is from 58% to 34%. Table 8 also shows that racial differences in the rates of nonreporting are apparent only in the youngest group, in which the rate of nonreporting for whites was higher than that for black/others (68% versus 58%).

Table 9 examines the joint effect that family income and the race of the head of the household have on rates of nonreporting for household burglary. The table shows that there is a tendency among both racial groups for rates of nonreporting to decrease gradually as income increases. For whites, the rate of nonreporting falls from 52% in the lowest income group to 40% in the highest; for black/others the pattern is comparable, except that there is an upturn in the

Table 9. ESTIMATED PERCENTAGE OF NONREPORTED HOUSEHOLD BURGLARIES, BY RACE AND FAMILY INCOME, EIGHT CITY AGGREGATE[a]

	White	Black/Other	Total
Under $3,000	52%	44%	48%
	(18,250)	(20,620)	(38,870)
$3,000-$7,499	47%	44%	46%
	(33,650)	(32,780)	(66,430)
$7,500-$9,999	49%	40%	46%
	(15,990)	(8,960)	(24,950)
$10,000-$14,999	45%	34%	42%
	(26,470)	(11,730)	(38,200)
$15,000-$24,999	47%	35%	44%
	(16,720)	(5,420)	(22,140)
$25,000 or more	40%	40%	40%
	(8,690)	(720)	(9,410)
Total	47%	41%	45%
	(119,770)	(80,230)	(200,000)

a. Subtotals may not sum to total due to rounding.

Table 10. ESTIMATED PERCENTAGE OF NONREPORTED PERSONAL
          VICTIMIZATIONS BY PRIOR RELATIONSHIP BETWEEN VICTIM
          AND OFFENDER, EIGHT CITIES AGGREGATE

	Stranger	*Nonstranger*
Rape	48%	52%
	(2,490)	(840)
Robbery	46%	50%
	(27,790)	(2,970)
Assault		
Aggravated	48%	48%
	(16,470)	(7,340)
Simple	68%	64%
	(25,410)	(11,860)
Larceny With Contact	58%	74%
	(29,060)	(1,030)

rate of nonreporting for the highest income group.[12] Racial comparisons within income categories show, in general, that whites have a slightly higher rate of nonreporting for burglary than do black/others.

One final characteristic of personal victimizations that may be a correlate of nonreporting is the prior relationship between the victim and the offender. Offenders in all victimizations reported to the survey interviewers were categorized as either "strangers" or "nonstrangers." Strangers were those offenders who were unknown to the victim or known by sight only.[13] Nonstrangers included those offenders who were relatives, well known, or casual acquaintances. Table 10 shows that for personal victimizations, with the exception of larceny with contact, there was no substantial relation between the prior relationship of the victim and the offender and the rates of nonreporting.

Overall, characteristics of the victim and the victim-offender relationship were found to be less strongly associated with nonreporting than were characteristics of the event. The victim's age was the victim characteristic most strongly related to nonreporting; the race and income of the victim were found to be only slightly related to nonreporting.[14]

DISCUSSION

The public opinion data presented in the first section of this paper can be summarized briefly. Between 1948 and 1972 the percentage of residents of large cities who viewed crime as their city's "worst problem" increased sharply. Further, by 1972 one-fifth of the men and three-fifths of the women reported that they were fearful of walking alone at night in areas as close to their homes as one mile. In 1964 nearly three-quarters, and in 1973 nearly one-half, of the

Americans polled believed that in the past year the crime rate in their own neighborhood had been increasing. All these findings indicate quite clearly that crime and its consequences are very salient to many Americans.

In light of this concern and the belief that crime in one's own neighborhood is increasing, it is not surprising that most Americans favor tougher responses by the police and other law enforcement agencies to "crime and lawlessness." These attitudes are consistent with the 1972 finding that 79% of a national sample reported that they would be likely to vote for a candidate who advocated tougher sentences for lawbreakers.

In view of these findings it may seem incongruous that the rates of nonreporting of personal and household victimizations to the police—as found in the LEAA-Census Bureau national victimization surveys—are so high. That is, if public concern about crime is so high, why is it that so many victims, when confronted with an opportunity to invoke the criminal justice process, fail to do so?

Among reasons for nonreporting, the reasons "nothing could be done" and "victimization not important enough" were the predominant reasons given for not reporting household and personal victimizations to the police. An examination of the *Uniform Crime Reports* clearance rates shows that clearances of all index offenses have been steadily declining. For example, between 1960 and 1973 the clearance rate for burglary fell from about 30% to less than 20%. For robbery the decline was from more than 40% to less than 25%, and for forcible rape the clearance rate fell from 70% to 50%. It seems to have become common public knowledge that for many types of victimizations—in particular, less serious victimizations—the police are unable to do anything more than take a report of the crime. Thus, the belief that "nothing could be done" may be quite realistic for many victimizations. If victims become increasingly dissatisfied with what the police are able to do, they may fail increasingly to report victimizations to the police. Although the LEAA-Census Bureau National Crime Panel surveys will shortly be able to provide trend data on the failure of victims to report victimization to the police, no strictly comparable statistics on this trend now exist. However, the NORC survey found that, in 1965-1966, robbery and aggravated assault had the same rates of nonreporting, 35%, while the LEAA-Census Bureau national survey in 1973 showed that both robbery and aggravated assault had rates of 47%. While there are many methodological differences between the two surveys, these findings are consonant with the hypothesis that rates of nonreporting—at least for these two crimes—are increasing. Confirmation of the hypothesis must await future National Crime Panel results.

The other major reason given for not reporting victimizations to the police was that the crime was not important enough. This subjective assessment by the victim appears to be borne out by our analysis of characteristics of the victimization that are associated with nonreporting. For example, victimizations that are not reported involve, disproportionately, attempted crimes or crimes without weapons, without loss, or without injury. In fact, it was found that these elements were more important in accounting for nonreporting than were characteristics of the victim or the prior relationship between the victim and the offender.

As was mentioned earlier in this chapter, increasing attention has been given to decisions made at various points in the criminal justice system and the effect that decisions made at prior points can have on subsequent processing. The flow of cases through the criminal justice system can be dramatically altered at any of the decision-points in the system. From this view it follows that decisions made at the earliest point in the system have the greatest potential for affecting the system. For this reason, in part, the police have been viewed by many as the most important link in the system because of the impact that their decisions can have on the rest of the system; in general, no subsequent decisions can be made about cases that the police choose not to process (LaFave, 1965; Goldstein, 1960). In viewing the total criminal justice system, however, it seems more appropriate to conceive of the victim, rather than the police, as the initial decision maker. The data on nonreporting presented here demonstrate that victims of assault and common theft exercise substantial discretion not to invoke the criminal justice process.

The importance of the victim's discretion whether to report a victimization to the police is enhanced by the finding that urban policing is much more reactive than proactive. For example, Reiss (1971:96) found in Chicago that about 95% of criminal incidents known to the police came to the attention of the police through citizen initiative. Data from the National Crime Panel victimization surveys are consistent with Reiss' finding regarding the reactive nature of policing. Of all victimizations reported to survey interviewers in the eight cities discussed above, only 3% came to the attention of the police as a result of the police being "on the scene." Clearly, for the vast majority of these victimizations, if it were not for the victim contacting the police, the criminal justice system would not become involved in the event.[15]

Reiss (1971:67-70) has argued that it is the "civic responsibility" of victims to report criminal matters to the police; otherwise, the system may be "subverted." It could be argued that it is the duty of citizens to report all victimizations to the police or that victims should have no discretion with regard to invoking the criminal process. While for "accounting" or measurement purposes it would certainly be beneficial to gauge precisely the parameters of criminal victimizations, full reporting would have serious negative consequences for the system of justice. Just as full enforcement by the police or full prosecution by district attorneys would hopelessly snarl the system, so too would complete reporting by victims—especially if victims expected the police to try to do something about the victimization. As with other criminal-justice decision makers, the question then becomes whether or not victims are appropriately exercising their discretion.

The victimization survey results indicate that less serious victimizations are disproportionately not reported to the police. If—other things being equal—a greater proportion of these less serious victimizations were to be reported to the police, the criminal justice system would be less able to deal efficiently and effectively with all reported crimes, even the most serious. Further, because of the competition for scarce resources, it would undoubtedly be the case that criminal-justice decision makers at each subsequent point in the system would disproportionately shunt these less serious cases out of the system.

The centrality of crime and criminal justice to the lives of many Americans seems to be increasing. The formal social control mechanisms which have been erected in response to the problem of crime continue to be strongly influenced by the public, not only through political processes but also through the public's willingness to invoke the criminal justice process.

NOTES

1. In the discussions of survey results that follow, all data apply to national probability samples, unless otherwise noted.

2. "Large cities" is not defined in the original report. For a reprint of the table giving the 1948 results, see Hindelang et al. (1975:171).

3. For the entire table, see Hindelang et al. (1975:176).

4. See Hindelang et al. (1975). The change from 73% to 48% in the 1964-1973 period is largely accounted for by a greater percentage of respondents in the latter year than in the former year who believed that the crime rate had remained the same.

5. See Hindelang et al. (1974). In this survey, 13% thought that the courts dealt "about right" with criminals and 10% had no opinion.

6. Because respondents could have given more than one reason, the percentages sum to more than 100%.

7. Proxy respondents are used for 12- and 13-year-old respondents and for respondents who are physically or mentally unable to respond for themselves.

8. In the national sample the reference period is the six months preceding the interview and in the city samples it is the twelve months preceding the interview.

9. The relevant figures may be found in Hindelang (1976:176). Analysis of some NCP city data, while not shown here, revealed no substantial differences in reasons given for not reporting victimizations to the police by such variables as age and race of respondent. Some fluctuation was found in such factors as attempted versus completed crimes, however; the

reason given for not reporting completed victimizations was less likely to be that the event was unimportant and more likely to be that nothing could be done about it.

10. An assault is categorized as "aggravated" if the offender had a weapon, whether or not an injury resulted. An assault is also categorized as "aggravated" if a serious injury resulted.

11. Because races other than black and white constitute too small a proportion of the total population in these eight cities to permit separate analyses, black and "other" races are combined for analytic purposes and are referred to as black/others. In these cities, blacks constitute more than 90% of the black/others group.

12. Note, however, that there are very few black/others in the highest income group.

13. If the victim did not know whether the offender was someone he or she knew—e.g., the offender was not seen by the victim—the offender was categorized as a "stranger."

14. Race and income were not as strongly related to nonreporting for other types of victimization as they were for burglary.

15. For other types of crimes, in particular those which are monitored by regulatory agencies, the victim's role as an initiator of the process may be less critical.

REFERENCES

American Institute of Public Opinion (1965). Study No. 709. Princeton, N.J.: Author.
——— (1972). Study No. 861. Princeton, N.J.: Author.
DRAPKIN, I., and VIANO, E. (1974). Victimology. Lexington, Mass.: D.C. Heath.
EDELHERTZ, H., and GEIS, G. (1974). Public compensation to victims of crime. New York: Praeger.
ENNIS, P.H. (1967). Criminal victimization in the United States (Field Survey II. A report of a National Survey. President's Commission on Law Enforcement and Administration of Justice). Washington, D.C.: U.S. Government Printing Office.
GOLDSTEIN, J. (1960). "Police discretion not to invoke the criminal process: Low-visibility decisions in the administration of justice." Yale Law Review, 69(March):543-588.
Harris, Louis, and Associates (1970). Study No. 2043. New York: Author.
HINDELANG, M.J. (1976). Criminal victimization in eight American cities: A descriptive analysis of common theft and assault. Cambridge, Mass.: Ballinger.
HINDELANG, M.J.; DUNN, C.S.; SUTTON, L.P.; and AUMICK, A.L. (1974). Sourcebook of criminal justice statistics, 1973. Washington, D.C.: U.S. Government Printing Office.
——— (1975). Sourcebook of criminal justice statistics, 1974. Washington, D.C.: U.S. Government Printing Office.
KELLEY, C. (1973). Crime in the United States. Washington, D.C.: Federal Bureau of Investigation.
LaFAVE, W.R. (1965). Arrest: The decision to take a suspect into custody. Boston: Little, Brown.
MULVIHILL, D.J.; TUMIN, M., and CURTIS, L. (1969). Crimes of violence. Vol. II, A staff report submitted to the National Commission on the Causes and Prevention of Violence. Washington, D.C.: U.S. Government Printing Office.
National Commission on Marijuana and Drug Abuse (1972). Marijuana: A signal of misunderstanding (Technical Papers of the First Report of the National Commission, Appendix, Vol. 2). Washington, D.C.: U.S. Government Printing Office.
President's Commission on Obscenity and Pornography (1971). Technical Report. Washington, D.C.: U.S. Government Printing Office.
REISS, A. (1971). The police and the public. New Haven, Conn.: Yale University Press.
SCHAFER, S. (1968). Victim and his criminal: A study in functional responsibility. New York: Random House.

Chapter 3

THE DECISION TO CALL THE POLICE:
REACTIONS TO BURGLARY

A. EMERSON SMITH and
DAL MANESS, Jr.

For years criminologists have known that the official statistics on the amount of crime in society underestimate the real number of crimes that occur. They have been aware that some unknown number of crimes are never reported to the police. In 1965 the President's crime commission sponsored the development of victim surveys (Biderman, 1967; Biderman and Reiss, 1967; Ennis, 1967). Since then, numerous additional victim surveys have been conducted. The primary purpose of all these surveys has been to try to shed some light on the "dark figure of crime," i.e., the amount of crime that does *not* get reported to the police.

Given this purpose, it is not surprising that these surveys have been one-sided in their questioning of victims. They have asked victims why they *did not* report their victimizations to the police; but they have neglected to ask victims why they *did* report their victimizations. Recently, however, researchers have begun to recognize the additional uses to which victim surveys can be put. In particular, they are recognizing the great potential of the victim survey as a

AUTHORS' NOTE: *This research was supported in part by Faculty Research Grant No. 20770-A000-54530 from the University of South Carolina. The authors wish to express their appreciation to the City of Columbia Police Department for their kindness in making the data available and to Jan Union for her advice and assistance.*

means of studying the interaction of victims and the criminal justice system (see McDonald, Chapter 1 in this volume). If this potential is to be exploited, however, the victim surveys will have to broaden their focus to include questions about why victims do report their victimizations. This chapter reports the findings of a victim survey which did ask that neglected question. It is a study of why victims of burglary *reported* their victimizations to the police.

PERSPECTIVE

Studies of why people call the police can be thought of as dealing with a specific class of a more generic phenomenon. The more general question is, "Why do people consult with *anyone* else—strangers, friends, relatives, government officials—about problems or experiences?" What events or behaviors lead people to seek out another person to talk about an event or behavior? In particular, under what circumstances do people ask for the assistance of a psychiatrist, a physician, a clergyman, Ann Landers, a friend, a Supreme Being, Mother, or a police officer? When and why do people resort to a third party when people perceive a conflict with other people?

The present study was done from a social interactionist perspective. As Blumer notes, there are three premises in the interactionist perspective (1969a:2): "(1) Human beings act toward things on the basis of the meanings that the things have for them. (2) The meaning of such things is derived from, or arises out of, the social interaction that one has with one's fellows. (3) These meanings are handled in, and modified through, an interpretive process used by the person in dealing with the things he encounters." In searching for the meaning that acts have for respondents, one must discover what kinds of acts respondents see as requiring intervention. The processes of interaction, its origins, maintenance, and consequences must be examined (see Phillipson, 1974:91).

In regard to why victims of burglary call the police it thus becomes important to have the respondent describe the act and events prior to his or her call. Was the respondent alone or with others when he or she discovered that the house had been "burglarized?" Did the respondent discuss the event with a friend in attempting to make sense of the situation, or did the respondent call the police so that they could assist in making sense of the events? The rationale for this line of questions is that, while people have some shared meanings for routine acts, the meaning of nonroutine events such as "burglary" has to be "created" or "discovered." What social events occur so that a person says "I've been burglarized!" and calls the police (who may or may not agree with the person's assertion of victimization)? In this process the setting which "occurs prior to the enforcement encounter and is quite distinct from it" (Hawkins, 1973:427) is a most crucial determinant of the definition that will be given to the situation.

It is also important to ask people why they made the decision to call for police intervention.[1] What meaning do people give to their calls to the police? What do they believe they are doing?

METHOD

This study is based on a sample of burglary victims from the city of Columbia, South Carolina. "Burglary" was operationally defined as a case contained in the police file labeled "housebreaking and burglary." The sample consisted of all cases for January and June of 1974. Burglaries of commercial establishments were excluded. The remaining 184 residential burglaries constituted the victimizations of interest to this study.

In July 1974, a letter on university stationery was mailed to the 184 burglary victims informing them that a study of citizen opinion about crime in Columbia was about to be done and that they would be contacted by telephone in the near future. In August and September of 1974, 116 telephone calls were completed to respondents. Three respondents indicated that they were not interested in participating and asked that their names be removed from the study. Sixty-seven other possible respondents were not contacted during the first round of telephoning because they had moved out of the city, had no telephone, had an unlisted telephone, or were not home.

During this first round of telephoning, respondents were asked "What do you think is the most important crime problem in Columbia?" Then they were asked, "During the past 12 months, have you been the victim of a crime?" If the respondent answered yes, he was asked "What happened?" Finally, the respondent was asked if we could contact him or her again should we need to ask further questions. In 10 of the 113 completed interviews the respondent indicated that he or she had *not* been the "victim of a crime." In several cases, the respondents who said that they had been "victims of crimes" in the past 12 months reported some event other than "housebreaking" or "burglary." During the second round of telephoning (approximately a year later) only 3 of the 10 respondents who indicated that they had not been "victims of a crime" persisted in that assertion even after the interviewer indicated that the respondent's name appeared in the police "victim" file.[2]

During August of 1975, the second round of telephone calls was made to all people for whom telephone numbers were available. This included some people not contacted during the first round. Ninety-one interviews were completed. Of the 94 people not contacted during the second round, 49 had moved out of the metropolitan area, 14 had not moved but had no phone, 11 had moved within the city and did not have a phone, 5 did not move but had unlisted phone numbers, and 3 who remained at their police file address said that they did not want to participate.[3]

Of the 91 completed interviews, 3 respondents indicated that they had not been the ones who had reported the burglaries to the police. Neighbors had called the police to report a "suspicious" person or activity at the respondent's home. Therefore, there were only 88 respondents for whom the question "Why did you call the police?" was appropriate.[4]

FINDINGS

Calling the Police: A Civic Duty

It is commonly held both in the criminological literature and in local police wisdom that the main reason why victims of burglary call the police is to make good their insurance claim. Conklin (1975:157), for example, refers to Reiss's studies (1967:99) of why people did not call the police and concluded that "people do not call the police unless they are seriously wronged or have something to gain—for example, being able to collect on an insurance policy if a crime is reported to the police. The gain must outweigh the effort of calling the police and the psychological cost of getting involved with the legal system; otherwise the call will not be made."

However, this belief is not confirmed by the present study. On the contrary, as Table 1 indicates, the reason that burglary victims most frequently gave for reporting their victimizations to the police was not "insurance" but "obligation." The latter category includes a variety of statements some of which include

Table 1. REASONS PEOPLE IN "HOUSEBREAKING AND BURGLARY" POLICE FILE GIVE FOR CALLING THE POLICE

Reason	Sequence for Multiple Reasons[a]				Percent Mentioning Reason at All[b]
	First	Second	Third	Fourth	
Obligation	38	5	1	—	50.0
Insurance	9	3	1	2	17.0
Recover property	7	8	5	—	22.7
Catch person	15	10	3	—	31.8
Personal protection	13	7	4	—	27.3
Protect neighborhood	3	6	3	—	13.6
Made me mad	1	1	—	—	2.3
Don't know	2	1	1	—	4.5
	N = 88				

a. Number of respondents giving one or more reasons.
b. Sume of percentages is greater than 100 since respondents may have given more than one reason in response to the question "Why did you call the police?"

clear references to civic duty while others refer to a more amorphous sense of obligation based simply on the fact that this is what one normally does or this is the custom. Examples of these statements are: "It's just the first thing you do." "It's the proper thing to do." "It's the natural thing to do." "It's the only way we can have law and order." "There was no one else to call." "It's required by law." "Newspapers had articles telling me that I should." "A friend told me that I should." "I want to cooperate with the police." "It should be reported."

The notion of civic duty was also evident in the second most frequently cited reason for reporting burglaries, namely, to help catch the criminal. Self-interest on the part of the victim was a prime motivator among those respondents who cited "personal protection," "insurance," and "recovering property" as their reasons. But, even then, it is noteworthy that of these three categories "insurance" was the least frequently cited. An additional finding further discredited the belief that when burglary victims do call the police it is for insurance reasons. Over one-third of the respondents did not even have insurance (assuming that what they told the researchers was accurate).

Among the respondents who did have insurance, 39.7% gave "obligation" as their first reason and 12.1% gave "insurance" as their first reason. Among the 34.1% of respondents who did *not* have insurance, 50% gave "obligation" as their first reason for calling the police. There was not much difference among the other reasons for calling the police between respondents who had or did not have insurance. Of those people who did have insurance, 22.4% had nothing taken from their homes. Of the people who had insurance and had something taken, 66% had property taken above deductable limits (if any) on their policies so that they received a settlement. Of all people who had insurance, nearly 50% did not have property taken,[5] did not have property valued above the deductable limit (usually $50-$100), or had property taken that was not covered (e.g., cash) by their insurance policy. For 58 out of 88 respondents who called the police, insurance policy requirements were not applicable.

Surely, one of the reasons that people give for calling the police may be related to insurance policy requirements that forcible entry be documented by a police officer or an insurance investigator. However, that requirement alone does not explain why people call the police after an event has occurred.

When respondents were divided on the basis of whether property was taken and an examination was made of the first reason each group gave for calling the police, it was found that 49.3% of those who had property taken gave "obligation" as their first reason for calling. In contrast, the most often cited reason (26.3%) for people who did not lose property was that police could provide protection for their homes and another attempt might not be made to enter their homes. Second to that, 21.2% of this group cited "obligation" as their primary reason.

Demographic Characteristics

Based on our social interactionist framework, it was expected that there would be no major difference in demographic characteristics between victims who called the police and the general adult population (see Blumer, 1969b). This expectation proved correct (at least for those victims who were being contacted by the survey). There were no differences between the respondents and the general population of Columbia, South Carolina, in terms of race (respondents were 70% white), in terms of whether the respondent lived alone or with others (23.1% of the respondents lived alone), or in terms of age or sex (respondents were 51.6% male).[6] It does not appear to be aggregate characteristics that make the difference on whether or not someone calls the police.

The police victim files contained two pieces of information on all people in the file—namely, the victim's sex and whether or not the victim owned or rented the residence. With respect to sex and home ownership, no significant differences were observed between the census population characteristics and the characteristics of all people who were in the police file (i.e., victims who reported their victimizations). The victims who cooperated with our survey were more likely to be homeowners and to be better educated than the general population. However, that is a function of the fact that many of the people who were unable to be contacted for one reason or another were renters. Although we did not have information on the educational attainment of nonrespondents, we have no reason to believe that the combined pattern of educational attainment for the poeple in the police file would differ from that of the general population (see Conklin, 1975:164).

Reporters Versus Nonreporters Compared

It is particularly interesting to see what differences exist between the beliefs of victims who do *not* report their victimizations to the police and the beliefs of those victims who *do* make reports. The reasons for not reporting have been given in previous studies (Ennis, 1967; Hindelang and Gottfredson, Chapter 2 in this volume; Richardson et al., 1972; Hawkins, 1973; and Law Enforcement Assistance Administration, 1974) and include, among other statements, that (1) there is little or nothing for the "victim to gain from calling the police." (2) the police can do nothing about it, (3) the "victim" does not see the act as a crime, and (4) the "victim" does not want to get involved in the police-court system.

In the present study it was found that the reasons for *calling* the police fall into four major categories: (1) the citizen has a personal obligation to call, (2) the police ought to find the person responsible for the event, (3) the caller could get restitution for loss or damage to property, and (4) the police will be alerted to pay more attention to protecting residential areas and provide personal protection services. Especially noteworthy is the fact that most of the respondents in this study felt there was little or nothing for them to gain from calling the police—in terms of their property being recovered. Most agreed with the statement that the police could do nothing about the event—other than make a record of the call.[7] Thus, it appears that nonreporting victims and reporting victims have similar views about the inefficacy of making a report, but the reporters notify the police anyhow out of some sense of civic duty. Perhaps this move provides some psychological benefit to the victim. It may give him or her a sense of closure to an event. Or the victim may feel that even if the probabilities of arrest and recovery are low, they are absolutely zero if no report is made. Or a call may help the victim feel that at least he is not to blame for the community's failure to stop crime. He did his part. Now it is the fault of the police, not of the citizen, that crime is not stopped.

In any event, one comes to the conclusion that knowing that a victim of burglary does not believe that the police will be able to do anything about it will not help predict whether that victim will or will not make a report to the police. Generally, those victims who do not report and those who do report are both inclined not to believe that the police will solve the problem.

The interactionist perspective suggests that it is the social interactions that occur from the time of the act being attended to by the respondent to the time of the call to the police, as well as the meanings given to such acts by the respondent, that may help explain the decision to call the police. If there is one thing that victimization surveys have shown, it is that the decision to call the police is related to particular events and not related to characteristics of the "victim." In general, for all "victimizations" (personal and property), people reported not calling the police because (1) force was not used, (2) property was not taken or damaged or (3) there was no personal injury resulting from the event. These were not the major reasons given, but rather correlates of event characteristics with whether the police were called. (See Hindelang and Gottfredson, Chapter 2 in this volume.)

FUTURE DIRECTIONS

Responses to questions of either "Why didn't you call the police?" or "Why did you call the police?" are not sufficient to answer research questions as to why people call the police. Asking people why they did or did not do something often leads to normative responses rather than statements that describe the events that led to the call. By confining oneself to such questions, the event is conceived in a snapshot fashion. The event is seen as a lone stimulus to which the respondent makes an immediate reaction: calling the police.

Of course, there are many events, behaviors, or interactions that occur from the time that an act comes to the attention of the potential caller until the call is made. In order to understand why people call the police attention must be directed at (1) the *time,* the interval between the initiation of the act and the call to the police, (2) the *interaction* among people present during the time interval, (3) the *intervention* by others asked to attend to the event prior to the police call, and (4) the *definition,* how acts take on the meaning of "wrongs" or "crimes" and require the attention of such people as a sherifff or police officer. Knowledge of these and other factors that tell us about the meaning that the event has for participants will lead to an understanding of calls and requests that people make to others for attention or intervention.

NOTES

1. Hawkins (1973:439) calls "calling the police" a "sanctioning initiation," indicating that people have similar objectives in making the call—namely, so that the culprit will be sanctioned. Our respondents had many reasons for calling the police, and we do not assume that calls to the police indicate a respondent's desire to invoke sanctions. The word "intervention" itself may not be adequate when all that respondents want is that the police have their call on record.

2. Two of these respondents still maintained that neither they nor anyone in their household had called the police for any reason during the 12-month period. The third respondent said that she had indeed called the police, but that she was not a "victim of crime." She reported that her husband had deserted her that day, and she thought first that someone had entered the house and stolen items belonging to her husband.

3. Whereas the response rate for the total group on file with the police is only 49.4% at this writing, it is expected that the final response rate will range upwards to a maximum of 71.7%, given that no more possible respondents move out of the metropolitan area.

4. Other questions asked were: "Did you have anything taken?" "Did the police recover anything?" "Did you have identification on any of your belongings at the time?" "Did you have property insurance?" (if yes, "Did you get a settlement on your insurance?"), "Have you at any other time called the police for any reason?" "Have you had any incident occur when you thought you should have called the police but for some reason didn't?" (if yes, "Did you call the police?"), "Have you moved since [January *or* June] 1974?"

5. Actually, one of the most common initial responses to the question, "Why did you call the police?" was a statement indicating that something had happened, such as "Because my house was broken into." Although respondents were asked to give reasons for calling the police, some respondents insited on giving descriptions of the events. When this occurred, respondents were pressed by the researchers to go beyond a mere description of the events and give a reason for their calling. We did not allow the respondents to say, in effect, that just because "something happened" to them that was enough justification for calling the police. Subsequently, we have realized that this pressuring of the respondent was quite inconsistent with our stated theoretical perspective.

6. This conclusion is based on 1970 U. S. Bureau of the Census reports.

7. Most respondents had their doubts about the probability of having their property returned or apprehending a suspect reinforced by the police. When they called to report their victimization, the police told them there was not much chance of recovering the property.

REFERENCES

BIDERMAN, A.D. (1967). "Surveys of population samples for estimating crime incidence." The Annals, 374(November):16-33.

BIDERMAN, A.D., and REISS, A.J., Jr. (1967). "On exploring the 'dark figure' of crime." The Annals, 374(November):1-15.

BLUMER, H. (1969a). "The methodological position of symbolic interactionism." Pp. 1-59 in H. Blumer (ed.), Symbolic interactionism: Perspective and method. Englewood Cliffs, N.J.: Prentice-Hall.

--- (1969b). "Public opinion and public opinion polling." Pp. 195-208 in H. Blumer (ed.), Symbolic interactionism: Perspective and method. Englewood Cliffs, N.J.: Prentice-Hall.

CONKLIN, J.E. (1975). The impact of crime. New York: Macmillan.

ENNIS, P.H. (1967). Criminal victimization in the United States. Washington, D.C.: U.S. Government Printing Office.

FURSTENBERG, F., Jr., and WELLFORD, C.F. (1973). "Calling the police: The evaluation of police service." Law and Society Review, 7(spring):393-406.

HAWKINS, R.O. (1973). "Who called the cops?: Decisions to report criminal victimization." Law and Society Review, 7(spring):427-444.

Law Enforcement Assistance Administration (1974). Crimes and victims: A report of the Dayton-San Jose Pilot survey of victimization. Washington, D.C.: Author, National Criminal Justice Information and Statistics Service.

PHILLIPSON, M. (1974). Understanding crime and delinquency: A sociological introduction. Chicago: Aldine.

President's Commission on Law Enforcement and Administration of Justice (1967). The challenge of crime in a free society. Washington, D.C.: U.S. Government Printing Office.

REISS, A.J. (1967). Field Studies III. Part 1 in President's Commission on Law Enforcement and Administration of Justice (ed.), Studies in crime and administration of justice. Washington, D.C.: U.S. Government Printing Office.

RICHARDSON, R.J.; WILLIAMS, O.; DENYER, T.; McGAUGHEY, S.; and WALKER, D. (1972). Perspectives on the legal justice system: Public attitudes and criminal victimization. Chapel Hill: Institute for Research in Social Science, University of North Carolina.

Chapter 4

THE ROLE OF ATTITUDES IN THE DECISION TO
REPORT CRIMES TO THE POLICE

A N N E   L.   S C H N E I D E R
J A N I E   M.   B U R C A R T   a n d
L.   A.   W I L S O N   I I

It is generally recognized that many persons who are the victims of crime do not report the incidents to the police. The National Crime Panel (NCP) surveys of the Law Enforcement Assistance Administation (LEAA) show that nearly half the victims of assault, robbery, burglary, and larceny of $50 or more did not report the incidents to the police. For property crimes involving less than $50, the nonreporting rate was about 80% (LEAA, 1974). The NCP surveys do not differ from their predecessors in this respect: every victimization survey conducted since 1967 has shown that total crime is two to three times as high as the amount of crime known to the police.

It appears that two points of view may be developing concerning the response which the criminal justice system should make in light of the high rates of unreported crimes. One point of view is that the criminal justice system does not

AUTHORS' NOTE: *Funding for this report and research was provided by Grant No. 74-NI-99-0016-G from the Oregon Law Enforcement Council and the National Institute of Law Enforcement in Criminal Justice, Law Enforcement Assistance Administration, Department of Justice, Washington, D.C. Points of view or opinions stated in this document are those of the authors and do not necessarily represent the official position or policies of the Department of Justice.*

need to be overly concerned about the fact that many victims do not report the incidents. This point of view might be warranted if it is established that unreported incidents are minor, trivial crimes, if the lack of reporting reflects the lack of importance of the incident rather than lack of confidence in the criminal justice system, and if the nonreporting rate is relatively constant across different time points and different geographical areas.

If these statements are true, then the official crime statistics can be "corrected" simply by recognizing that real crime is two or three times as great as reported crime, and criminal justice officials would not need to give any additional consideration to the problem.

An alternative point of view is that the nonreporting of crimes to the police should be a major concern for the criminal justice system. This point of view would be warranted if it is shown that many serious incidents never become known to the police. In addition, this point of view would be warranted if the nonreporting of incidents represents a lack of trust in the police or is produced by feelings of alienation and isolation from the community as a whole. The first factor, if it indeed is reflected in low reporting rates, is important since it reflects on the performance of the criminal justice system itself. The second factor, if it too is related to nonreporting, is important because many persons believe that the breakdown of community and family not only results in the nonreporting of crimes but also is associated with the types of values and orientations which result in rising crime rates. Criminal justice planning and evaluation agencies also are concerned about nonreporting rates because of the potential effect on the accuracy and reliability of the data used by the agencies. If nonreporting rates vary from area to area or change from one time period to another, then the data used to generate plans and to evaluate programs may be inaccurate. Evidence has been presented suggesting that the Uniform Crime Reports were unreliable indicators of burglary trends in Portland, Oregon (Schneider, 1975b). More important than any of these, however, is the fact that an offender who is quite confident that the crime will not be reported can be rather certain that he or she will not be apprehended for the crime. Thus, the nonreporting of incidents could contribute to rising crime rates.

Donald Santarelli, former director of the LEAA, reacted to the National Crime Panel survey by observing that "the statistics have uncovered in minute detail the sobering fact that a great many people do not report crime because they are turned off by the criminal justice system and its clanking process. It shows that there is an obvious need to turn the citizen on to the criminal justice system through citizen action programs" (LEAA, 1974).

The purpose of this report is to provide an exploratory analysis of reporting and nonreporting of incidents in order to ascertain the reasons for nonreporting.

CONCEPTUALIZING THE PROBLEM

In order to understand why a person might decide to report a crime to the police or not report it, one must begin with some intuitive ideas concerning what a person might gain or lose if the crime were reported to the police.

Beginning first with property crimes, the following list is proposed as a parsimonious statement of what a person might perceive as desirable outcomes in the aftermath of a property crime:

(1) Recovery of the stolen property or compensation, through insurance or other means.

(2) Avoidance of future victimizations by the same person(s).

(3) Avoidance of future victimizations by other offenders.

(4) Assistance to the neighborhood and community so that others may be less apt to be victimized.

(5) Revenge.

After a property crime has been committed, the individual could be interested in achieving one or more of the goals listed above. There are basically three strategies available to the person for achieving these goals. One would be to report the crime to the police. This should increase the chance that the property will be returned, if it is recovered; and most insurance claims will not be honored unless the crime has been reported. In addition, reporting to the police should alert the police to the specific offender (if known) and alert them to the fact that a crime of a particular type has occurred in a specific place. Thus, reporting to the police could, under ideal circumstances, reduce the likelihood that the same offender will victimize the person again. If the police increase their surveillance of the area, it should reduce the probability of victimization not only for the resident who has already been victimized but for others as well. Further, if potential criminals believe that victims in a particular area *will* report incidents, it could provide an incentive for them to cease committing crimes in that area.

A second strategy is for the individual to take private action to prevent a recurrence of the incident and to recover the property. This strategy could be effective if the offender is known to the victim and if the victim has some means of control over the offender. A strategy of this type might seem reasonable for incidents committed by juveniles who live in the area and whose parents, or other adults, could reverse the criminal behavior. The strategy might also be effective if a relative or other well-known person is the offender. Private action to prevent a recurrence also can involve simple "gate locking" activities such as locking doors, not leaving items outside the house, and so on.

The third strategy is to do nothing at all. This, of course, would not achieve any of the goals mentioned above, but it would prevent the victim from incurring any of the costs of reporting crimes to the police (such as time, energy, and possibly the harassment which might accompany reporting). In addition, the victim would avoid retaliation by the offender, which, for some persons, might be viewed as more serious than another property crime.

Given the goals mentioned above, it follows that the incentive to do something about a crime (rather than nothing) should be greater if the monetary loss from the crime was greater. In addition, the incentive to do something should be greater dependent upon how serious a crime *might* have been. That is, a loss of $10 from an automobile while parked downtown may be monetarily equal to a loss of $10 from a bedroom drawer in the middle of the night, but the incentive for action depends not only on recovering the monetary loss, but on preventing future offenses, and the offense at home *could* have been much more serious. Thus there would be greater incentive to prevent a recurrence of it than to prevent a recurrence of the incident in the parking lot.

Summarizing the discussion to this point, the incentive for a victim to take some type of action about a property crime depends on the seriousness of the crime as measured both by the monetary loss and an estimate of how serious a similar crime might be if committed again. The question, then, is what type of action the victim is most apt to take: reporting it to the police or taking personal action against the offender.

First, if the victim does not know who the offender is, then the chance of taking effective private action against the offender is very slim. Thus, crimes committed by strangers should be more often reported to the police than are crimes committed by persons known to the victim.

Second, if the person is insured, the crime is more apt to be reported to the police because this should result in recovery of at least part of the loss (disregarding the vagaries of insurance companies, which of course would not be known to the victim until after an attempt to collect).

The third factor which should be of some importance in the victim's decision pertains to his or her subjective estimate of whether it will do any good to report the event to the police, or whether reporting will just be a waste of time and energy. Some persons might not report the incident if they fear embarrassment or harassment from the police or if they think the police would not believe them or would not try to solve the crime. Some may have an aversion to having the police come into their home or place of business. Some may not want increased police surveillance in the area. Attitudes of trust and confidence in the police, then, should provide an incentive to report. In addition, victims should be more apt to report the incident if they believe that there is some possibility of recovering the property, or some possibility that the police will catch the person, or some possibility that the courts will punish the offender if he is caught, and so on.

Attitudes and orientations of the person to the local governing institutions could also impinge on the decision to report. Those who do not believe that they can be effective in their relationships with either the police or other local officials may be less apt to report incidents to the police.

As pointed out above, one of the possible goals that a person might have in mind is to prevent the offender from victimizing others in the community and/or to increase police attention and surveillance in an area for the benefit of everyone who lives there. An individual may believe that he or she can take effective action, personally, to prevent the crime from being repeated—such as putting a new lock on the door, keeping the bicycles inside the house, installing an alarm, and so on. These actions, however, are of no benefit to the neighbors and community. Thus, it seems reasonable to expect that persons who are more involved in their community or who are more concerned about assisting in a neighborhood or city-wide crime prevention effort will be more apt to report crimes to the police.

The latter factor differs from the others in one important respect: We are assuming that any reasonable person wishes to recover lost property and wishes to prevent future crimes against himself, but we do not assume that everyone is "community oriented."

Personal Crimes

The rationale for taking action in the aftermath of a personal crime differs from that of property crimes in two ways. First, many personal crimes do not involve any monetary loss, and, therefore, there is less incentive to take action in order to recover monetary losses for personal crimes, as a whole, than for property crimes, as a whole. Second, losses due to injuries, the psychological trauma accompanying an encounter with an assailant, and so on, cannot be measured in monetary terms and cannot be recovered in any way at all. Nevertheless, the logic underlying the decision to take action, as well as the type of action to take, is basically the same as for property crimes.

First, the individual is more apt to take some kind of action if there was a monetary loss (in order to recover it), and he is more apt to take some kind of action as a direct function of how serious the crime *could* have been. In particular, the use of a weapon or a threat to use a weapon or seriously injure the person is more apt to provide an incentive for action than is a personal incident not involving a weapon or a threat to use one. The person is also more apt to take action in direct relation to the seriousness of the injury. If the victim knows the offender, then there may be a greater chance that the victim might attempt to handle the offender personally than if the offender were a stranger. Insurance would provide additional incentive to report the crime to the police only if a property loss accompanied the incident. As before, the victim's attitudes toward the police and other local officials should be important, as should the extent of community involvement.

This discussion suggests that the following propositions should be supported from the data:

(1) If the seriousness of the crime is greater, the probability of reporting is greater.

(2) If the victim has more positive attitudes toward the police, is more trusting of the police, then the probability of reporting is greater.

(3) If the victim believes the police and other law enforcement institutions are effective, then the probability of reporting is greater.

(4) If the victim is more involved in the community, more integrated into the community, then the probability of reporting is greater.

(5) In the event of property loss, if the lost items were insured, then the probability of reporting is greater.

(6) If the offender is a stranger, then the probability of reporting is greater.

These propositions will be tested separately for property and for personal crimes because of the noncomparability of monetary loss and other aspects of seriousness across the two categories. It is possible that the motivation for reporting an incident could differ dependent upon the seriousness of the crime. For example, the victim's estimate of the likelihood that the police will catch the person or recover the property could be more important motivations for reporting serious crimes than for reporting minor ones. For this reason, the attitudinal variables and community-involvement indicators will be examined *within* each category of crime seriousness whenever it is feasible to do so, given the limited number of incidents in some categories.

It is obvious that the theory sketched above and the propositions do not suggest that socioeconomic characteristics of individuals should be important in decisions to report or not report incidents to the police. Characteristics of victims such as income or race are omitted because, if these are related to reporting, it should be through the effect of some other attribute of the individual. That is, persons with higher incomes may be more apt to report crimes to the police, but, if so, it would be because they lost more in the crime or differed in some other way from low income persons. If blacks are less apt to report than whites, it might be because they are less trusting of the police. In other words, socioeconomic variables should not be important in the decision to report except insofar as they are surrogate indicators of some attitudinal characteristic.

METHODOLOGY

The data for this analysis are from more than 3,900 face-to-face interviews of a random sample of residents of the Portland, Oregon, area. The interviewing was done in the summer of 1974. Although more than 1,700 offenses were reported to the interviewers, only approximately 900 different persons were victims of one or more target offenses during the 12-month recall period.

The purpose of the analysis is to examine the strength of the relationship between reporting crimes and selected independent variables, as well as to ascertain the statistical significance of the observed relationships. The dependent variable (reporting) is dichotomous, with scores of 1 given to nonreporting, and scores of 2 to reporting. Most of the independent variables are ordinal scales. There is, of course, an ongoing controversy about whether to use correlation-regression analysis on ordinal data or whether to employ one or more of the nonparametric statistics designed for use with ordinal data.

The argument that correlation analysis should be confined to interval data will not be reviewed here. It has been shown that Pearson's correlation coefficient r is quite robust even though the data are not intervally scaled. That is, correlation analysis is not apt to show that a relationship exists when one in fact does not exist, even though the data are ordinal rather than interval. Rutherford has shown that Pearson's r, in fact, consistently *underestimates* the true strength of the relationship when used on ordinal and/or nominal data (Rutherford, 1972).

Thus, it seems that there is no danger in using correlation analysis except that it may underestimate the strength of the relationship. Rutherford's work indicates that several nonparametric statistics, including gamma, are more accurate than Pearson's r for estimating the "true" strength of association on ordinal data.

The choice of statistics to be used here, then, consists of the use of gamma and Pearson's r for examining the bivariate relationships. In the final section of this paper, a multivariate analysis using discriminant function analysis and multiple correlation-regression will be presented.

Table 1. PROPERTY AND PERSONAL INCIDENTS

Type of Crime	Number of Incidents	% in Each Seriousness Category	Definitions
Property Crimes			
Low seriousness	283	35	Lowest possible score on serious was 1, and all cases with this score are considered "low." Incidents in this category involve no loss at all or loss not greater than $10, and in no instance is a forcible entry involved.
Moderate seriousness	352	44	Score of 2 on the scale. Incidents include those with loss of $10 to $250 *not* involving forcible entry, or loss of less than $10 *with* forcible entry.
High seriousness	171	21	Score of 3 or higher on the scale. Incidents include loss greater than $250 (with or without forcible entry), or forcible entry with a loss of $10 or more.
Personal Crimes			
Low seriousness	42	53	Scores of 1, 2, or 3 on the seriousness scale. No incident in this category involved use of a weapon, none involved injury requiring doctor's treatment, none were sex offenses, and none involved loss of more than $250. These incidents, then, involve a combination of verbal threats, small losses, minor injuries.
High seriousness	38	47	Scores of 4 or higher. In this category are rapes, any offense involving a dangerous weapon, any injury requiring doctor's treatment, any monetary loss of $250 or more, and combinations involving threat of harm with any monetary loss or involving threat of harm and minor injury with any monetary loss.

RESULTS OF BIVARIATE ANALYSIS

The dependent variable for the analysis is the reporting or nonreporting of victimization incidents. Only those incidents committed against the respondent, or the household, in the 12-month recall period were used. If the person did not answer the question concerning whether the incident was reported to the police, or if the person said that he or she did not know whether or not it was reported, the incident was counted as an "unreported" incident. There were only a few nonresponses and only a few "don't know" answers. It should be emphasized that all the data are from the survey respondents. The term "reported to the police" refers to the *respondent's* statement to the interviewer that the incident was reported. It does not refer to actual police data from official records.

The relationships between reporting crime and each of the following independent variables will be examined: (1) seriousness of the crime, (2) attitudes toward the police, (3) effectiveness of the police and courts, (4) community involvement and integration, (5) insurance, (6) strangers as offenders.

Seriousness of the Crime

The seriousness scale used in the analysis is a replication of Sellin and Wolfgang's 1964 index (see the Appendix to this chapter for the exact questions and scoring procedures). For personal crimes, the index includes an injury component, sex-offense component, weapon component, and intimidation component, and, if there was any monetary loss, this also was considered in the scaling. For property crimes, the total loss is the major component, and the type of entry to the home (if any) is the second component. By definition, a property crime could not involve injury, use of a dangerous weapon, and so on.

Because of the low frequency of crimes in the very high seriousness categories, the incidents were regrouped in order to provide greater stability to the statistical analysis. For property crimes the incidents were grouped into three categories (low, moderate, and high seriousness). As indicated in Table 1, 35% of the crimes were of very low seriousness, 44% were in the moderate category, and 21% were considered quite serious. The definitions of each category are also shown in Table 1.

Personal crimes were divided into two categories as shown in Table 1. Because of the small number of persons who were the victims of personal crimes, most of the analysis for these incidents will be done without dividing the sample.

As expected, the seriousness of the crime is one of the most important factors explaining why some crimes are reported and others are not (see Table 2). When property and personal crimes are combined, the percentage reported goes from

Table 2. CRIME SERIOUSNESS AND REPORTING

Type of Crime	N	% Not Reported	% Reported	Strength of Relationship
Property Crimes				
Low seriousness	283	75	25	Gamma = .65
Moderate seriousness	352	51	49	Pearson's r = .43
High seriousness	171	16	84	
Personal Crimes				
Low-Moderate seriousness	42	47	52	Gamma = .52
High seriousness	38	22	77	Pearson's r = .26
All Crimes Combined				
Low seriousness	290	76	24	Gamma = .65
Moderate seriousness	357	51	49	Pearson's r = .43
High seriousness	239	20	80	

24% in the low seriousness category to 49% for the moderately serious to 80% for the crimes designated as highly serious. Gamma estimates the strength of relationship at .64, and the correlation coefficient (Pearson) is .43. For property crimes alone, 24% of the minor ones were reported, 49% of the ones with an intermediate (moderate) seriousness level were reported, and 84% of the highly serious incidents were reported. (It should be pointed out again that information about whether the incident was reported or not comes from the respondent and not from an independent check on the police records.) The seriousness of personal crimes also influences reporting: 52% of the less serious ones are reported, compared to 77% of the highly serious.

Attitudes and Orientations Toward the Police and the Criminal Justice System

Trust in Police. A scale involving five attitudinal items was developed to reflect an overall measure of trust in the police (see the Appendix to this chapter for the exact questions and scoring procedures). The five questions involved the following major attitudinal components: (1) the police would give serious attention to them if they contacted the police; (2) they would be treated as well as anyone else by the police; (3) the police would believe their account of what happened if they reported a crime to the police; (4) the police would try to find out who committed the crime they reported; (5) generally, attitudes toward the police are favorable. All of the questions had responses which could be divided into two main categories of favorable versus unfavorable.

The distribution of respondents on the trust scale, as well as the percentage of persons in each category who reported crimes to the police, is shown in Table 3.

The first column in Table 3 shows the number and percentage of persons in each of the trust categories. Most persons have favorable attitudes toward the police, because 57% are in the high trust category, compared to 23% of the crime victims who had low trust scores and 20% who had moderate scores. The high trust category includes persons who gave positive responses to all five questions which formed the scale. Individuals in the moderate category gave one negative response on the five questions, and individuals in the low trust group gave two or more negative responses.

Although the results are somewhat uneven, the percentage of victims who report incidents to the police tends to be higher if the victims had higher scores on the trust scale. Of the persons who were victims of minor property crimes, 14% reported these incidents if they tended to distrust the police, whereas 30% of those who scored in the high trust category reported the minor incidents. (The percentages are computed on the basis of the number of persons in each cell. For example, there were 49 persons who were the victims of a minor property crime and who also had low trust scores. Of these, 14% reported the incidents, and 86% did not. The latter figure is not shown in the table.) The same pattern exists for property crimes of moderate seriousness: victims who distrust the police are less apt to report the incidents (42% reporting) than victims who are more trusting (56% reporting). The relationship does not hold for serious property crimes, however.

A relationship between trust and reporting also was found for personal crimes. When all were analyzed together, disregarding seriousness, 55% of the personal crime victims with low trust scores reported the incidents, compared with a 74% reporting rate for victims with high trust scores. When the personal crimes are divided into less and more serious categories, the same pattern holds, but the relationship is not as steady across the trust categories. Generally, however, personal crimes are more apt to be reported by persons who trust the police than by those who do not.

Police-Community Relations. Respondents were asked to rate the quality of the relationship between the police and community. As shown in the first column of Table 3, most persons said the relationship was good (48%), and 13% said it was very good. This indicator of victims' attitudes toward the police generally was not very important in terms of reporting crimes with the exception of minor property offenses. For these, the persons who live in areas which they say have poor relationships with the police are not at all likely to report the minor property offenses (10% reporting rate, 90% nonreporting). In contrast, 38% of the minor property crime victims who say the relationship with the police is very good report the crimes.

Belief in Police Effectiveness. Most of the respondents are not very optimistic

Table 3. PERCENTAGE OF VICTIMS REPORTING INCIDENTS TO THE POLICE BY ATTITUDES

Independent Variable	Distribution of Responses		Property Crime Victims Seriousness			Personal Crime Victims Seriousness		
	N	%	Low % Rep.	Moderate % Rep.	High % Rep.	All % Rep.	Low % Rep.	High % Rep.
1. Trust in Police								
Low trust	180	23	14	42	86	55	42	63
Moderate trust	155	20	21	38	81	64	37	100
High trust	440	57	30	56	89	74	68	81
2. Police-Community Relations								
Poor	141	19	10	45	88	61	55	69
Fair	155	21	21	47	73			
Good	360	48	30	55	88	53	55	—
Very good	101	13	38	48	89	64	40	81
3. Chance Police Catch Offender								
Poor	146	17	25	44	76	56	44	69
Fairly poor	181	21	20	46	83			
Even	270	31	26	47	83	74	65	84
Good	267	31	24	57	93	62	50	77
4. Chance Police Recover Property								
Poor	388	44	25	49	82	62	54	71
Fairly poor	237	27	25	46	89			
Even	172	20	29	52	75	90	50	93
Good	82	9	15	50	99			
5. Chance Court Punish Offender								
Very poor	120	14	22	53	85	52	40	69
Poor	169	20	28	44	99			
Even	277	32	22	44	78	74	69	78
Good	300	37	28	53	83	70	63	85

	N							
6. Attitudes Toward Court								
Very unfavorable	69	8	23	56	79	42	83	63
Unfavorable	182	21	23	45	81			
Neutral	230	26	23	46	87	38	77	58
Good	391	45	26	50	84	64	74	70
7. Understanding of Local Issues								
Understand few, none	502	57	20	45	85	56	43	73
Understand most	376	43	32	53	83	79	72	85
8. Length of Residence								
Less than 1 year			17	53	77	55	40	76
1 to 6 years			26	42	83	70	61	90
More than 6 years			31	49	90	60	65	61
9. Involvement in CPB Program								
None	427	48	21	39	84	60	47	79
1 activity	286	32	23	50	77	77	84	72
2 activities	120	13	42	64	98	58	–	–
3 or more	54	6	37	76	86	54	40	87
10. Insurance								
None	228	26	22	47	78	64	53	76
Insured	658	74	26	49	86	65	52	79
11. Identity of Offender								
Well known	24	4	39	32	77	64	47	84
Slightly known	28	3	15	38	67	81	–	–
Stranger	754	93	25	49	85	62	53	74

about the chance of the police catching the offender and are even less optimistic that the police would be able to recover property lost in a burglary. (These questions were asked of all respondents in relation to a hypothetical offense. The responses shown in Table 3 are only for the persons who were victims of some type of crime, however.) Slightly more than 30% believe that the chances are better than even that the police would catch an offender, and only 9% believe that the chances are better than even that the police would be able to recover the property. Persons who believe that the police have a good or fairly good chance of catching the offender are more apt to report a serious crime than are persons who think the police will not catch the person (Table 3). The belief (or lack of it) is not important in a person's decision to report minor property crimes and has a slight effect on those in the moderate seriousness category.

The belief that the police will (or will not) recover the stolen property has very little effect on reporting of property crimes regardless of whether the incident is very minor or quite serious. This lack of relationship should not be taken to mean that a belief in police effectiveness would never impinge on a person's decision to report a crime, however, because there are very few persons in the sample who think that the odds are greater than 50-50 that the police would be able to recover the property.

Attitudes Toward the Courts. Two questions about the court system were included on the questionnaire. One question concerns the respondent's subjective estimate of whether the court would punish an offender if the offender were caught. The other is a general question concerning whether the respondent's attitudes toward the courts are favorable or not.

As shown in entries 5 and 6 of Table 3, a majority of persons believe that the chances are even or less than even that the court would punish an offender if he were caught. On the other hand, slightly more persons (37%) believe the courts would punish an offender than believe the police would catch him.

For property crimes, persons who think the court is more apt to punish the offender are no more likely to report the incident than are persons who think the court would not punish the person. For property crimes, there is no difference in reporting rates for persons with favorable rather than unfavorable attitudes. The victims of personal crimes, however, are somewhat more likely to report the incident if they think the court would punish the offender than if they do not believe the court would take action.

Community Involvement and Integration

Several indicators of community involvement and integration were available to test the relationship between this aspect and the reporting of crimes. One indication that a person is *not* integrated into the community or has a sense of localized "anomie" in relation to the community is his response to a question asking whether he is able to understand most of the local issues or only a few of them (see the Appendix to this chapter for the actual question).

The length of residence in the community was used as an additional, more objective, estimate of community integration—on the assumption that persons who have lived in an area longer will feel more a part of it.

The final scale relating to the general community-orientation dimension was formed from four items concerning community and/or city-based crime prevention involvement. The only active crime prevention program in the city is a burglary prevention program by the Crime Prevention Bureau. Individuals were given one point for each of the following activities: (1) having heard about the crime prevention programs, (2) engraving their property, (3) displaying an antiburglary sticker, (4) having attended a block meeting concerning the antiburglary program or some other crime prevention program. The scores range from zero for persons who had done none of the above, to 4 for persons who responded affirmatively to all four items. The distribution of respondents on these variables, and the percentage of victims in each category who reported the incidents to the police, are shown in entries 7-10 of Table 3.

The person's ability to understand local political issues is one of the most consistent indicators of whether an individual will report a crime or not. Persons who say they cannot understand local issues are less apt to report minor property crimes, moderately serious ones, the less serious personal crimes, and the more serious personal crimes. Particularly striking is the difference in percentage reporting for the less serious personal crimes, where 43% of the victims who do not understand the nature of local issues report, compared to 72% of those who are able to understand issues. It is interesting to note, as well, that 57% of the victims say that they generally are not able to understand local issues.

Length of residence at the person's current address is not a consistent predictor of decisions to report crimes, although persons who have lived at the same address for more than 6 years are more apt to report minor property offenses and major ones than are the more transient victims.

Involvement in the Portland Crime Prevention Bureau's antiburglary program is another very consistent predictor of decisions to report property offenses, especially the minor and moderately serious ones.

The final two entries in Table 3 concern whether the victim was insured or not, and whether the offender was a stranger or someone known to the victim. Persons with insurance are more apt to report property offenses, but the percentage differences are not very great. For minor offenses, 22% of the persons without insurance report, compared to 26% of the persons with

Table 4. STRENGTH OF RELATIONSHIP BETWEEN ATTITUDES AND DECISIONS TO REPORT CRIMES[a]

| | Property Crimes Seriousness | | | | | | Personal Crimes All | |
| | Low | | Moderate | | High | | | |
Independent Variable	gamma	r	gamma	r	gamma	r	gamma	r
1. Trust in Police	.32	.15*	.25	.14*	.15	.05	.31	.18+
2. Police-Community Relations	.32	.18*	.08	.04	.13	.04	.11	.04
3. Chance Police Catch Offender	.02	.01	.14	.09*	.32	.16*	.08	.06
4. Chance Police Recover Property	-.04	-.03	.02	.02	.07	.03	.32	.15+
5. Chance Court Punish Offender	.10	.07	.04	.03	-.28	-.13*	.25	.16*
6. Attitudes Toward Court	.10	.06	.03	.01	.07	.04	.12	.07
7. Understand Local Issues	.30	.14*	.17	.08+	-.07	-.03	.48	.23*
8. Length of Residence	.11	.05	-.09	-.04	.34	.18*	.08	.06
9. Involvement in CPB Program	.24	.14*	.35	.22*	.09	.06	.04	.01
10. Insurance	.10	.05	.05	.04	.25	.12*	.08	.07
11. Identity of Offender	.02	.02	.29	.14*	.40	.22*	.08	.05

a. Tests of significance for the gamma values are not readily available and were not conducted. The Pearson correlation significance levels are shown. An asterisk indicates significance at .05 or better, and a plus sign indicates significance between .05 and .10.

insurance. In the moderate category, 47% of the noninsured report, compared to 49% of the insured. And for the more serious property crimes, 78% of the noninsured report, compared to 86% of the insured. Only the latter difference is great enough to be statistically significant. The cliché that property crimes are reported because of insurance is much too simple to constitute an explanation of the reporting of property crimes.

Most of the crimes were committed by strangers, and victims were less apt to report moderate or serious property crimes if they knew the identity of the offender.

Strength of the Relationships

The correlation coefficients and gamma values relating each of the independent variables to reporting are shown in Table 4. These statistics make it easier to summarize the relationships observed in the percentages of Table 3.

Minor property crimes, involving no forced entry and no loss greater than $10, are more apt to be reported to the police if the victim (a) is more trusting of the police, rather than less trusting, (b) lives in an area where the police enjoy good relationships with the community, (c) is more integrated into the community in the sense that he or she is able to understand most of the local issues rather than only a few or none of them, (d) has participated in more activities sponsored by the Crime Prevention Bureau antiburglary team.

It is also interesting to notice that, for the minor crimes, beliefs about the ability of the police to catch the offender or recover the property are not important factors in a victim's decision to report incidents, and neither are attitudes toward the courts. In addition, whether the offender is a stranger or not seems to be irrelevant, as is also the question of whether the property was insured.

The pattern changes in an interesting way for property crimes that fall into the most serious category. Serious property crimes are more apt to be reported if the victim (a) believes that the police will be able to catch the offender, (b) has lived in the city for a longer period of time, (c) has insurance on the stolen items, (d) thinks that the offense was committed by a stranger.

Again, a belief that the police will be able to find the stolen property is not important, and neither are attitudes toward the court. The negative relationship between reporting of serious property crimes and the question of the person's belief that the court would punish the offender indicates that victims who think the likelihood of punishment is small are more apt to report incidents than those who are more confident that the court will punish the offender. This is just the opposite from what we suggested in the propositions stated earlier. Perhaps the statement should be made with the direction of causality reversed: Persons who have reported incidents to the police are less confident the courts will punish the offender than are persons who were victimized but did not report the incident.

Personal crimes are more apt to be reported if the victim (a) has greater trust in the police rather than less trust, (b) believes that the courts are more apt to punish the offender if he is caught, (c) is better able to understand local issues, (d) believes that the police have a better chance of recovering lost property.

RESULTS OF MULTIVARIATE ANALYSIS

The multivariate analysis has two major purposes. The first is to determine whether any of the relationships observed previously change when the other major independent variables are controlled. The second purpose is to show the predictive power of the independent variables and to ascertain the proportion of victims who are accurately classified into the reporting and nonreporting categories.

Two types of multivariate analysis are used. One is multiple regression-correlation analysis, and the other is discriminant function analysis. The results of the two are virtually identical, as shown in Tables 5 and 6. In conducting the analysis, the independent variables were entered into the equation in order of the additional explanatory power which they would add.

Table 5. REPORTING PROPERTY CRIMES: MULTIVARIATE ANALYSIS

	Discriminant Function Coefficient	F	Partial Regression Coefficients	F
Seriousness	.73	96	.39	96
Participation in CPB Program	.34	22	.18	21.5
Trust in Police	.18	6.6	.10	5.0
Understand Local Issues	.17	5.0	.09	5.1
Police-Community Relations	.14	2.2	.07	2.88
Belief Police Catch Person	−.12	2.4	.07	2.5

Canonical correlation = .466; R = .465; % of cases correctly classified = 71%

PREDICTION RESULTS FROM DISCUSSANT FUNCTIONS

Actual Group	No. of Cases	Predicted Group Group 1	Membership Group 2
1. Nonreporters	268	198 74%	70 26%
2. Reporters	254	83 33%	171 67%

Six variables have statistically significant relationships with reporting property crimes when each of the other variables is statistically controlled (Table 5). The seriousness of the crime is the strongest predictor, followed by participation in the Crime Prevention Bureau antiburglary program. In addition, trust in the police, understanding local issues and the quality of police-community relationships contribute to reporting. The negative relationship between the final variable (belief that police will catch the person) indicates that the correlation is in the wrong direction. The canonical correlation from the discriminant function is .466, and the multiple R from the regression analysis is .465. The discriminant function analysis indicates that 71% of the property crime victims were correctly classified as reporters or nonreporters using the linear discriminant function. At the bottom of Table 5, the proportion correctly classified is shown. Of those who did not report the incident, information on the six independent variables results in 74% of these being correctly classified as nonreporters. Seventy persons (26%) were incorrectly classified. Of those who did report the crime, the linear combination of the independent variables placed 67% in the correct category, and 33% were wrongly classified.

From the previous analysis, it is clear that the minor and moderately serious property crimes tended to dominate the multivariate analysis, since most of the

Table 6. REPORTING PERSONAL CRIMES: MULTIVARIATE ANALYSIS[a]

	Discriminant Function Coefficient	F	Partial Regression Coefficients	F
Understand Local Issues	.64	7.6	.44	12.9
Seriousness	.51	6.6	.34	8
Belief Police Catch Person	.24	4.5	.17	1.7
Belief Police Recover Property	.55	1.8	.21	2.7
Belief Courts Punish Offender	.33	2.8	.34	6.8

Canonical correlation = .62; R = .62; % correct = 81%

a. Any case with missing data on any variable used in the analysis had to be excluded, reducing the N considerably from that used in the bivariate analysis.

PREDICTION RESULTS FROM DISCRIMINANT FUNCTION

Actual Group	No. of Cases	Predicted Group Group 1	Membership Group 2
1. Nonreporters	23	19 81%	4 19%
2. Reporters	28	5 19%	23 81%

variables showing significant relationships are those which were important in the reporting of minor and/or moderate incidents.

The results for personal crime victims are shown in Table 6. The ability to understand local issues is the strongest single predictor variable, followed by the seriousness of the incident. In addition, the victim's belief in the effectiveness of the criminal justice system—as indicated by the three variables pertaining to the chance that the police will catch the person, the police will recover the property, and the court will punish the offender—add additional explanatory power. The multiple correlation is .62, and 81% of the victims are correctly classified using these five independent variables. It should be pointed out that the variable representing trust in the police did not enter the analysis. However, a reanalysis of the data indicates that the trust in the police variable could be entered in place of any one of the three indicators of effectiveness, and the results would be virtually identical to those shown in Table 6.

CONCLUSIONS

The seriousness of a property crime is the single most important factor in a victim's decision to report or not report an incident to the police. For personal crimes, the victim's ability to understand the nature of local issues is the single most important factor in the victim's decision to report incidents, although the seriousness of the crime is also a good predictor of whether the incident will be reported or not.

When the victims are divided into groups corresponding to the type of crime and its seriousness, it is apparent that attitudinal variables are more important factors in the decision to report for victims of minor and moderately serious property crimes and for all victims of personal crimes (assaults, rapes, and robberies). Attitudinal variables are not as important in the reporting by victims of serious property crimes. Combining the bivariate and multivariate analysis reported earlier, all crimes *except* serious offenses are more apt to be reported if (a) the victim is more integrated into the community as evidenced by the person's ability to understand most of the local issues in the community and/or his involvement in community crime prevention activities, (b) the victim believes that there is a fairly good chance that the police will be able to catch the offender, and (c) the victim has more positive attitudes toward the police and is more trusting of them. In relation to the latter point, it should be recalled that the scale of police trust was formed from questions concerning the respondent's statement that he thinks he would be treated with equal fairness by the police, that the police would believe his account of an incident, and so on. The trust scale did not include any statements concerning the victim's belief in the effectiveness of the police.

In addition to the above factors, the victim of a personal crime also is more apt to report it if he thinks the court would punish the offender and if he believes the police would be able to recover lost property.

Serious property crimes are most apt to be reported, and the reasons for reporting or not reporting them are not as tied to attitudinal variables as are the other types of crimes. Only one attitudinal measure—the belief that the police would be able to catch the offender—correlates with higher reporting rates for victims of serious property crimes. The other variables which tend to be associated with higher reporting are insurance, longer residence in the city, and a crime which was committed by a stranger.

One implication of these results is that intensive efforts to improve residents' attitudes toward the police probably will increase the proportion of minor property crimes which are reported, as well as the proportion of personal crimes that are reported. Increased perceptions by residents that the police will be effective probably will have the same effect. One of the most important variables, however, was the individual's ability to understand local issues. This was a stronger predictor of reporting for personal crimes than any other—including seriousness. Our interpretation is that an individual's response to the question about local issues taps a dimension of anomie or alienation from the community—a sense of rootlessness and lack of belonging. Persons who feel alienated and isolated from their community are not as apt to report crimes. Efforts by the police to increase their effectiveness or increase citizens' trust of them may increase reporting tendencies for some persons, but others may still fail to report even the more serious personal crimes because of their sense of isolation and alienation from the community. It is possible that some police and civilian activities to increase involvement in crime prevention may, as a side product, increase the sense of belonging to a community or neighborhood.

The implication of this study for the measurement of crime rates with official crime statistics also should not be overlooked. A change in the proportion of victims who report incidents to the police can produce changes in the official crime rate, even though the actual volume of crime may not change at all. If residents become more trusting of the police and more involved in local crime prevention and if the police become more effective, then the *reporting rate* may increase, producing an apparent increase in the crime rate. Further, comparisons of official crime statistics from one city to another could be complicated by the fact that the citizens of one city may have more positive orientations toward the police and a higher reporting rate. Thus, the official crime rate may not be an accurate indication of the comparative amount of crime in different cities. More important, when official crime statistics are used to measure the effectiveness of the criminal justice system, they may produce quite misleading results, since citizens who trust the police and believe tham to be more effective tend to report more crimes than citizens who do not have these attitudes. An increase in the effectiveness of the criminal justice system—as measured by citizen trust and perceptions of effectiveness—could produce an apparent decrease in effectiveness as measured by the official crime statistics.

Thus, the results of the study provide support for the contention made by Biderman and Reiss (1967) that "attempts at improving police-community relations conceivably could produce sharp 'paper increases' in some classes of crime." And the results call into question the generality of the conclusion drawn by Hawkins in a previous study (1973) that decisions to report victimizations are not influenced by attitudes toward the police.

REFERENCES

BIDERMAN, A.D. (1967). Surveys of population samples for estimating crime incidence. The Annals, 374:16-33.
BIDERMAN, A.D.; JOHNSON, L.A.; McINTYRE, J.; and WEIR, A.W. (1967). Report on a pilot study in the District of Columbia on victimization and attitudes toward law enforcement. Washington, D.C.: Bureau of Social Science Research.
BIDERMAN, A.D., and REISS, A.J., Jr. (1967). "On exploring the 'dark figure' of crime." The Annals, 374:1-15.
ENNIS, P.H. (1967). Criminal victimization in the United States: A report of a national survey (President's Commission on Law Enforcement and Administration of Justice, Field Survey II). Washington, D.C.: U.S. Government Printing Office.
HAWKINS, R.O. (1973). "Who called the cops? Decisions to report criminal victimization." Law and Society Review, 7(spring):427-444.
Law Enforcement Assistance Administration (1974). Newsletter, 3(11):1, 9, 11.
RUTHERFORD, B.R. (1972). "The accuracy, robustness and relationships among correlational models for social analysis: A Monte Carlo simulation." Paper presented at the annual meeting of the American Political Science Association.
SCHNEIDER, A. (1975a). Crime and victimization in Portland: Analysis of trends, 1971-1974 (Occasional papers in Applied Policy Research). Eugene: Oregon Research Institute.
––– (1975b). Evaluation of the Portland neighborhood-based anti-burglary program (Occasional papers in Applied Policy Research). Eugene: Oregon Research Institute.
––– (1975c). Methodological approaches to measuring short-term victimization trends (Occasional papers in Applied Policy Research). Eugene: Oregon Research Institute.
SELLIN, T., and WOLFGANG, M.E. (1964). The measurement of delinquency. New York: Wiley.
SKOGAN, W.G. (1974). "Measurement problems in official and survey crime rates." Paper presented at the annual meeting of the American Statistical Association.
SMITH, P.E., and HAWKINS, R.O. (1973). "Victimization, types of citizen-police contacts, and attitudes toward the police." Law and Society Review, 7:135-152.

APPENDIX

SCALES USED IN THE REPORTING AND NONREPORTING ANALYSIS

1. Seriousness of the Crime

The seriousness scale used in the analysis is a replication of Sellin and Wolfgang's 1964 index.

a. Injury Component

Question (INC069): (If victim was injured): Did you receive treatment at a hospital, at a doctor's office, or what type of treatment did you receive?

Scoring:	Score
Blank (indicates no injury)	0
1. No treatment	1
2. Treated in doctor's office	4
3. Treated in emergency room	4
4. Overnight at hospital, or more	7

b. Sex Offense

(Crime codes of 120000 through 129999 are rape.)

Rape	8

c. Weapon Intimidation

Question (INC030): Did the person(s) have a weapon such as a gun or knife, or something he used as a weapon, such as a bottle or wrench?

Scoring:	Score
1. No	0
2. Yes, gun	4
3. Knife	4
4. Gun and knife	4
5. Other dangerous weapons	4
9. Don't know	0

d. Physical or Verbal Intimidation

Question (INC031): Did the person(s) threaten you with harm in any way?

Scoring:	Score
1. No	0
2. Yes	2
9. Don't know	0
Blank	0

e. Forcible Entry

Question (INC021): Was there any evidence that the offender(s) forced his way in or tried to force his way into the building, such as a broken lock, broken window, forced door, forced window, or slashed screen?

Scoring:	Score
1. Blank or no	0
2. through 8. Other evidence	1
9. Don't know	0

f. Costs and Losses

(Questions concerning losses are called COST1, COST2, COST3 . . . COST6 and represent, in order, money lost, dollar value of items lost and dollar value of damages, none of which was recovered; insurance paid, value paid by offender, value paid by anyone else. The sum of these represents the total value of the loss.)

Scoring:	Score
Under $10	1
$10-$250	2
$251-$2,000	3
$2,001-$9,000	4
$9,001-$30,000	5
$30,001-$80,000	6
$80,001-highest	7

(note: values of 88,888 represent refusal to name the amount, and values of 99,999 represent don't know. These were set to a score of 1.)

Several alternatives to the Sellin seriousness scale were also tried, but none of these had greater explanatory power for reporting than the Sellin index. The revised seriousness scores included all the above indicators, plus one additional point if the crime was committed by a stranger, or if it occurred at night, or if it was closer to the person's home, or if all of these were characteristics of the crime. None of these additions improved the correlation between seriousness and reporting.

2. Seriousness of Property versus Personal Crimes

The seriousness of a property crime (burglary or larceny) was computed exactly as above except, by definition, there were no injuries, etc. The only indicators, then, are cost and whether the entry was forcible or not. For personal crimes, all the indicators are used because personal crimes could involve monetary losses.

3. Confidence, Trust in Police

(VAR077, VAR078, VAR138, VAR139, VAR144)

Questions:

1. If you explained your point of view to the police, what effect do you think it would have? Would they give your point of view serious consideration, would they pay some attention or only a little attention, or would they ignore what you had to say?

Scoring:

1. Serious } = 1
2. Some
3. Little   } = 2
4. Ignore
9. Don't know

Questions:

2. If you had some trouble with the police—a traffic violation, maybe, or being accused of a minor offense—do you think you would be given equal treatment? That is, would you be treated as well as anyone else?

3. Suppose you reported a crime to the local police department. Generally speaking, do you think they would believe your account of what happened? Do you think they would definitely believe you, probably believe you, probably *not* believe you, or definitely *not* believe you?

4. Would the police *try* to find out who committed the crime you reported? Do you think that they definitely would try, probably would try, probably would not try, or definitely would not try to find out who committed the crime?

5. Generally speaking, how would you characterize your attitude toward the police?

Scoring:

1. Yes = 1
2. No = 2
9. Don't know

1. Definitely   } = 1
2. Probably
3. Probably not } = 2
4. Definitely not
5. Depends on
9. Don't know

1. Definitely   } = 1
2. Probably
3. Probably not } = 2
4. Definitely not
5. Depends on
9. Don't know

1. Very favorable   } = 1
2. Favorable
3. Neutral
4. Unfavorable   } = 2
5. Very unfavorable
9. Don't know

Chapter 5

THE VICTIM IN THE
ADMINISTRATION OF CRIMINAL JUSTICE:
PROBLEMS AND PERCEPTIONS

RICHARD D. KNUDTEN
ANTHONY MEADE
MARY KNUDTEN and
WILLIAM DOERNER

While substantive criminal law focuses exclusively upon harm experienced as a result of an unlawful act or omission, the overall costs of crime victimization to an individual are not limited to the crime incident alone. Once a case enters the criminal court system, the victim-witness becomes susceptible to a myriad of problems and needs. In his critical review of the criminal justice system's treatment of witnesses, Ash (1972:397) has labeled these problems "victim-ization by administrative runaround." A prosecuting attorney himself, Ash (p. 407) puts much of the blame on the court system which

> exhibits the natural human tendency to favor "insider interests" at the expense of "outsider interests." Wherever minor inconvenience to "in-siders" (judges, lawyers, court clerks, etc.) is to be balanced against major inconvenience to outsiders (witnesses, jurors, etc.) and the balancing is to be performed by insiders, insider interests will invariably prevail.

He also points to the paucity of hard data documenting these problems.

AUTHORS' NOTE: *This paper was prepared under grant no. 75-NI-99-0018-G from the National Institute of Law Enforcement and Criminal Justice, Law Enforcement Assistance Administration, U.S. Department of Justice. Points of view or opinions stated in this document are those of the authors and do not necessarily represent the official position or policies of the U.S. Department of Justice.*

This chapter reports the initial findings of a study intended to supply that documentation. It examines the extent to which various types of problems are experienced by victims in the course of their assisting with the administration of justice.

METHOD

A saturation sample of victims actively participating in the criminal justice process in Milwaukee, Wisconsin, was interviewed. The victims were contacted as their cases were processed at any one of four stages in the criminal justice process: (1) the screening conference in a district attorney's office, where a decision to charge or not charge an offender is arrived at; (2) the preliminary hearing in front of a circuit court judge, where evidence is reviewed to determine if it meets the probable cause criterion that determines whether or not the case will proceed to the felony trial stage; (3) the misdemeanor trial; and (4) the felony trial.

While the study design necessitated the gathering of data over a 48-week period, the data presented in this chapter refer only to those victims contacted during the first quarter (12 weeks) of the study. During that interval, interviews of 386 crime victims were completed; 65% of the interviews were conducted on site, while 35% were completed over the telephone when time or convenience did not permit questioning at the appropriate location. In terms of stages, 37% of those questioned were contacted at the screening conference, 30% at the misdemeanor trial, 18% at the preliminary hearing, and 15% at the time of the felony trial stage. These percentages not only indicate representation of victims at different junctures of the criminal justice process, but also tend to reflect the relative volume of "business" carried out within the respective levels during the period under analysis. Victimizations were classified into categories of *personal offense* (42%), *property offense* (45%), and *other offense* (13%). Personal offenses referred to those incidents in which the victim was either injured or threatened with injury. Property offenses included those cases involving theft of or damage to the victim's possessions as well as cases of attempted theft or damage. Other offenses were primarily family problem or disorderly conduct cases.

THE SAMPLE

One of the interesting findings of victimization survey research is that those same demographic groups which are overrepresented among offenders in arrest statistics (FBI, 1974:124-135) are also overrepresented in the victimized

Table 1. DEMOGRAPHIC COMPARISON OF MILWAUKEE COUNTY POPULATION
15 YEARS OF AGE AND OLDER WITH STUDY SAMPLE (Percentages)

Demographic Characteristic of Victim	County Population	Study Sample
Sex		
Male	47[a]	54
Female	53	46
Race		
White	92	70
Black	8	30
Age		
15-20	12	17
21-29	21	36
30-49	31	30
50 and over	36	17
Education		
Some high school or less	45	30
High school graduate	34	41
Some college	21	29

a. Percentages rounded to nearest whole number.

population (LEAA, 1974; Ennis, 1967). As can be seen in Table 1, results in the present study are consistent with these findings. When compared with the general population of Milwaukee County, males, blacks, and persons under 30 years of age are overrepresented among victims of crime (Beverstock and Stuckert, 1972).

FINDINGS

This section of the chapter is organized into six subsections: (1) victim satisfaction with and other ratings of criminal justice personnel; (2) the costs to the victim and others of participating in the administration of justice; (3) a summary presentation of the data regarding the problems that victims experienced in connection with their participation in the system; (4) an analysis of those problems by demographic characteristics of the victim; (5) an analysis of those problems by the stage in the criminal process; (6) an analysis of those problems by factors related to the offense.

Victim Satisfaction

Given what Ash (1972) and others have reported about the callous, indifferent, and exploitative treatment which victims receive from the criminal justice system (see the chapters by McDonald, Lynch, and Ziegenhagen in this volume), our findings regarding the satisfaction of victims with their treatment

Table 2. OVERALL VICTIM SATISFACTION WITH HANDLING OF THEIR CASE
BY SYSTEM PERSONNEL GROUPS (Percentages)

| | Type of System Representative | | |
Victim Response	Police	District Attorney	Judge
Very satisfied	41	27	24
Satisfied	40	48	42
Dissatisfied	10	9	9
Very dissatisfied	3	6	5
No opinion	6	10	20

and other victim opinions about the criminal justice system are surprising. A
large majority of the victims in this study were not critical of the criminal justice
officials. As reported in Table 2, 8 out of 10 crime victims who had contact with
the police indicated that they were generally either "satisfied" or "very
satisfied" with the handling of their case by the police. The district attorneys
were rated almost as highly with 75% of the victims indicating overall
satisfaction. Of those victims who had an experience with a judge, two-thirds
were either "satisfied" or "very satisfied" with the judge's overall performance.

Also surprising is the finding that approximately 70% of the victims felt that
police, prosecutors, and judges, respectively, "are interested in helping victims of
crime."

However, there is one finding which seems to be in line with what critics of
the criminal justice system's handling of victims would lead one to expect.
Victims who experienced two or more adjournments during the prosecution of
their cases were less likely (55%) than those who had no adjournments or only
one adjournment (71%) to be satisfied or very satisfied with the judge.

Thus, victim satisfaction with the performance of one criminal justice
official—namely, the judge—seems to decline as the "administrative runaround"
takes its toll. However, this finding is most curious because it holds only for the
judge, not for the police or the district attorney—as Ash and others would lead
one to expect. Things become even more complex when the data are analyzed

Table 3. RATINGS OF POLICE BY VICTIMS (Percentages)

| | Criterion | | |
Rating	Effort	Effectiveness	Courteousness
Excellent	50	42	60
Good	23	28	26
Fair	15	16	8
Poor	9	9	3
No opinion	3	5	3

Table 4. RATINGS OF DISTRICT ATTORNEY BY VICTIMS (Percentages)

| | Criterion | | |
Rating	Effort	Effectiveness	Courteousness
Excellent	37	29	55
Good	34	32	32
Fair	15	18	7
Poor	8	7	2
No opinion	6	14	4

by the four stages in the process at which victims were interviewed. Victims who have reached the felony trial stage had experienced (as one would expect) more adjournments and days lost than victims at the other three stages (initial screening, preliminary hearing, and misdemeanor trial). Yet the felony-trial-stage victims were the group most likely to indicate satisfaction with the police and the district attorney. In contrast, misdemeanor-trial-stage victims were less likely than either felony-trial-stage or preliminary-hearing-stage victims to indicate overall satisfaction. In addition, misdemeanor-trial-stage victims were least likely to agree that police and prosecutors are interested in helping victims.

These results suggest several unanticipated, tentative conclusions. It appears that the "administrative runaround" does lead to victim dissatisfaction but that dissatisfaction is not generalized to all criminal justice officials. Rather it ends up being focused only on the judge. Furthermore, it seems that the difference in the kind of involvement that the victim has in the administration of justice affects the relationship between "administrative runaround" (at least as measured by repeated adjournments) and victim dissatisfaction. The more involved the victim gets in assisting in the administration of justice the less likely he is to be dissatisfied even though he experiences a large number of adjournments and loses considerable personal income. Felony-trial-stage victims are more involved in their cases in the sense that there is longer, more intense, and more personalized contact between those victims and the prosecutors and policemen involved in their cases than are victims at any of the other three stages of the

Table 5. RATINGS OF JUDGE BY VICTIMS (Percentages)

| | Criterion | | |
Rating	Effort	Effectiveness	Courteousness
Excellent	33	31	43
Good	33	29	32
Fair	13	13	8
Poor	5	6	2
No opinion	16	21	15

Table 6. SUMMARY DATA ON SYSTEM-RELATED VICTIM PROBLEMS

Problem	Percentage Answering "Yes"	Incidence Level*	Percentage Experiencing Problem Who Rated It as		Intensity Level (VS + S)**
			Very Serious	Serious	
Did you make unneeded or excessive trips to the police station, courthouse, or safety building?	33	(moderate)	41	34	(high)
Did you have difficulty finding the correct building, office, or courtroom?	23	(low)	16	21	(moderate)
Was it difficult for you to get transportation?	12	(low)	42	25	(high)
Did you have difficulty finding parking space?	28	(low)	28	36	(moderate)
Did you have to pay for transportation or parking?	87	(high)	12	25	(moderate)
Did you lose time from work or school?	63	(high)	41	27	(high)
Did you lose income?	40	(moderate)	52	26	(high)
Was it difficult or necessary to find some way of taking care of your children?	16	(low)	33	40	(high)
Did you have difficulty finding out what you were supposed to do once you got there?	16	(low)	33	37	(high)
Did you have to spend a long time waiting?	56	(high)	33	35	(high)
Were the waiting conditions uncomfortable?	30	(low)	29	30	(moderate)
Were you exposed to threatening or upsetting persons?	11	(low)	39	27	(high)
Was some of your property kept as evidence?	18	(low)	13	15	(low)

*If a problem was indicated by at least one-third (33%) of the respondents, it was classified as low on incidence, while a figure of 50% or more was rated high. A lesser percentage was rated moderate.

**With respect to intensity, the lower cutting point of 33% was again used, though the upper cutting point of 33% was increased to 66% or more. This more demanding criterion for high intensity was selected so that respondents had the opportunity of indicating at least two levels of seriousness.

process—all of which typically involve considerably less interaction between the victims and the police and prosecutors. Apparently, as a result of this greater involvement, the victim tends to be more tolerant of the inconveniences and expenses to himself and more convinced that the police and prosecutors with whom he is working are indeed interested in helping him. In contrast, the victims in misdemeanor trials do not receive the same kind or intensity of attention from prosecutors and police and consequently go away less satisfied with the experience.

If it is true that victim dissatisfaction is reversed by the intimate relations established during the course of a felony trial, this is an interesting but not too encouraging finding. It is interesting because it suggests that the disaffection which the administration of justice breeds among participating victims can be countered under certain circumstances. It is not encouraging because most criminal cases are not disposed of by felony trials. Those particular circumstances which are conducive to counteracting victim disaffection are not going to have an opportunity to operate in most criminal cases.

In addition to rating their general satisfaction, victims were asked to give ratings of the police, prosecutors, and judges on three more specific criteria —namely, effort, effectiveness, and courteousness. Again, the findings are surprising (see Tables 3, 4, and 5). The majority of victims rated all three types of criminal justice agents as good or excellent on all three criteria. The criterion on which there was most agreement among victims that criminal justice officials were doing a "good" or "excellent" job was courteousness. In contrast, the least agreement about "good" or "excellent" performance was over effectiveness.

Also, there were some differences in the ratings. The police were given high ratings for effectiveness more frequently than were the district attorneys or the judges. The police were also given high ratings for courteousness more frequently than were judges.

Costs to Victims and Others

There are two types of costs associated with being a crime victim: the costs associated with victimization itself and those additional costs associated with cooperating with the administration of justice. The latter costs are of particular interest to the theme of this book.

Of all the study victims, 62% lost one day or less from work or school as a result of their involvement in the administration of justice. Another 26% lost between two and three days. The median income loss was $44, with 137 victims totaling $13,344 in lost income. Where actual waiting time was concerned—i.e., the difference between the time the victim was asked to appear and the time at which the case proceedings began—the 386 victims showed a total wait of about

Table 7. TIME PROBLEMS BY VICTIM CHARACTERISTIC: UNNECESSARY TRIPS AND ADJOURNMENTS
(Number and Percentage)[a]

Demographic Characteristic of Victim	Those Indicating Unnecessary Trips as a Problem	Those Experiencing Problem Who Rated It as Very Serious or Serious	Number of Adjournments			
			0	1	2	3+
Sex						
Male	(76) 36	(57) 75	(60) 44	(33) 24	(20) 15	(13) 17
Female	(51) 29	(38) 74	(41) 44	(26) 28	(9) 10	(17) 18
Race						
White	(88) 34	(63) 72	(72) 46	(38) 24	(22) 14	(26) 16
Black	(37) 32	(31) 84	(28) 41	(20) 29	(7) 10	(14) 20
Age						
15-20	(17) 26	(13) 76	(22) 58	(8) 21	(3) 8	(5) 13
21-29	(49) 35	(35) 71	(30) 38	(22) 28	(10) 12	(18) 22
39-49	(39) 34	(29) 74	(26) 38	(18) 26	(13) 19	(11) 16
50 and over	(22) 34	(17) 77	(24) 54	(12) 27	(2) 4	(6) 14
Education						
Some high school or less	(33) 29	(23) 70	(23) 37	(22) 36	(7) 11	(10) 16
High school graduate	(49) 31	(40) 82	(44) 46	(18) 19	(13) 14	(21) 22
Some college	(45) 40	(31) 69	(35) 49	(20) 28	(8) 11	(9) 12

a. Number in parentheses

495 hours. The median time spent waiting was one hour, with 11 victims not having to wait at all and one victim experiencing a wait in excess of eight hours. Income loss was the problem most likely to be given a rating of "very serious." When simultaneously considering incident-related and system-related costs, the total monetary consequences of victimization observed for these 386 respondents was more than $180,000, probably a conservative estimate of ultimate victimization financial impact inasmuch as many of these respondents will be required to make further appearances as their respective cases progress toward termination.

The victim's participation in the administration of justice results in financial and other costs and inconveniences not only to himself but also to other people who are a part of his network of social relations. Thus, 37% of the victims indicated that at least one "close" associate had been "seriously inconvenienced" as a result of the respondent's victimization. Also, 17% of the victims said that at least one person who is close to them had experienced "serious financial consequences," and 30% stated that at least one had known "serious mental or emotional suffering" as a consequence of the present victimization.

Victim Problems Experienced: A Summary

Study victims were asked what kinds of problems they had experienced as a result of their case coming to the attention of the district attorney's office. Results for 13 problem items are presented in Table 6. The selection of items was made after a review of Ash's work (1972) and after extensive direct observation of the victim-witness experience within the court system under study. Respondents were also asked to rate the relative seriousness of their problems as they perceived them.

In the paragraphs below the problems experienced by victims are analyzed in greater detail. For convenience, the problems experienced by victims have been divided into four categories: (1) *time-related* problems (including unnecessary trips; long waiting time; time lost from work or school; the number of adjournments experienced; length of time spent waiting for the case to be handled on the day of the interview contact; and the total number of days lost from work or school since the case came to the attention of the district attorney's office); (2) *financial* problems (lost income; transportation and parking costs); (3) *court-setting* problems (including difficulties in where to go; finding out what to do once one arrives; discomfort because of unpleasant waiting conditions; and anxiety because of exposure to threatening or unsettling persons); (4) *personal* problems (such as child care, arranging transportation, and having one's property kept as evidence).

The analysis of these problems is done in three parts: by demographic

Table 8. TIME PROBLEMS BY VICTIM CHARACTERISTICS: WAITING TIME (Number and Percentage)[a]

Demographic Characteristic of Victim	Those Indicating Waiting Time as a Problem	Those Experiencing Problem Who Rated It as Very Serious or Serious	Minutes Spent Waiting				
			0-30	31-60	61-90	91-120	121+
Sex							
Male	(126) 60	(89) 71	(34) 18	(55) 29	(32) 17	(32) 17	(37) 20
Female	(90) 52	(59) 66	(42) 28	(55) 36	(16) 10	(17) 11	(23) 15
Race							
White	(154) 59	(103) 67	(49) 20	(84) 35	(29) 12	(34) 14	(45) 19
Black	(59) 51	(43) 73	(27) 27	(26) 26	(17) 17	(14) 14	(15) 15
Age							
15-20	(32) 49	(20) 62	(10) 17	(23) 39	(6) 10	(11) 19	(9) 15
21-29	(86) 61	(61) 71	(30) 24	(33) 27	(24) 20	(13) 11	(23) 19
30-49	(61) 53	(39) 64	(27) 26	(34) 32	(13) 12	(13) 12	(18) 17
50 and over	(37) 58	(29) 78	(8) 14	(21) 38	(5) 9	(12) 21	(10) 18
Education							
Some high school or less	(58) 51	(39) 67	(23) 23	(35) 35	(7) 7	(16) 16	(18) 18
High school graduate	(98) 61	(70) 71	(30) 20	(40) 27	(25) 17	(24) 16	(27) 18
Some college	(60) 54	(40) 67	(22) 22	(36) 37	(16) 16	(9) 9	(15) 15

a. Number in parentheses.

characteristics of the victim; by stage in the criminal process at which the victim was interviewed; and by factors related to the offense.

Victim Problems Experienced: By Demographic Characteristics

Time-Related Problems. The extent to which time-related problems were differentially perceived or experienced by demographically classified victim groups is indicated in Tables 7 through 10. While it was the college group which demonstrated the highest percentage indicating unnecessary trips as a problem (40%), the high school graduate group, as noted in Table 7, was more likely than either of the other educational groups to rate the making of unnecessary trips as a very serious or serious problem (82% as compared to 70% and 69%). These results appear consistent with the finding that the high school graduate group was also the educational group most likely (55%) to have had cases adjourned on two or more occasions. Similarly, the age group 15-20 was less likely than the older age groups to have experienced an adjournment and, as would be expected, was the age group least likely (26%) to have specified unnecessary trips as a problem. Although the results with respect to adjournment experiences and the percentage specifying unnecessary trips as a problem were essentially the same for white and black respondents, blacks (84%) were more likely than whites (72%) to rate their unnecessary trip problem as serious. ("Serious," throughout our discussion, combines both the serious and the very serious ratings.) Males were somewhat more likely than females to designate unnecessary trips as a problematic experience, though there was no indication that males experienced adjournments to a greater degree than did females.

Among age groups, the oldest group had the highest percentage (78%) perceiving their waiting-time problem as serious (see Table 8). This finding is understandable in that the 50-and-over category was both least likely to have a short wait (30 minutes or less) and most likely to have a long wait (more than 90 minutes). As was the case for unnecessary trips, males were somewhat more likely than females to indicate that waiting was a problem. Male victims also were considerably more likely than female victims (a difference of 18 percentage units) to have experienced a wait in excess of one hour. The high school graduate category was more likely than either of the other educational groups to indicate that waiting time was a problem and was also more likely to have had a wait of more than one hour. White victims were more likely than black victims to identify waiting time as a problem.

As seen in Table 9, males (26%) were more likely than females (17%) to have had a time loss of three days or more away from normal activities. Though males indicated time loss as a problematic experience more often than females, there was essentially no difference between the percentage of males and females who

Table 9. TIME PROBLEMS BY VICTIM CHARACTERISTICS: TIME LOST FROM NORMAL ACTIVITIES (Number and Percentage)[a]

Demographic Characteristic of Victim	Those Indicating Time Lost from Normal Activities as a Problem	Those Experiencing Problem Who Rated It as Very Serious or Serious	Number of Days Lost			
			1	2	3	4+
Sex						
Male	(147) 71	(102) 69	(85) 60	(19) 13	(19) 13	(19) 13
Female	(92) 53	(65) 71	(59) 66	(15) 17	(5) 6	(10) 11
Race						
White	(177) 68	(115) 65	(105) 62	(29) 17	(14) 8	(22) 13
Black	(58) 50	(50) 86	(35) 61	((5) 5	(10) 18	(7) 12
Age						
15-20	(40) 62	(25) 62	(30) 77	(4) 10	(2) 5	(3) 8
21-29	(88) 63	(57) 65	(46) 55	(11) 13	(12) 14	(15) 18
30-49	(73) 64	(56) 77	(42) 59	(16) 22	(19) 13	(4) 6
50 and over	(38) 61	(29) 76	(26) 70	(3) 8	(2) 5	(6) 16
Education						
Some high school or less	(53) 48	(36) 68	(34) 67	(5) 10	(6) 12	(6) 12
High school graduate	(99) 62	(74) 75	(55) 58	(18) 19	(10) 10	(12) 13
Some college	(87) 78	(57) 66	(55) 65	(11) 13	(9) 11	(10) 12

a. Number in parentheses.

perceived their problem as serious. Whites were more likely than blacks (a difference of 18 percentage units) to regard their problem as serious even though blacks were more likely than whites to have experienced a three-day-or-more time loss. Among those who specified loss of time as a problem experience, the two oldest age groups were more likely than either the 15-20 or 21-29 age groups to rate their problem as serious. While those having had some college were more likely than the other educational backgrounds to have viewed lost time as a problem, it was the high school graduate group that was most likely to rate it as serious when they experienced it.

Certain consistencies emerged when time-related inconveniences were compared in relation to demographic characteristics of victims. First, high school graduates, blacks, and persons aged 30 and over tended to rate their time-related problems as serious to a greater extent than their respective comparison groups. Analysis of the more quantitative indices did not always support the subjective, seriousness-rating results, however. Second, male victims were more likely than female victims to indicate the experiencing of time-related inconveniences.

Table 10. FINANCIAL PROBLEMS BY VICTIM CHARACTERISTICS: INCOME LOSS (Number and Percentage)[a]

Demographic Characteristics of Victim	Those Indicating Income Loss as a Problem	Those Experiencing Problem Who Rated It as Very Serious or Serious	Income Loss in Dollars		
			25 or less	26-100	101+
Sex					
Male	(90) 44	(67) 74	(10) 74	(35) 50	(25) 36
Female	(60) 35	(50) 83	(25) 48	(23) 44	(4) 8
Race					
White	(112) 44	(82) 73	(26) 29	(41) 46	(22) 25
Black	(36) 32	(34) 94	(19) 29	(15) 48	(7) 23
Age					
15-20	(20) 32	(16) 80	(10) 59	(6) 35	(1) 6
21-29	(58) 42	(43) 74	(14) 29	(21) 44	(13) 27
30-49	(54) 48	(46) 85	(9) 20	(23) 50	(14) 30
50 and over	(18) 30	(12) 67	(2) 18	(7) 64	(2) 18
Education					
Some high school or less	(34) 31	(29) 85	(11) 37	(13) 43	(6) 20
High school graduate	(72) 45	(56) 78	(17) 28	(30) 50	(13) 22
Some college	(44) 41	(32) 73	(7) 22	(14) 44	(11) 34

a. Number in parentheses.

Examination of the quantitative data showed that males also experienced inconveniences of a greater magnitude in terms of minutes spent waiting and days lost from work or school than did females. It should be emphasized that demographically classified victim groups may regularly experience problems at different rates and/or perceive them with different degrees of intensity. Thus, sensitivity to such experiential continuums and the distribution of their empirical referents among victim types ought to be a major priority for criminal justice planners and professionals.

Financial Problems. The results of the analysis of system-related financial problems are presented in Tables 10 and 11. While female victims and black victims were less likely than male victims and white victims, respectively, to have specified income loss as a problem, those within each of the former groups who did so were more likely to rate their problem as serious. Somewhat inconsistent with the above is the fact that males were more likely than females (a difference of 34 percentage units) to have had an income loss greater than $25. There was no difference between the percentage of black and white victims having lost income in excess of $25. Among age groups, the 50-and-over category showed the lowest percentage indicating income loss as a problem and also the lowest percentage giving this problem a serious rating when it was experienced. In this context, it is interesting to note that when income loss was specified as a

Table 11. FINANCIAL PROBLEMS BY VICTIM CHARACTERISTICS:
TRANSPORTATION AND PARKING COSTS (Number and Percentage)[a]

Demographic Characteristic of Victim	Those Indicating Paying for Transportation or Parking as a Problem	Those Experiencing Problem Who Rated It as Very Serious or Serious
Sex		
Male	(187) 90	(72) 38
Female	(144) 83	(52) 36
Race		
White	(229) 87	(79) 34
Black	(97) 84	(45) 46
Age		
15-20	(48) 74	(14) 29
21-29	(123) 88	(60) 49
30-49	(100) 87	(28) 28
50 and over	(61) 95	(22) 36
Education		
Some high school or less	(98) 86	(36) 37
High school graduate	(139) 87	(61) 44
Some college	(95) 86	(27) 28

a. Number in parentheses.

problem, the 50-and-over group was the age category most likely to have known a loss greater than $25. The subjective importance attached to a loss of income appears, then, to be lowest for the oldest age group. Those respondents having had some high school or less, although not as likely to indicate income loss as a problem, were more likely than either of the other educational groups to rate the problem as serious once it had been experienced. The fact that the high school nongraduate group was the educational unit least likely to have noted a loss of more than $25 suggests that it attached greater subjective importance to a loss of income than did those respondent groups with more education.

Among those respondents who designated transportation and parking costs as a problem, blacks (46%) were more likely than whites (34%) to perceive the problem as serious. While the percentage indicating transportation and parking costs as a problematic experience basically increased with victim age level, the 21-29 group, as seen in Table 11, was considerably more likely than the other groups to rate their experience as serious. Especially when compared to the college group, the high school graduate group was more likely than the other

Table 12. COURT-SETTING PROBLEMS BY VICTIM CHARACTERISTICS
(Number and Percentage)[a]

Demographic Characteristic of Victim	Those Indicating Waiting Conditions as a Problem	Those Experiencing Problem Who Rated It as Very Serious or Serious	Those Indicating Exposure to Threatening or Upsetting Persons as a Problem	Those Experiencing Problem Who Rated It as Very Serious or Serious
Sex				
Male	(62) 30	(38) 61	(18) 9	(12) 67
Female	(52) 30	(30) 58	(23) 13	(15) 65
Race				
White	(65) 25	(34) 52	(31) 12	(19) 61
Black	(46) 40	(33) 72	(28) 9	(8) 80
Age				
15-20	(19) 29	(9) 47	(19) 14	(7) 78
21-29	(55) 39	(36) 65	(25) 18	(16) 64
30-49	(25) 22	(13) 52	(5) 4	(3) 60
50 and over	(15) 24	(10) 67	(2) 3	(1) 50
Education				
Some high school or less	(34) 30	(18) 53	(10) 9	(7) 70
High school graduate	(58) 36	(34) 59	(21) 13	(13) 62
Some college	(22) 20	(16) 73	(10) 9	(7) 70

a. Number in parentheses.

educational groups to perceive their transportation and parking cost problems as serious, although there were essentially no intergroup differences with respect to the percentages indicating such costs as a problem. One thing that stands out in Tables 10 and 11 is the fact that black victims are clearly more likely than white victims to view their system-related financial costs as a serious problem.

Court-Related Problems. Results regarding court-setting problems are presented in Tables 12 and 13. Black victims, as recorded in Table 12, were much more likely than white victims (40% as compared to 25%) to indicate uncomfortable waiting conditions as a problem and were also more likely to regard these conditions as a serious concern. Blacks were not more likely than whites to specify exposure to threatening or upsetting persons as a problem, but when they did give this indication, a greater percentage rated it as serious. Thus, the tendency for black victims to more often judge their problematic experience as serious was again observed. Victims under 30 years of age were more likely than those 30 and over to specify uncomfortable waiting conditions and exposure to upsetting persons as problems. The percentage of respondents rating the latter problem as serious decreased as the victim age-level increased. With

Table 13. COURT-SETTING PROBLEMS BY VICTIM CHARACTERISTICS
(Number and Percentage)[a]

Demographic Characteristic of Victim	Those Indicating Finding Out Where to Go as a Problem	Those Experiencing Problem Who Rated It as Very Serious or Serious	Those Indicating Finding Out What to Do as a Problem	Those Experiencing Problem Who Rated It as Very Serious or Serious
Sex				
Male	(42) 20	(14) 33	(26) 12	(18) 69
Female	(44) 25	(18) 41	(37) 21	(26) 70
Race				
White	(56) 21	(18) 32	(48) 18	(32) 67
Black	(28) 24	(14) 50	(14) 12	(12) 86
Age				
15-20	(20) 31	(4) 20	(15) 23	(6) 40
21-29	(33) 23	(12) 36	(14) 17	(18) 75
30-49	(24) 21	(12) 50	(19) 17	(16) 84
50 and over	(10) 16	(4) 40	(5) 8	(4) 80
Education				
Some high school or less	(28) 25	(10) 36	(19) 17	(14) 74
High school graduate	(39) 24	(15) 38	(24) 15	(15) 62
Some college	(20) 18	(7) 35	(20) 18	(15) 75

a. Number in parentheses.

respect to educational distinctions, victims with some college background were less likely than the other two groups to specify uncomfortable waiting conditions as a problem. However, the college group was the education group most likely to rate this problem as serious when it was experienced.

The percentage of respondents indicating that finding out where to go and what to do were problems clearly decreased with victim age-level, although those 30 and over were more likely than those under 30 to rate these problems as serious. A pattern which emerged from the court-setting problem data was the tendency for the percentage of respondents rating their difficulties as serious to increase with victim age-level.

Personal Problems. As indicated in Table 14, females more often than males, and blacks more often than whites, indicated that they had some difficulty in arranging transportation. Black victims were again considerably more likely than white victims to regard the problem as serious (a difference of 20 percentage units). The percentage of victims specifying transportation difficulties as a problem tended to decrease with both age and educational level. Victims 30 and over, however, were more likely than those under 30 to perceive their transportation problem in serious terms.

With regard to the problem of the nonreturn of victim property that has been held as evidence, males were more likely than females to have indicated that this was a problem. What is more, as the age and educational level of the victim increased, the percentage of victims indicating that this was a problem also increased. Among those having had property kept as evidence, black victims were more likely than white victims to rate this as a serious problem, and the high school graduate group was clearly more apt to perceive this concern as serious than were the other two educational groups.

As expected, female victims were more likely than male victims to indicate child care as a problem. Also as expected, middle-aged victims were more likely than young or old victims to indicate child care as a problem. Among the educational groups, the high school graduate group was most likely to indicate this as a problem.

Victim Problems Experienced: By Stage in the Criminal Process

The extent to which problematic experiences for victims vary by stage of involvement in the criminal justice process is presented in Tables 15 through 20.

Time-Related Problems. As expected, victims interviewed at the later stages (preliminary hearing, misdemeanor trial, and felony trial) were more likely than those interviewed at the earliest stage (the district attorney screening stage) to indicate unnecessary trips as a problem (see Table 15). Trial-stage respondents (both misdemeanor and felony) were considerably more likely than preliminary-

Table 14. PERSONAL PROBLEMS BY VICTIM CHARACTERISTICS (Number and Percentage)[a]

Demographic Characteristics of Victim	Those Indicating Getting Transportation as a Problem	Those Experiencing Problem Who Rated It as Very Serious or Serious	Those Indicating Property Kept as Evidence as a Problem	Those Experiencing Problem Who Rated It as Very Serious or Serious	Those Indicating Child Care as a Problem	Those Experiencing Problem Who Rated It as Very Serious or Serious
Sex						
Male	(16) 8	(10) 62	(44) 21	(12) 27	(11) 5	(8) 73
Female	(32) 18	(22) 69	(23) 13	(7) 30	(39) 28	(36) 74
Race						
White	(23) 9	(13) 56	(48) 18	(12) 25	(35) 14	(26) 74
Black	(25) 22	(19) 76	(19) 16	(7) 37	(22) 19	(16) 73
Age						
15-20	(12) 18	(6) 50	(8) 12	(3) 38	(5) 8	(4) 80
21-29	(17) 12	(11) 65	(26) 18	(8) 31	(33) 23	(23) 70
30-49	(15) 13	(12) 80	(21) 18	(4) 19	(21) 19	(16) 76
50 and over	(4) 6	(3) 75	(13) 20	(5) 38	(1) 2	(1)100
Education						
Some high school or less	(17) 15	(11) 65	(11) 10	(2) 18	(16) 14	(12) 75
High school graduate	(22) 14	(16) 73	(31) 19	(14) 45	(34) 22	(25) 74
Some college	(9) 8	(5) 56	(26) 23	(4) 15	(10) 9	(7) 70

a. Number in parentheses.

Table 15. TIME PROBLEMS BY STAGE AT WHICH INTERVIEW WAS CONDUCTED: UNNECESSARY TRIPS AND ADJOURNMENTS (Number and Percentage)[a]

System Stage of Involvement	Those Indicating Unnecessary Trips as a Problem	Those Experiencing Problem Who Rated It as Very Serious or Serious	Number of Adjournments[b]			
			0	1	2	3+
Screening hearing	(22) 16	(15) 62				
Preliminary hearing	(19) 32	(15) 79	(36) 65	(14) 26	(3) 5	(2) 4
Misdemeanor trial	(56) 48	(44) 79	(50) 45	(30) 27	(17) 15	(15) 13
Felony trial	(31) 44	(21) 68	(16) 25	(16) 25	(9) 14	(23) 36

a. Number in parentheses.
b. There are no adjournments at the screening hearing stage.

Table 16. TIME PROBLEMS BY STAGE AT WHICH INTERVIEW WAS CONDUCTED: WAITING TIME
(Number and Percentage)[a]

System Stage of Involvement	Those Indicating Waiting Time as a Problem	Those Experiencing Problem Who Rated It as Very Serious or Serious	Minutes Spent Waiting				
			0-30	31-60	61-90	91-120	121+
Screening hearing	(35) 40	(21) 60	(29) 24	(43) 37	(16) 14	(15) 13	(14) 12
Preliminary hearing	(77) 59	(61) 79	(6) 11	(22) 42	(10) 19	(7) 13	(8) 15
Misdemeanor trial	(49) 66	(31) 63	(23) 21	(25) 23	(17) 16	(16) 15	(27) 25
Felony trial	(56) 70	(36) 64	(18) 26	(21) 32	(5) 8	(11) 17	(11) 17

a. Number in parentheses.

Table 17. TIME PROBLEMS BY STAGE AT WHICH INTERVIEW WAS CONDUCTED: TIME LOST FROM NORMAL ACTIVITIES
(Number and Percentage)[a]

System Stage of Involvement	Those Indicating Time Lost from Normal Activities as a Problem	Those Experiencing Problem Who Rated It as Very Serious or Serious	Number of Days Lost			
			1	2	3	4+
Screening hearing	(75) 54	(50) 67	(67) 89	(3) 4	(3) 4	(2) 3
Preliminary hearing	(32) 54	(22) 69	(21) 66	(7) 22	(2) 6	(2) 6
Misdemeanor trial	(77) 68	(58) 75	(36) 50	(15) 21	(11) 16	(9) 13
Felony trial	(56) 82	(38) 68	(20) 36	(9) 17	(9) 17	(16) 30

a. Number in parentheses.

[135]

hearing respondents (32%) to designate this as a problem. But preliminary-hearing respondents were equally likely as misdemeanor-trial-stage respondents and more likely than felony-trial-stage respondents to rate the problem as serious. However, objectively it was the felony-trial group that experienced the greatest number of adjournments.

With regard to time spent waiting for proceedings to begin, the two trial groups, as noted in Table 16, were more likely than the preliminary-hearing and the screening groups to indicate that this was a problem. The preliminary-hearing group had the greatest percentage giving this problem a serious rating upon experiencing it, though it was the misdemeanor-trial group which showed the greatest likelihood of experiencing a wait in excess of 90 minutes.

With regard to time lost from normal activities, trial-stage respondents, especially those involved in felony trials, were, as would be expected, more likely than the other two groups to indicate time lost from normal activities as a problem (Table 17). Also as expected, victims involved in felony trials were more likely than victims at any other stage to have lost at least three days from work or school. In summary, trial-stage respondents demonstrated the greatest degree of time-based inconvenience in terms of both that accumulated over the history of the case (unnecessary trips, adjournments, and days lost from normal activities) and that involving the immediate situation (minutes spent waiting).

Financial Problems. Again as would be expected, proportionately more trial-stage respondents indicated income loss as a problem than did the other two groups (Table 18). Negligible interstage differences were observed when comparing the percentages of those specifying income loss as a problem who, in turn, rated it as serious in nature. This latter finding is surprising in light of the fact that victims involved in felony-level cases (felony trial and preliminary hearing) were more likely than either those in misdemeanor trials or those at the screening stage to have experienced income losses in excess of $100.

Table 18. FINANCIAL PROBLEMS BY STAGE AT WHICH INTERVIEW WAS CONDUCTED: INCOME LOSS (Number and Percentage)[a]

System Stage of Involvement	Those Indicating Income Loss as a Problem	Those Experiencing Problem Who Rated It as Very Serious or Serious	Income Loss in Dollars		
			25 or less	26-100	101+
Screening hearing	(43) 32	(33) 77	(15) 44	(13) 38	(6) 18
Preliminary hearing	(15) 26	(12) 80	(1) 10	(4) 40	(5) 50
Misdemeanor trial	(53) 46	(44) 83	(14) 32	(22) 50	(8) 18
Felony trial	(40) 60	(29) 77	(5) 14	(19) 54	(11) 32

a. Number in parentheses.

Table 19. COURT-SETTING PROBLEMS BY STAGE AT WHICH INTERVIEW WAS CONDUCTED (Number and Percentage)[a]

System Stage of Involvement	Those Indicating Waiting Conditions as a Problem	Those Experiencing Problem Who Rated It as Very Serious or Serious	Those Indicating Exposure to Threatening or Upsetting Persons as a Problem	Those Experiencing Problem Who Rated It as Very Serious or Serious
Screening hearing	(13) 24	(8) 62	(16) 11	(9) 56
Preliminary hearing	(42) 22	(26) 62	(2) 3	(1) 50
Misdemeanor trial	(25) 36	(18) 72	(10) 9	(8) 80
Felony trial	(34) 36	(16) 47	(14) 20	(10) 71

a. Number in parentheses.

Court-Setting Problems. Trial-stage respondents, more often than the other two groups, indicated uncomfortable waiting conditions as a problem (see Table 19). However, among those who regarded waiting conditions as a problem, felony-trial victims were least likely to rate this as serious. In contrast, victims involved in misdemeanor trials were the group most likely to rate this problem as serious. Victims involved in felony trials were most likely to indicate exposure to upsetting persons as a problem. Both misdemeanor-stage and felony-stage victims were considerably more likely than the screening- or preliminary-hearing groups to rate this problem as serious.

Personal Problems. As Table 20 shows, victims involved in felony cases at the court level (preliminary hearing or felony trial) were considerably more likely than the victims at the other two stages to indicate property confiscation as a problem. But victims involved in felony trials were least likely to rate it as a serious concern. Perhaps victims at this stage have come to appreciate the relevance of property as evidence for the prosecution. It was the misdemeanor trial group (44%) that was most likely to give this problem a serious rating.

Table 20. PERSONAL PROBLEM BY STAGE AT WHICH INTERVIEW WAS CONDUCTED (Number and Percentage)[a]

System Stage of Involvement	Those Indicating Property Kept as Evidence as a Problem	Those Experiencing Problem Who Rated It as Very Serious or Serious
Screening hearing	(11) 8	(3) 27
Preliminary hearing	(22) 37	(8) 36
Misdemeanor trial	(9) 8	(4) 44
Felony trial	(26) 37	(5) 19

a. Number in parentheses.

Table 21. TIME PROBLEMS BY OFFENSE FACTORS: UNNECESSARY TRIPS AND ADJOURNMENTS
(Number and Percentage)[a]

Offense Factors	Those Indicating Unnecessary Trips as a Problem	Those Experiencing Problem Who Rated It as Very Serious or Serious	Number of Adjournments			
			0	1	2	3+
Victim Perception of Offense Seriousness						
Very serious	(63) 37	(48) 76	(39) 39	(22) 22	(18) 18	(22) 22
Serious	(52) 32	(39) 75	(51) 50	(27) 26	(7) 7	(17) 17
Not too serious or not serious at all	(12) 26	(7) 58	(12) 44	(10) 37	(4) 15	(1) 4
Victim Perception of Penalty						
Lenient	(41) 39	(36) 88	(35) 44	(14) 18	(15) 19	(16) 20
Fair or harsh	(31) 30	(19) 61	(39) 49	(20) 25	(7) 9	(14) 18

a. Number in parentheses.

Victim Problems Experienced: By Offense-Related Factors

Selected victim problems were analyzed by two offense-related factors, namely, the victim's perception of the seriousness of the offense and the victim's perception of the leniency of the penalty received by the offender.

Time Problems. As the perceived seriousness of the offense increased so did the percentage of victims who indicated that unnecessary trips were a problem (see Table 21). Similarly, while 58% of those perceiving the offense as of low seriousness rated their unnecessary trip experience as a serious problem, the comparative figure for those victims perceiving the offense as serious or very serious was about 75%. However, these two findings may be explained by the fact that the percentage of respondents having experienced two or more adjournments increased directly with victim perception of the seriousness of the offense.

Victims who regarded the offender's penalty as lenient were more likely to have indicated unnecessary trips as a problem, and they were more likely to define their unnecessary trip problem as serious. But, again, these two findings may be explained at least partly by the fact that those victims who regarded the penalty as lenient were also more likely to have experienced two or more adjournments than had victims who regarded the penalty as fair or harsh.

With regard to the problem of time spent waiting for a hearing, there were no notable differences in the frequency of experiencing this problem by perception of offense seriousness or by perception of leniency of the penalty (see Table 22). But again the victim's subjective rating of the seriousness of this problem tended to be higher among victims who perceived the offense as of higher seriousness and among victims who perceived the penalty as lenient. However, once again, both of these findings may be explained in part by the objective situation. That is, the percentage of respondents experiencing waits in excess of 90 minutes also increased with perceived seriousness of the offense, and victims who perceived the penalty as lenient were more likely to have experienced a wait of more than 90 minutes.

Thus, in summary, it appears that if victims believe that the crime is not serious or if they regard the sentence imposed as too lenient they are more likely to regard their participation in the administration of justice as a heavier burden than do victims who do not have these perceptions. But further analysis will have to be made of these relationships with other relevant variables controlled before these conclusions can be regarded as anything more than tentative.

Court-Setting Problems. Victims who felt that the penalty was lenient were more likely to have found all five court-setting experiences as problematic, as Tables 23 and 24 indicate. In only two instances (finding parking and finding out what to do), however, could it be said with any confidence that those

Table 22. TIME PROBLEMS BY OFFENSE FACTORS: WAITING TIME
(Number and Percentage)[a]

Offense Factors	Those Indicating Waiting Time as a Problem	Those Experiencing Problem Who Rated It as Very Serious or Serious	Minutes Spent Waiting				
			0-30	31-60	61-90	91-120	121+
Victim Perception of Offense Seriousness							
Very serious	(100) 58	(70) 70	(27) 18	(46) 30	(23) 15	(29) 19	(28) 18
Serious	(90) 54	(62) 69	(40) 27	(47) 32	(16) 11	(15) 10	(29) 20
Not too serious or not serious at all	(26) 55	(16) 62	(8) 20	(17) 41	(8) 20	(5) 12	(3) 7
Victim Perception of Penalty							
Lenient	(67) 64	(51) 76	(14) 14	(29) 30	(15) 15	(20) 20	(20) 20
Fair or harsh	(65) 64	(39) 60	(18) 19	(37) 39	(14) 15	(9) 9	(17) 18

a. Number in parentheses.

Table 23. COURT-SETTING PROBLEMS BY OFFENSE FACTORS (Number and Percentage)[a]

Offense Factors	Those Indicating Finding Parking as a Problem	Those Experiencing Problem Who Rated It as Very Serious or Serious	Those Indicating Finding Out Where to Go as a Problem	Those Experiencing Problem Who Rated It as Very Serious or Serious	Those Indicating Finding Out What to Do as a Problem	Those Experiencing Problem Who Rated It as Very Serious or Serious
Victim Perception of Offense Seriousness						
Very serious	(44) 26	(23) 52	(38) 22	(19) 50	(32) 19	(23) 72
Serious	(49) 30	(36) 74	(39) 24	(10) 26	(24) 14	(18) 75
Not too serious or not serious at all	(14) 30	(9) 64	(10) 21	(3) 30	(7) 15	(3) 43
Victim Perception of Penalty						
Lenient	(40) 38	(28) 70	(30) 29	(11) 37	(22) 21	(16) 73
Fair or harsh	(25) 24	(13) 52	(15) 15	(6) 40	(13) 13	(8) 62

a. Number in parentheses.

Table 24. COURT-SETTING PROBLEMS BY OFFENSE FACTORS
(Number and Percentage)[a]

Offense Factors	Those Indicating Waiting Conditions as a Problem	Those Experiencing Problem Who Rated It as Very Serious or Serious	Those Indicating Exposure to Threatening or Upsetting Persons as a Problem	Those Experiencing Problem Who Rated It as Very Serious or Serious
Victim Perception of Offense Seriousness				
Very serious	(60) 35	(41) 68	(24) 14	(18) 75
Serious	(38) 23	(20) 53	(15) 9	(8) 53
Not too serious or not serious at all	(16) 34	(7) 44	(3) 6	(2) 67
Victim Perception of Penalty				
Lenient	(45) 43	(28) 62	(23) 22	(16) 70
Fair or harsh	(27) 26	(18) 67	(11) 11	(7) 64

a. Number in parentheses.

judging an offender's penalty as lenient were more likely to rate their problem as serious.

The tendency for the percentage of these indicating a problematic experience to increase with perceived seriousness of an offense was observed for only one court-setting experience (exposure to upsetting persons). The positive pattern of association between the victims' perception of the seriousness of the offense and the percentage of those rating a problematic experience as serious was less marked for court-related problems than was the case for time-related problems. Those holding an offense to be very serious were, however, more likely to rate their problem as serious in four out of five comparisons (finding out where to go, finding out what to do, uncomfortable waiting conditions, and exposure to upsetting persons).

Personal Problems. For all three personal problems (see Table 25), it was observed that victims who perceived an offender's penalty as lenient tended to be more likely to rate a personal problem (babysitting, transportation, getting property returned) as serious upon experiencing it. Also, the association between the victims' perception of the seriousness of the offense and the percentage experiencing a problem who rated it as serious was again observed. The percentage rating both transportation and property kept as evidence as serious increased with the perceived seriousness of the offense, and the group that rated child care as not too serious or not serious at all was clearly the group least likely to rate their problem as serious.

IMPLICATIONS

A hue and cry has gone out for improving the criminal justice system's treatment of victims. Remedial action programs are already being established (see the chapters by McDonald, Lynch, and Ziegenhagen in this volume). However, these programs are moving blindly into the problem. Except for the present study there has been no systematic, empirical analysis of the problems actually experienced by victims as they participate in the administration of justice.

What, then, are the actual problems and needs of victims and witnesses and what reliable guidance can be given to reformers? The findings of the present study tentatively suggest that in designing improvements in the criminal justice treatment of victims the following points be taken into consideration:

1. There are several types of system-related problematic experiences whose overall impact can be cumulative. This suggests that a thorough description of the victim or witness situation requires a holistic and inclusive accounting system.

2. In a cumulative sense, no particular grouping of persons appears to monopolize problematic experiences. Certain groups, however, are more likely than others to perceive their problems as serious. Although problems are perceived in personal or idiosyncratic terms, service and assistance programs for victims and witnesses should not be so narrow in scope that they are primarily oriented to specific target groups such as blacks, women, or the elderly. Programs should be geared to types of problems rather than types of persons.

3. It is unlikely that any single program could respond to all the kinds of problems and needs expressed by victims and witnesses. Primary focus, therefore, should be placed upon common and high-intensity problems.

4. Effective programs to serve victims and witnesses will have to be multifaceted and interorganizational. They must be founded upon interagency cooperation.

5. Significant assistance to victims and witnesses can be rendered by changing the administrative procedures of the criminal justice system. For example, time-related inconvenience is a major problem that could be minimized by administrative reforms.

6. Victims and witnesses are apparently far more satisfied with the performance of criminal justice officials than reformers have believed. Thus, programs of victim-witness assistance will have to find their justifications on grounds other than improving the victim-witness opinion of criminal justice officials.

7. There are substantial financial losses to direct and indirect victims of crime

Table 25. PERSONAL PROBLEMS BY OFFENSE FACTORS (Number and Percentage)[a]

Offense Factors	Those Indicating Child Care as a Problem	Those Experiencing Problem Who Rated It as Very Serious or Serious	Those Indicating Getting Transportation as a Problem	Those Experiencing Problem Who Rated It as Very Serious or Serious	Those Indicating Property Kept as Evidence as a Problem	Those Experiencing Problem Who Rated It as Very Serious or Serious
Victim Perception of Offense Seriousness						
Very serious	(29) 17	(20) 69	(25) 15	(18) 72	(36) 21	(14) 39
Serious	(24) 15	(20) 83	(19) 12	(12) 63	(24) 14	(5) 21
Not too serious or not serious at all	(6) 13	(3) 50	(4) 8	(2) 50	(8) 17	(1) 12
Victim Perception of Penalty						
Lenient	(13) 13	(11) 85	(11) 11	(7) 64	(14) 14	(5) 36
Fair or harsh	(16) 16	(9) 56	(11) 11	(6) 55	(36) 35	(9) 25

a. Number in parentheses.

as well as to witnesses. Thus, victim compensation programs should consider the possibility of broadening their scope and compensating these individuals if their losses are not otherwise covered.

CONCLUSION

The results of this study indicate that significant assistance may be given to victims and witnesses by reducing the financial and time losses that they encounter during the processing of criminal cases. It implies the need for a reduced number of postponements, improved prosecutorial preparedness, more effective use of judicial court operations, and enhanced cross-agency coopera-tion. In essence, it supports the creation of a criminal justice equilibrium which would take into consideration the needs of all parties involved in the resolution and disposition of criminal justice cases. But this is easier said than done.

Although the system-related needs of the victims and witnesses may be best met when justice is speedy and certain, the defendant is not always served by a speedy trial. Thus, balancing the interests of the victim-witness against those of the defendant represents a critical issue for the future. The present imbalance implies a need for structural change and programming modification such that victims and witnesses can assume their legitimate place within the criminal justice resolution procedure. Other tinkering within the system is likely to be largely superficial in its impact until these important actors are returned to the point of centrality on the stage of criminal justice and until the system is modified to enhance their participation.

REFERENCES

ASH, M. (1972). "On witnesses: A radical critique of criminal court procedures." Notre Dame Lawyer, 48(December):386-425.

BEVERSTOCK, F., and STUCKERT, R. (eds., 1972). Metropolitan Milwaukee fact book: 1970. Milwaukee: Milwaukee Urban Observatory.

EDELHERTZ, H., and GEIS, G. (1974). Public compensation to victims of crime. New York: Praeger.

ENNIS, P.H. (1967). Criminal victimization in the United States: A report of a national survey. Washington, D.C.: U.S. Government Printing Office.

Federal Bureau of Investigation (1974). Uniform crime reports for the United States, 1973. Washington, D.C.: U.S. Department of Justice.

HALL, J. (1960). General principles of criminal law. New York: Bobbs-Merrill.

KNUDTEN, M.; KNUDTEN, R.D.; DOERNER, W.G.; and MEADE, A.G. (1975). "Will anyone be left to testify? Disenchantment with the criminal justice system." Paper presented at the annual meeting of the American Sociological Association, San Francisco.

Law Enforcement Assistance Administration (1974). Crime in eight American cities:
    Advance report (July). Washington, D.C.: U.S. Department of Justice.
ROTHSTEIN, P.F. (1974). "How the Uniform Crime Victims Reparations Act works."
    American Bar Association Journal, 60(December):1531-1535.

Chapter 6

PATTERNS OF VICTIM ADVOCACY

FREDRIC L. DuBOW and
THEODORE M. BECKER

This chapter considers the role of victim advocacy in legal proceedings involving crimes. By "advocacy" we mean attempts to argue for or otherwise promote the interests of victims in legal proceedings.

At one time in history the victim of crime exercised significant influence over the administration of justice. Over the centuries, however, the defendant and the state have evolved as the two parties that have legal standing in Anglo-American criminal proceedings. Except in states where private prosecutor laws still exist, the victim has no standing as an advocate of his own interests in a criminal trial. He may appear as a witness at a trial, but he otherwise must defer to the prosecutor, and it is not always the case that the prosecutor promotes the victim's interests. There exists for the victim no institutionalized way of controlling decisions regarding the prosecution or disposition of a case.

HISTORICAL DEVELOPMENTS IN THE
PROSECUTION OF CRIMINAL CASES

The use of specialized non-kin representatives in the settlement of disputes is a common characteristic of legal systems in urbanized societies (Rueschemeyer, 1973). However, in a great number of societies with simpler political and

AUTHORS' NOTE: *This paper is based, in part, on research supported by the American Bar Foundation. The views expressed here are those of the authors and not the American Bar Foundation.*

economic organizations and even in some settings in complex societies, self-representation is the usual form of legal participation (Schwartz and Miller, 1964). With self-representation, the involvement of parties in determining their legal fate is direct and often extensive. Proceedings tend to be less formal than those in which legal representatives are present. When representatives are introduced they begin by assisting parties in the pursuit of their own ends. Representatives begin by *standing in* for persons who cannot be present and by *speaking for* those who are. By virtue of their oratorical skills, their experience in dealing with legal proceedings, and their knowledge of the law, legal representatives serve as advisors or advocates. Although legal professionals have played a wide variety of roles (Nonet and Carlin, 1968), this discussion will focus on their roles as advocates.

The presence of legal professionals in the capacity of attorneys, judges, and scholars has been associated with the creation of legal forms and proceedings that are more complex and less accessible to the layman. The knowledge required to participate effectively in legal proceedings becomes more specialized and arcane. Whereas legal representatives began as aids to parties, they gradually became indispensable to the pursuit or protection of interests by legal means.[1] Inherent in the position of legal intermediary is the possibility that the representatives may respond to concerns other than those of the party when participating in legal proceedings.[2]

The development of the role of the prosecutor can be viewed as a *special* case of the emergence of legal representatives. In the course of the development of state political institutions, there comes a point where the state asserts its responsibility for the enforcement and prosecution of wrongs which formerly were the responsibility of local legal institutions (DuBow, 1974). Wrongs that were previously defined as disputes between private parties are redefined as wrongs against the state. Settlement processes that were formerly restitutive in character are replaced by legal proceedings under state authority that are increasingly punitive. The proportion of payments defined as fines belonging to the state enlarges as payments to the victim and his kin diminish and eventually disappear.[3] The state also seeks to enforce laws, such as those having to do with taxation, which define wrongs that private citizens do not experience as personal harms. In the case of the latter offenses, it is necessary for the state to employ agents to initiate prosecutions since private citizens do not have the sense of victimization as an incentive for action.

First in the realm of serious conduct and eventually over a broad range of minor offenses, a prosecutor employed by the state is introduced to present the case against an accused offender in court. The prosecutor enters the case as an advocate, but his principle client is the state, not the direct victim of the crime.

The victim's status as a party to the case is weakened and his influence on the course of the proceeding wanes. The victim may still have the possibility to seek restitution through other procedures, but the introduction of the state diminishes the effectiveness of such recourse. Restitutively oriented proceedings may find themselves in competition with the state for the settlement of action for personal wrongs.

Before the advent of the criminal process, the prospect of punitive sanctions was a distant threat to compel the offender to pay restitution to the victim. Once punishment in the state courts became more prominent, offenders predictably are less willing to undertake negotiations for restitution. Restitution under such conditions would be in addition to, rather than in place of, the punishment he already receives. The state's limitation on recourse to collective violence by private citizens limits the ability of local groups to coerce those who prove unwilling to restitute.[4]

The task of prosecuting state cases is initially performed by officials who have other executive or judicial functions. These may be sheriffs, tax collectors, or lay justices of the peace. The needs of central state institutions to review the implementation of state policies in lower courts leads to an emphasis on written records and standardized court procedures (Langbein, 1974). These require-ments, along with the pressure from an increasing number of state cases, contributes to the development of a specialized officer of the court responsible for prosecutions.[5]

CONTEMPORARY RELATIONS BETWEEN PROSECUTORS AND VICTIMS

With the establishment of the prosecutor the conditions for the general alienation of the victim from the legal process further increase. The victim is deprived of his ability to determine the course of a case and is deprived of the ability to gain restitution from the proceedings. Under such conditions the incentives to report crime and to cooperate with the prosecution diminish. As the importance of the prosecution increases, the role of victim is transformed from principal actor to a resource that may be used at the prosecutor's discretion. The principal form of power left to the victim is the negative one of not reporting the crime or not cooperating in its prosecution. The importance of the prosecutor has increased as more and more courts are staffed by legal professionals and are subjected to statewide standards of procedure.

Recent analyses of the social organization of prosecutor's offices reveal further aspects of the differentiation of prosecutorial and victim interests. Besides carrying out the state's interest in prosecution, the prosecutor has developed his other goals and priorities that have supplanted a concern for the victim. Prosecutors, like judges and defense attorneys, work in a setting where the disposition of cases is accomplished in a manner that accommodates ongoing relationships with the other regular actors in the criminal justice system (Feeley, 1973; Cole, 1970). Decisions as to when to dismiss, when to plea bargain, or when to go to trial and seek harsh penalties are made according to criteria that only occasionally involve the victim of the crime. The victim, to an even greater extent than the offender, is the outsider to the criminal justice system. The incentives for the prosecutor to be highly responsive to the victim's point of view are minimal, beyond assuring his cooperation when necessary. Where a case can be disposed of in a manner acceptable to the prosecutor, a victim may never be interviewed or asked to appear. In some cases the victim is not even informed about the disposition of the case; in others, the victim's contribution is limited to a hurried interview immediately before a hearing or summary proceeding.

The typical processes by which most criminal cases are disposed of through plea bargaining or dismissal have been described elsewhere (Blumberg, 1967; Alschuler, 1968; Casper, 1972). Such bargains generally produce sentences that are significantly less than could be received under the law (Newman, 1966).[6] If the victim is interested in retribution, he may be frustrated by the imposition of a low sentence without explanation of the reasons for leniency or the opportunity to participate meaningfully in the process of reaching a disposition. If the victim is not interested in retribution, there is little other satisfaction to be gained. Victims seldom get an apology, seldom are reconciled with the offender, and seldom receive restitution.

There are certain types of cases in which the prosecutor's concern for a disposition leads to an outcome in which the victim's interests are also served. In cases of embezzlement and bad checks, restitution may be made a prerequisite in the disposition. The victims in such cases tend to be businesses and organizations rather than private individuals. Restitution may also be an aspect of probationary sentence where individuals have been harmed, especially by juveniles. For most victims, the system of prosecution in large urban court systems in the United States deprives them of a sense of involvement or understanding of what will occur.

The prospect for victims who report a crime is such that many feel unmotivated to make the effort required to have a case prosecuted. Victimization studies demonstrate that a majority of the victims of even serious crimes do not report their victimization to the police (Ennis, 1967; LEAA, 1974; Skogan, 1975), but even among those who do, many will decide that the requirements of multiple appearances in court with little hope of influencing what transpires is too heavy a price to pay. A recent study of victims who were serving as witnesses at different stages of criminal proceedings found that the more experience a person had with the courts, the greater the reluctance expressed about getting involved again (Knudten et al., 1975). Most victim-witnesses objected to the slowness, inefficiency, and leniency of the courts. Recent studies have noted the high rate of criminal case dismissals due to the nonappearance of the complaining witness (Institute for Law and Social Research, 1975). Police witnesses tend to be more cooperative and effective than private citizens, but they are subject to many of the same limitations and frustrations. They are given little opportunity to influence prosecutorial decisions and they experience the same pattern of repeated delays in court.

NONADVOCACY PROGRAMMATIC RESPONSES

Many new programs have been established to assist victims of crime; most of them are designed to provide various kinds of service to the victim.[7] At this juncture most victim-witness aid programs are too new to have been formally evaluated. We suggest, however, that what is missing from programs like those described above is a conception of the victim as a person deprived of an ability to influence the outcome of the legal proceedings other than by providing the information requested by the prosecution and police. The existing programs concentrate on helping the victims to participate in ways determined by prosecutors. The unmet needs of the victim are defined as a lack of understanding of criminal proceedings and of services to deal with the out-of-court consequences of his or her victimization. Programs seek to increase the victims' involvement by ameliorating their worst grievances and making them feel more committed, but without giving them more of an opportunity to influence the way the case is handled or the sentencing imposed.

Where programs are designed and administered by police or prosecutorial personnel it is understandable that they would encourage modes of citizen participation that would not interject new and potentially conflicting interests and perspectives.

The prosecutor-victim relationship remains the same except perhaps that prosecutors take more seriously their need to keep their witness cooperative. The divergence of interests that is likely to be found among prosecutors, other actors in the criminal justice system, and the victim is unchanged.

RETURNING POWER TO THE VICTIM: TWO CASE STUDIES

While the typical contemporary victim has no institutionalized method of influencing prosecutorial or judicial decision making, some victims do try to apply pressure to have their views and feelings influence the dispostion of cases. This is usually done on a case-by-case basis, and its success is unknown. In Chicago, two citizens' groups, the Hyde Park community group and the Early Ardmore Group, established programs to apply this pressure in a more sustained way. Both programs were designed to inform the prosecutors of the communities' concern about specific victimizations—as opposed to crime in general. What follows is an analysis of the experiences of those two groups.

The Early Ardmore Group in Chicago's Edgewater Area

In 1973, a group of neighbors on the north side of Chicago joined together in response to what they collectively experienced as harassment and victimization by a local gang. When one of the neighbors was assaulted by a gang member—after an argument—a number of residents decided to exert pressure on the courts and police to respond to the situation. In the past, residents of the area who claimed to be victims of the gang had often declined to press charges for fear of reprisals. When residents did file complaints, they found that their cases were handled in the same manner as lesser criminal offenses. Dismissals, frequent continuances, and lenient sentences were typical. The residents called and visited the prosecutors and the police in an effort to get more severe dispositions. They tried to demonstrate to prosecutors that, although each of the cases was minor, they were all part of a pattern of gang harassment that was serious. The police provided some assistance, but the prosecutors proved little help to either the residents or the police.

In Chicago different assistant district attorneys are assigned to each stage of a case. This has meant that residents rarely dealt with the same prosecutor twice. There was no one prosecutor who was in a position to identify these gang cases and treat them with a special concern at each stage of the proceedings. Furthermore, prosecutors had too little time to spend on each case to allow for significant inputs from victims or other residents.[8] Over a period of 6 months, the residents became more organized and developed a sense of identity—calling themselves the Early Ardmore Group. They pressed more than half a dozen cases against members of the gang. When there were hearings on these cases, the group would muster a carload or more of neighbors to accompany the victims. On several occasions over 40 residents appeared in court. When gang-related cases were called, the residents would rise and move to stand at the railing separating the audience from the working court area. Their presence was obvious, and defense attorneys sometimes objected to their actions. However, the judges allowed them to remain as long as they obeyed the rules of the court. There is no systematic evidence on the effects of these efforts, but prosecutors and judges appeared less willing to grant continuances and dismissals when the group was present.

For a while, morale and membership in the group was high. Monthly meetings were held at which police, judges and prosecutors were invited to speak. The group later began to encounter problems in mobilizing support for the endless series of hearings. Their activities were further undermined when the gang filed a large damage suit against the local police and some members of the neighborhood group for violating their civil rights.

The Ardmore strategy has been tried in communities elsewhere, though rarely with the degree of effort displayed here. Such activity may have a limited effect on prosecutors in getting them to take into account the community's and the victim's point of view. However, it appears that these kinds of efforts are difficult to sustain. Courts are highly resilient organizations and are able to function in terms of their own priorities and accommodations; they are able to resist change (Jacob and Eisenstein, 1974; Feeley, 1973). The Early Ardmore Group was, in a disorganized way, asserting its standing[9] as a class of victims and potential victims who had an interest in the outcome of the cases. Because informal pressure on prosecutors was ineffective, a more direct role in the proceedings was sought. However, without a legal right to participate directly in criminal-justice decision making, they were unable to exert an influence beyond the indirect pressure of being present in the courtroom and creating a heightened sense of public accountability among criminal-justice decision makers.

SECC Program in Chicago's Hyde Park

What would happen if a victim was represented in court by his own counsel? Would it be possible for him to alter the way in which a case was processed? Would the case be less vulnerable to attrition? These are the kinds of questions that get asked when victims get even more serious about finding ways to effectively and more directly exert influence over criminal case dispositions. They are also the questions which guided our analysis of a second victim advocate program. This program—located in the Hyde Park area of Chicago—involved supplying individual victims with private attorneys who assisted them in their efforts to make criminal justice officials responsive to their wishes. The analysis was conducted during 1974. It was a field study in which interviews, participant operation, and archival analysis were used to study the program's operation and impact. The program was sponsored by the South East Chicago Commission (SECC).[10] SECC's program to assist victims of crime employed a lawyer to act as "victim advocate." The lawyer's role and his mode of operation were not clearly defined in the formative stages of the program; they evolved during the first year. In developing the program and defining priorities, the SECC lawyer arranged meetings with community leaders who acted in an advisory capacity. The nature of their advice or the extent of their influence on the program's ultimate development cannot be accurately assessed from documentary evidence or individual recollections, but it appears that SECC's "victim advocate program" evolved out of the general concern with the crime problem.

By the end of the first year of the program, the victim advocate concentrated on representing individual victims within the community in their contacts with the criminal adjudication process.[11] Cases were referred to the victim advocate, SECC's director, or SECC's staff sociologist and fell into two broad categories. First were those cases thought to require the immediate and concentrated efforts of the victim advocate. Cases of this type involved serious incidents or victims who were influential community members or special in some other sense. Referrals concerning such cases were made directly by telephone, in person, or by written communication.

The other general category of referrals concerned more routine incidents and came to the advocate's attention through incident reports that he received from the city and campus police. The police carried forms which described the victim advocate's function and indicated his readiness to help in a variety of ways. They gave these out to most victims and complaining witnesses at the time that interviews for police reports were conducted. Also, forms were sometimes handed out by the staff of the emergency room at the university hospital.

In some of the cases, the advocate would initiate contact with the victim. He might do this when sources at the University of Chicago (which is located in Hyde Park) referred an unusual case or when the case presented a situation coincident with the advocate's research and law-reform interests. The staff sociologist had analyzed community crime data for Hyde Park for many years. As a result of this work he was able to identify crime trends by blocks and had developed files on repeated offenders. If such persons were defendants in a case, the advocate would make a special effort to assist the victim in pressing the case. He would give particular attention to cases of probation violation because he believed that the probation system needed to be changed and he wanted to give special consideration to cases that had the potential for getting attention from the news media.

The advocate's initial contact with the victim was made usually within a short time after the crime. The advocate explained who he was, attempted to obtain the victim's own account of the incident, and briefly explained how the procedural events would unfold and how long the case might take. The advocate personally contacted approximately 25% of the victims; the others he talked with by telephone. In our subsequent interview with these victims, they expressed favorable opinions of the advocate's efforts, though total satisfaction was expressed by very few. The greatest satisfaction was reported by those victims whose initial meeting with the advocate occurred soon after the offense. After the victim's appearance at the preliminary hearing, the advocate followed the common practice of the state's attorneys office of telling victims not to come to court until the case was ready for trial—a period of 3 months to 2 years. If necessary and feasible, the advocate would transport the victims to their first courtroom appearance.

A good portion of the advocate's daily work was devoted to making and receiving calls concerning the status of pending cases. Most of his advocacy was carried out in telephone conversations with prosecutors and police. Certain policemen and prosecutors would inform him of the events that had transpired in certain cases; many would not. When he expected that the courtroom appearance would be merely a continuance or the filing of some discovery motions, the victim advocate would not attend and would instead rely on the report of the policeman involved in the case or on consultation with an assistant state's attorney. Sometimes, the victim advocate was misinformed or guessed wrong about the events that would transpire.[12] The advocate's relationship with the assistant state's attorneys varied tremendously. Some shouted at him when he entered their office or were cautious in their encounters with him. Others had very good relationships with him. The advocate's relations with police seemed on the whole to be more favorable than his relations with prosecutors.

The victim advocate would appear in court, but he made no attempt to take an active part in the proceedings. If he had tried, there would have been objections raised, for there is no formal role designated for a representative of the victim. The advocate had to consider the ways in which a defense attorney might exploit his presence. One danger of overt participation or excessive intervention by the advocate surfaced during the trial of a rape offender. The victim, during her cross-examination, was subjected to extensive inquiry concerning her pretrial contacts with the advocate and the possibility that he had helped her rehearse her testimony or had otherwise influenced her. The advocate had assisted in this rape case by transporting the victim to court on several occasions and had conversed with a university psychiatrist and the victim's psychiatrist concerning the victim's ability to testify at trial. He also had arranged with the prosecution for payment of the corroborating witness's travel expenses from New York in order to assure his testimony, and he had gathered and relayed to the prosecution information concerning the prior criminal record of the offender. The victim advocate appeared to walk a fine line between acceptance and rejection by other actors in the criminal adjudicative process. He might seek to influence prosecutors, but we never observed an attempt to participate in plea negotiations, and we believe that he did not do so. He also deferred to the trial prosecutor the task of preparing the witness to testify.

At times the advocate's work was impaired by court scheduling. Unlike prosecutors and defense lawyers, he found himself relatively powerless to arrange to have a case called at a time convenient to him. If he was unacquainted or on bad terms with the court prosecutor, the time involved in getting one case called often precluded his participation in cases scheduled in other courtrooms for the same morning or afternoon. This problem might have been avoided if he had acceded to the demands of court clerks and others to purchase raffle or "golf-outing" tickets, the proceeds of which went to the sponsoring political party. He felt, however, that his role and SECC connections precluded any such activity.

The victim advocate worked primarily behind the scenes. The advocate believed that behind-the-scene advocacy was a more effective method of dealing with cases than actual participation onstage in the courtroom. He would, on occasion, approach the judges in chambers and express the concern of SECC in preserving order in Hyde Park. He might offer the judge extrinsic facts not brought out in the hearing, such as that the defendant was a repeater.

He often attempted to apply pressure through avenues outside the context of the courtroom. He wrote numerous letters to the elected state's attorney, severely criticizing some assistant state's attorneys who he decided were not performing in the interests of crime control. When the response from the state's attorney was not satisfactory—and it seldom was—the victim advocate, through SECC's director Julian Levi,[13] would go to the newspapers. SECC experienced a large measure of success in procuring editorial coverage of cases in which the system had erred on what might be interpreted as the side of leniency. Some state's attorneys felt that the advocate's demands went too far when he denigrated the types of compromises that the assistants sometimes felt compelled to make by virtue of their ongoing relationships with defense lawyers and judges.

One striking example of the victim advocate's concerns came during the preliminary hearing on a case in which one of the defendants had been involved in an attack on one of the university's upper-echelon administrators. The victim advocate persistently requested that the prosecutor ask the court to fashion an order barring the youthful attacker from traversing an area that the advocate defined as the "University," despite the fact that the youth lived within two blocks of the boundary that the advocate set as the south side of this area. The prosecutor flatly refused, stating his opinion that it would be an impossible condition to enforce and that he believed it had serious constitutional implications.

After conviction, when the individual victim's participation no longer was required by the adjudicative process, the victim advocate often pursued individual offenders. This was particularly true in cases in which the offender had been granted a term of probation. Many of the news items that the advocate "leaked" to the papers concerned violations of probation by offenders whose victims he had represented.

Thus, while some researchers have noted a marked lack of conflict between defense counsel and prosecutor in a great number of cases, we observe instances of genuine conflict between prosecutors and the victim advocate. The advocate took a consistent approach to his cases. He would always emphasize the prosecutorial side of the case, but often he demanded higher bonds, fewer continuances, and harsher penalties than the prosecutors themselves. We did not observe a single request for leniency tendered by the advocate. If victims wanted to drop charges, the advocate generally would seek to dissuade them. He would remind them of their responsibility to the community: by having the offender punished, he would argue, the community might be spared a future victimization. In other cases, the advocate might argue for sanctions heavier than victims thought necessary. Such differences reveal an important aspect of the advocate's role as a representative. He might claim to represent victim interests, but when these clashed with SECC's strategy for fighting crime, the advocate would assume a more adversarial stance toward the victim. The advocate might speak in terms of the community's interests, but he had no constituency or accountability other than SECC. This program spoke in the name of victims, but it could not accurately be said to be their voice.[14]

We hasten to point out that the advocate felt that SECC's stance toward victim representation was the proper approach for the ultimate improvement of the victim's position in the Chicago courts and for reducing crime in Hyde Park. The advocate was concerned with representing Hyde Park victims as a class, as well as individuals. He looked upon tasks such as transporting victims to court, aiding them in recovering their property, briefing them on the forthcoming events and the like as "stop-gap" measures which hopefully would be rendered unnecessary if enough pressure could be placed upon the police, and particularly upon the prosecuting attorneys, to do what he considered was "properly their job." The victim advocate aided in the negotiations for the establishment of a victim-notification program, which used computerized means within the Chicago Police Department to notify witnesses of their court appearance dates.

As we have seen, depending on the circumstances, the victim advocate might find himself allying with, or opposing the interests of, victims, prosecutors, or judges. The advocate strove hardest to avoid outright confrontations with victims, but some report having felt pressured by him. The conflicts with prosecutors were more frequent and heated. There was less that the advocate could do for them and more that he could do to make their work difficult.

In some respects, the courtroom tactics of the advocate are similar to those of the Early Ardmore Group. They both sought to make their presence felt in court, but did not participate directly. Both stood silently behind the victims. Unlike the Ardmore group, the Hyde Park advocate had considerable effect through informal channels. His informal effectiveness had less to do with his skills as a lawyer than it did with the powerful position that he represented when he spoke for SECC and its president, Julian Levi. However, the dynamics of this influence process reduced the victim advocate's ability to represent individual victims.

ALTERNATIVES TO ADJUDICATIVE ADVOCACY

The SECC and Early Ardmore examples were both relatively unsuccessful efforts to promote victim and community advocacy within the criminal adjudicative process. Some programs for restoring the victim's influence over the criminal process deal with those matters that are handled in a nonadjudicative procedure. These programs involve either mediation or arbitration. They have been established in New York City, Rochester, Akron, Cleveland, Philadelphia, and Columbus.[15] In all of them, victims and offenders confront each other directly. No prosecutor is present, and, although legal representatives may participate, they rarely do.

The informality of the proceedings makes it easier for the parties to participate actively. Proceedings in the Columbus project were described in the following way (National Institute of Law Enforcement and Criminal Justice, 1974):

> Hearings are conducted . . . without regard to rules of evidence, burdens of proof or normal courtroom procedures. The complainant and respondent are ushered into a plain office. The hearing officer introduces himself and requests the complainant and then the respondent to state their cases. These are the only instructions given. Emotional outbursts are common.

Complainants and defendants decide what facts they will introduce and what arguments to make. What they say and do has a substantial impact on the case outcome. Whatever the outcome, they, at least, are likely to feel that they had a chance to articulate their points of view.

These programs are predicated on the assumption that most of their cases will involve conflicts between people who know each other—usually family members or friends. In such cases, it is often difficult to draw a line between offender and victim, and there is often more to be gained by restoring amicable relations and facilitating restitution than by sanctioning a wrongdoer. Cases may involve acts that would be defined as either felonies or misdemeanors if they were prosecuted in court. There is also some evidence that these proceedings can be effective when strangers are involved.

If a case cannot be settled, it is referred to court for prosecution. Early reports of the Philadelphia program (Hoff and Stein, 1974) and the Columbus program (National Institute of Law Enforcement and Criminal Justice, 1974) indicate that a high proportion of the cases do not go to court, and that there is a high success rate in arriving at a settlement. Out of 3,626 direct complaints filed between September 1972 and September 1973 in Columbus, only 84—that is, 2%—led to criminal complaints being filed. In Philadelphia, only 7% of the cases were forwarded to the court when a settlement could not be reached.

In Minnesota (Fogel et al., 1973) a limited number of convicted felons are being allowed to enter a program to make restitution in lieu of going to prison. Such victim restitution programs have been recommended on the basis of their potential for rehabilitating offenders (Schafer, 1968); an additional aspect of the programs is their responsiveness to victim interests especially in property offenses. The Minnesota program provides offenders with an opportunity to offer restitution, but it also contains the rarest of qualities—the chance for the victim to become directly involved in an aspect of the criminal justice system.

CONCLUSIONS

The power of the victim to influence criminal case dispositions has declined historically. He presently has no meaningful control over the prosecution of his case—except for his option to refuse to cooperate with the prosecutor. The problem of victim-witness noncooperation is substantial and may be regarded as an indication of the degree to which victims regard the costs of participation as exceeding the benefits.

Most present programs of victim assistance seek to reduce these costs and make the victim's participation as a witness less arduous. These programs, however, stop short of recognizing the interest of the victim as a party to the case or of increasing the influence of victims in the proceedings. They are attempts by the criminal justice system to co-opt the victim-witness.

Unlike the victim assistance programs, the Early Ardmore and Hyde Park programs were committed to advocacy goals, but were limited by the difficulties of identifying an acceptable mode of participation in the court. Many of the problems encountered by the Hyde Park advocate, as well as his consistent "hard-line" approach to law enforcement, may be explained by the failure of the criminal justice system to accord him standing in the adjudicative process. By the same token, his efforts to enhance his impact, and that of the victim, via channels outside the legal process—such as newspaper publicity—have often served to further impair his effectiveness within the process. Ironically, when in some cases the advocate pressed harder through outside channels, the victim was recognized to a lesser degree by the prosecutor and judge.

While the Early Ardmore approach did seem to increase the victim's influence over prosecutorial decision making, this arrangement is not available to most victims. The Hyde Park program inserts yet another legal representative between the victim and the proceedings. Like other representatives, the Hyde Park victim advocate balanced the desires of the victim-client against a number of other interests. In his case, these were primarily the interests of SECC. There are possibilities for victim representation to be improved, but some of the limits of this approach are already foreseeable.

Historically, courts of equity evolved in response to the cumbersome rules of procedure in courts of law that deprived many potential litigants of standing to press claims to a disposition that the parties would view as reasonable. Eventually, the equitable system of law and procedure, which had for so long been considered apart from the courts of law, merged with law to create a system wherein litigants have standing to assert a broad range of claims and theories of relief.

Perhaps a parallel development is occurring with regards to victims and the criminal justice system. The mediation-arbitration programs now under way manifest an effort to serve a broader range of victim interests than the court process is equipped, in its present form, to handle. There may, however, exist limitations on the type of crimes to which the mediation-arbitration model can effectively be applied. For example, it has yet to be shown how effective it can be in serious cases involving parties who are strangers. The arbitration proceedings that are being used are also less suited to the protection of offender rights and to the application of retributive sanctions when they are needed.

NOTES

1. Even in a country like the United States with the highest ratio of lawyers to population of any country in the world (Galanter, 1968:205) there are still a large number of persons who appear in court unrepresented. Whether by choice or by necessity, these unrepresented parties are generally disadvantaged when faced with a represented adversary (Galanter, 1975:361).

2. Writers in both the criminal and the civil law area have described the tensions in the lawyer-client relationship. Among the concerns that may lead a lawyer to act less like an advocate and more in his own self-interest are considerations of fees and his ongoing relationships with court personnel and other attorneys (Ross, 1970; Blumberg, 1967; Skolnick, 1967; Lobenthal, 1970).

3. The state seeks to preserve the sense of legal continuity by interpreting a fine or other type of punishment as "paying," i.e., restituting a "debt to society." There are some

societies in which the demise of restitution as a formal element in a criminal trial has not been complete. In France, the victim may appear as the *partie civile,* thereby joining his civil suit to the criminal case (Howard, 1958). The Tanzanian primary court magistrate is formally empowered to allow restitution as part of a criminal sentence (DuBow, 1973). In the United States, the discretionary power of judges is broad enough to allow the use of restitutive elements in criminal sentences, but restitution is not given recognition in statutes, and, hence, victims have no standing to request its use (Holman, 1975:7). To date, there have been no studies that have detailed the frequency and patterning of this discretionary restitution.

4. The state's increased involvement and redefinition of private wrongs in criminal terms appeared at a somewhat later period in the courts of America. Whereas some European states were heavily involved in the adjudication and prosecution of serious criminal cases by the time of the Renaissance in England, France, and Germany (Langbein, 1974), the major introduction of such actions in the American courts did not occur until the years after the American Revolution (Nelson, 1967).

5. Langbein (1974) argues that in England, France, and Germany the office of the prosecutor develops from that of a judicial officer who is given responsibility for evaluating the evidence in a criminal case prior to the indictment.

6. Whether most plea bargains are "good deals" is not as clear. Sentences handed down in bench and jury trials are generally lighter than the law allows as well. Therefore, guilty plea dispositions should be compared with trial outcomes rather than the upper limits as stated in the law. We have little systematic comparisons of this type.

7. Illustrative of the kinds of services being provided by these new victim programs is the proposed Brooklyn Victim-Witness Assistance Program (Vera Institute of Justice, 1974). This program will operate a complaint room in the Brooklyn Courthouse designed to familiarize victim-witnesses with what to expect in court proceedings and to provide more adequate facilities for interviewing witnesses. There will be a courtesy center to provide a more comfortable place in which witnesses can await their court appearance. There will also be more complete witness notification by mail and phone as to when they are required to appear. This notification system will be combined with a computerized case management plan to reduce delays by balancing out the scheduling of cases. Transportation will be provided to enable victims to make complaints and to appear in court, and referrals will be made to welfare, medical, counseling, and other sources of aid to victims. In addition, simple repairs will be made to victim residences damaged in burglaries. Finally, an attempt will be made to reduce the delay in returning victims' property that is held as evidence.

Programs in other cities have many or all of the components listed above. The National District Attorneys Association is sponsoring Victim-Witness Programs in eight cities. In some cities there are private citizens' groups such as Americans United Against Crime in Philadelphia and Aid to Crime Victims, Inc., in St. Louis, which are undertaking similar activities. Police departments in many cities also are seeking to redesign their procedures for dealing with victims of crime. The most concentrated efforts have been aimed at improving the treatment of rape victims. These programs may have a person known as the "victim advocate," as in Sacramento, California, but such an individual does not perform the function of legal advocacy as we have defined it. (See also Baluss, 1975; McDonald, Chapter 1 in this volume.)

8. As a response to the difficulties experienced by the Early Ardmore Group and by other citizens who had contact with the court, the Organization of the Northeast (ONE) began a campaign aimed at getting the state's attorney to open a local branch of his office.

Residents of the area felt that a prosecutor who worked in the neighborhood could be more responsive to their concerns than one who worked out of the main office of the prosecutor in the criminal courts downtown. After considerable pressure, a neighborhood office was established in the Uptown area. Community activists report that having their "own" prosecutor had led to speedier and more effective prosecutions.

9. "Standing" as defined by Webster, is "a position from which one may assert or enforce legal rights and duties." If an individual or group lacks standing, the court will refuse to hear their arguments. The community efforts bear some similarity to the ideas embodied in class action suits. However, efforts to establish a "community of victims" right to be heard are unlikely to make headway until the rights of individual victims are enlarged.

10. SECC, the sponsor of the program, has been in the forefront of the massive urban renewal program in Hyde Park and can generally be said to support the interests of the University of Chicago in maintaining the community surrounding it. In the years prior to the program, there had been growing concern in Hyde Park about the crime problem. A significant number of residents had left the area, even when it meant commuting daily to Hyde Park or leaving positions at the university. Many remaining Hyde Park residents were committed to finding effective responses to the problem of crime. Programmatic responses to crime were instituted, such as an innovative crime-reporting program known as Operation WhistleSTOP and the widely used Operation Identification.

11. The reasons for this decision are unclear. Our information concerning the formative year is not first-hand, but none of the minutes from block meetings sponsored by SECC tend to evidence explicit requests for this type of activity on the part of the victim advocate.

12. At times he claimed he had purposefully been misinformed. At first, we concluded from viewing the files that the victim advocate went to court on every case. In fact, for the majority of the appearances he received the information secondhand or else made a biweekly trip to the court-records file room to update his own files.

13. Julian Levi is an influential figure in Hyde Park and Chicago. He is the brother of Edward Levi, the former president of the University of Chicago and the Attorney General of the United States under President Ford.

14. While not directly analogous, the scenario of competing interests of client (victim) and lawyer (advocate) is reminiscent of that observed by Mather (1974) with regard to defense counsel and client.

15. The New York City program was recently initiated by the Institute for Mediation and Conflict Resolution in an area on the upper west side of Manhattan. The Rochester, Akron, and Cleveland programs, like the Philadelphia one, were started in cooperation with the National Center for Dispute Resolution of the American Arbitration Association. In Boston, an innovative victim mediation program has been funded and will soon begin operation in conjunction with a victim-witness service program.

REFERENCES

ALSCHULER, A.W. (1968). "The prosecutor's role in plea bargaining." University of Chicago Law Review, 36:50-112.
BALUSS, M. (1975). Integrated services for victims of crime. Washington, D.C.: National Association of Counties.
BLUMBERG, A. (1967). Criminal justice. Chicago: Quadrangle.

CASPER, J. (1972). American criminal justice: The defendant's perspective. Englewood Cliffs, N.J.: Prentice-Hall.

COLE, G. (1970). "The decision to prosecute." Law and Society Review, 4(February): 313-343.

DRAPKIN, I., and VIANO, E. (eds., 1974). Victimology: A new focus. Lexington, Mass.: D.C. Heath.

DuBOW, F.L. (1973). "Justice for people: Law and politics in the lower courts of Tanzania." Unpublished Ph.D. dissertation, University of California, Berkeley.

––– (1974). "Nation-building and the imposition of criminal law." Paper presented at the annual meeting of the American Sociological Association, Montreal, August.

ENNIS, P.H. (1967). "Criminal victimization in the United States: A report of a national survey" (May). Chicago: National Opinion Research Center, University of Chicago.

FEELEY, M. (1973). "Two models of the criminal justice system: An organizational perspective." Law and Society Review, 7(spring):407-426.

FOGEL, D.; GALAWAY, B.; and HUDSON, J. (1973). "Restitution in criminal justice: A Minnesota experiment." Criminal Law Bulletin, 8(8):681-691.

GALANTER, M. (1968). "Introduction: The study of the Indian legal profession." Law and Society Review, 3(November-February):201-217.

––– (1975). "Afterward: Explaining litigation." Law and Society Review, 9(winter): 347-368.

HOFF, B.H., and STEIN, J.H. (1974). "Interim evaluation report: Philadelphia 4-A Program arbitration as an alternative to criminal courts." Unpublished paper.

HOLMAN, N.A.G. (1975). "Criminal sentencing-victim compensation legislation–Where is the victim?" Paper presented at the International Advanced Study Institute on Victimology and the Needs of Contemporary Society, Bellagio, Italy, July 1-12.

HOWARD, C. (1958). "Compensation in French criminal procedure." Modern Law Review, 21:387-393.

Institute for Law and Social Research (1975). Witness Cooperation Project summary report. Washington, D.C.: Author.

JACOB, H., and EISENSTEIN, J. (1974). "Sentences and other sanctions imposed on felony defendants in Baltimore, Chicago, and Detroit." Paper presented at the annual meeting of the American Political Science Association, Chicago.

KNUDTEN, M.; KNUDTEN, R.; and MEADE, A. (1975). "Crime victims and witnesses as victims of the administration of justice." Unpublished paper. Milwaukee: Center for Criminal Justice and Social Policy, Marquette University.

LANGBEIN, J.H. (1974). Prosecuting crime in the Renaissance: England, Germany, France. Cambridge, Mass.: Harvard University Press.

Law Enforcement Assistance Administration (1974). "Criminal victimization in the United States" (Vol. 1). Washington, D.C.: U.S. Department of Justice.

LOBENTHAL, J.S., Jr. (1970). Power and put on: The law in America. New York: Outerbridge and Dienstfrey.

MATHER, L.M. (1974). "The outsider in the courtroom: An alternative role for the defense." Pp. 263-289 in H. Jacob (ed.), The Potential for Reform of Criminal Justice. Beverly Hills, Calif.: Sage.

National Institute of Law Enforcement and Criminal Justice (1974). "Citizen dispute settlement: The Night Prosecutor Program of Columbus, Ohio." Washington, D.C.: U.S. Department of Justice.

NELSON, W.E. (1967). "Emerging notions of modern criminal law in the Revolutionary Era: An historical perspective." New York University Law Review, 42(May):450-482.

NEWMAN, D.J. (1966). Conviction. Boston: Little, Brown.

NONET, P., and CARLIN, J. (1968). "The legal profession." International Encyclopedia of the Social Sciences, 9:66-72. New York: Macmillan.

ROSS, H.L. (1970). Settled out of court: The social process of insurance claims adjustments. Chicago: Aldine.

RUESCHEMEYER, D. (1973). Lawyers and their society: A comparative study of the legal profession in Germany and the United States. Cambridge, Mass.: Harvard University Press.

SAMAHA, J. (1974). Law and order in historical perspective: The case of Elizabethan Essex. New York: Academic Press.

SCHAFER, S. (1968). The victim and his criminal: A study of functional responsibility. New York: Random House.

SCHWARTZ, R.D., and MILLER, J.C. (1964). "Legal evolution and societal complexity." American Journal of Sociology, 70(September):159-169.

SKOGAN, W.G. (1975). "Citizen reporting of crime: Some national panel data." Unpublished paper.

SKOLNICK, J. (1967). "Social control in the adversary system." Journal of Conflict Resolution, 11:51.

Vera Institute of Justice (1974). "The Brooklyn Victim-Witness Assistance Project." Unpublished paper. New York: Author.

WEBER, M. (1954). On law in economy and society (Max Rheinstein, ed.). Cambridge, Mass.: Harvard University Press.

Chapter 7

IMPROVING THE TREATMENT OF VICTIMS:
SOME GUIDES FOR ACTION

RICHARD P. LYNCH

Police, prosecutors, judges, and the public at large should examine the possible ramifications of long-term citizen frustration with the criminal justice system. What do citizens do when their faith in the fairness, effectiveness, and adequacy of the criminal justice system is minimal or nonexistent? This question has not been answered yet by hard research data. But the victimization surveys suggest that a lack of confidence in the system at least results in not reporting crime to the police. Other less systematic evidence suggests an even more ominous conclusion. Consider, for example, the following account of a recent crime in Chicago (Fitzpatrick, 1974):

> "For three nights now it all comes back to me in my dreams," Juan Matos said. "Maybe those dreams will never go away. I see everything that happened last Friday night when those three colored men came in to hold up my store. I feel the fear in my stomach when I see the gun pointed at me. But I see more than that. I see myself chasing them down an alley, and shooting at them with my pistol. I see one holdup man fall and I see myself rush up and grab him in the alley. Then I see the worst of it. The mob charges upon us. I think maybe there are 40 of them. They want to help me. They keep shouting: 'Kill him! Let's show them they can't rob us. Kill him!'

"I try to tell them not to keep stabbing the holdup man all over. They stab him in the stomach and the chest and the neck and the face. I try to put my body over his to save his life because I want the holdup man to tell me where the others have gone with my money but the mob won't listen. Finally, we are alone on Division St., the holdup man and me. He is unconscious and blood is pouring out of many parts of his body. And then a policeman comes up to me and asks what happened."

[Says Juan's brother and partner Francisco:] "The first thing you must realize is that the Latin people are always being made the victims in these crimes. The police cannot help us. It is always the same no matter what store you are talking about. They come in with guns. They take our money. Maybe they shoot us. They board their cars and drive away. They are never caught."

What prosecutors and other law enforcement officials must decide is whether an incident like this is merely an aberration or whether it is the natural and logical culmination of public frustration. We think that prosecutors would be wise to view such incidents as serious evidence of a failed—or failing—philosophy of criminal justice administration. To be a crime victim in all too many jurisdictions means that one will do more than suffer the immediate consequences of a criminal act. In all too many cases the victim who suffers the criminal act is then subjected to indifferent treatment from law enforcement and criminal justice agencies. The treatment of victims and witnesses can be indifferent for a number of reasons, many of which may be beyond the power of district attorneys to rectify.

One area which can be addressed by district attorneys concerns a reordering or reshaping of the criminal justice bureaucracy. Bureaucracy, insofar as it insulates us all from reality, can frustrate and confound an institution's capacity to respond to a victim's most essential needs.

Consider the following example involving a rape victim. First she was the victim of a brutal assault—then she became the victim of a bureaucratic system which seemed to have an almost independent existence unrelated to the victims whom it was supposed to be serving. Unfortunately, the example is not untypical. Her case has been pending in the courts for 16 months. Her alleged attacker, released on bail, has raped and shot another woman. The victim (Juris Doctor, 1974) described her treatment from the criminal justice system as follows:

The police took me to the hospital. I was kept waiting, and the intern was very rude. A few months later I saw his report; there was no mention of my facial cuts and he had written that I appeared calm.

After the hospital examination, I went down to the police station and gave my statement. I hadn't been back to sleep or even taken a shower when a detective arrived to dust for prints. A few minutes later the district attorney's office called and told me to come in right away for a preliminary hearing. I told my story for the third time that morning. He was there, with his lawyer, and I was very nervous because they made me give my name and address.

The next day I told the story again—to the grand jury. It was easier, though, because he wasn't there. One of the cops was really nice. He knew I'd be alone, so he brought his wife along. Everyone looked bored out of their minds, and no one bothered to tell me what was going on.

In September, I got a subpoena. I panicked. I didn't know what it meant. An assistant district attorney told me I had to appear before the grand jury. He wouldn't believe that I had already done that. He asked me questions like what I had been wearing on the night of the rape. When I said a nightgown, he asked, "Was that all?" Finally, he discovered that I had been before the grand jury and sent me home.

I inquired about my case in October, but couldn't get any information. I began to think I was a lunatic. I kept telling my story over and over, but nobody seemed to be listening. I just wanted to drop the whole thing.

In December, I called the D.A. and told him I was going home to California for Christmas. He told me not to go because my case might come up. I didn't want to give him my parents number because they didn't know about the rape. We wound up hanging up on each other.

Then a new assistant district attorney took over my case. This one started to collect evidence, but it had been several months since the crime and there weren't too many witnesses left in the area. He had the defendant investigated by a private detective, who discovered that he had raped and shot another woman while he was out on bail.

The trial was delayed by the defense attorney's constant excuses. He claimed he was sick or busy with another case. The judge found out that there was no such case. The lawyer had just been stalling.

I believe that a rapist has every right to be defended, but I don't believe he should win his case by not showing up. The judge has finally ordered the attorney and defendant to appear in court. After 16 months, my case will finally be heard. I hope it is over soon; my nightmares keep getting worse. If the defense attorney goes into my sexual history, I don't think I'll be able to handle it. I think I might fall apart.

VICTIM WITNESS ASSISTANCE PROGRAMS

In October 1974 the National District Attorneys Association—with the aid of a one million dollar grant from the U.S. Department of Justice—created the Commission on Victim Witness Assistance. The commission decided that its attack on the existing "nonsystem" of treatment and assistance for crime victims and witnesses should be a three-pronged attack. First, the commission reasoned, district attorneys needed to have empirical data to support intuitive judgments about the problems encountered by victims and witnesses as they moved through the criminal justice system. Second, the commission decided that it should not limit its endeavors to research studies, but should move simultaneously to institute a variety of pilot assistance programs within its eight participating district attorneys' offices. And, finally, the commission, recognizing the general lack of physical facilities to accommodate crime victims and witnesses, decided that at least some of the commission's participating offices should create Victim Witness Reception Centers.

The National District Attorneys Association was by no means the only organization conducting a victim-witness assistance program. Indeed, in July 1975, the commission compiled a list of some 33 significant local victim-witness assistance programs operating in 17 states. On the other hand, the National District Attorneys Association Commission on Victim Witness Assistance was the only program in the fall of 1974 which was operating on a nationwide basis. It was also the only program which was attempting to use its local pilot jurisdictions as "laboratories," with the hope that those successful laboratory programs could be transferred to other jurisdictions across the country.

In all cases the Commission on Victim Witness Assistance tried to tie its action programs to its survey research findings, and in all cases it attempted to design programs which could be operated inexpensively. It would be instructive to describe some of the commission's programs in order to demonstrate what other district attorneys and other criminal justice agencies can—and should—do to aid crime victims and witnesses. First, from its beginning, the commission recognized the need to conduct both public and professional information campaigns.

Public and Professional Information Program

Crime victims receive less than adequate treatment in the criminal justice system. Crime victims know it. People who work in the criminal justice system know it, but heretofore their "knowledge" has not compelled the system to alter the treatment accorded to those victims. Thus, one of the first tasks to be undertaken by an organization established to improve the lot of crime victims is to point out to victims and criminal justice workers alike that *things can be better*. The Commission on Victim Witness Assistance did this in several ways. First, it undertook an aggressive public information campaign to publicize the fact that Victim Witness Assistance Units were operating in the commission's field jurisdictions. This was more than a self-serving advertising campaign designed to make district attorneys "look good." No service can be effective if its prospective clients are unaware of its existence. The commission's participating district attorneys sought media coverage, appeared on television programs, and—with the assistance of materials produced by the commission staff—distributed thousands of brochures, pamphlets, buttons, and other materials designed to tell people about available services. In addition to producing public information materials which would inform and advise citizens of victim-witness assistance programs within the commission's operating jurisdictions, several professional information documents were produced. The commission published and distributed 10,000 copies of a pamphlet entitled "16 Ideas to Help District Attorneys Help the Victims of Crime." This pamphlet emphasized the fact that modest, inexpensive programs could be operated by almost any district attorney. It also stressed the fact that the prime requisites for instituting such programs were not money and additional personnel but rather imagination and commitment. The "16 ideas" included such suggested programs as the institution of child care services for witnesses, the use of senior citizen volunteers to operate a telephone court appearance notification system for victims and witnesses, and the suggestion that district attorneys lobby their local public transportation authorities for the creation of a free transport system for crime victims and witnesses responding to subpoenas.

Next, the commission produced a "Social Service Referral Card." The card, a copy of which appears here (front and back), is designed to encourage the formal referral of crime victims and witnesses to existing social service agencies. It does so with the imprimatur of the district attorney.

The Social Service Referral Card shown here was distributed to each district attorney participating in the commission's program. And, to encourage other district attorneys to adopt the concept, the commission produced a "Social Service Referral" pamphlet which was distributed to district attorneys and other criminal justice agencies. The pamphlet's introduction succinctly states the case for providing social service referral:

> The victims of crime are often in need of social service assistance. While in recent years many programs have offered social service assistance to criminal offenders, the needs of crime victims have remained largely ignored.

SOCIAL SERVICE REFERRAL CARD

FRONT

TO: _____

_____

_____

FROM: District Attorney Harry F. Connick, a participant in the National District Attorneys Association Commission on Victim Witness Assistance funded by the Law Enforcement Assistance Administration.

VICTIM-WITNESS   504-822-2414
ASSISTANCE PROGRAM   Ext. 214

BACK

The bearer of this card was recently the victim of a crime. Initial interviews with our legal staff indicate that _____

_____

is in urgent need of services provided by your agency.

Please extend every courtesy and make every effort to promptly provide all services for which _____ is eligible.

Thank you.

Harry Connick

Harry F. Connick
District Attorney
New Orleans, Louisiana

No criminal justice official—with the exception of police—has more frequent contact with crime victims than does the district attorney. This special publication suggests to district attorneys that a creative and well planned Social Service Referral Program can be operated by district attorneys at a modest cost by utilizing existing facilities and services. We urge district attorneys to consider the merits of this program through which we think that they can provide tangible assistance to the victims of crime.

Finally, as part of its national effort to improve the services offered to crime victims and witnesses, the commission published "A Primer for Model Victim Witness Assistance Centers." The "Primer" contained architectural drawings, renderings, and floor plans for Victim Witness Reception Centers which would be appropriate for small, medium, and large prosecutor's offices. Moreover, the primer contained carefully prepared budgets to apprise district attorneys of the possible costs involved in creating formal reception centers. The concluding page of this special publication provides the commission's rationale for urging the creation of such facilities for crime victims and witnesses:

This publication has provided plans and recommendations for the structuring and furnishing of Victim Witness Assistance Centers which could cost from $23,800 to $117,395. These sums are, of course, only estimates and District Attorneys may well find that total costs exceed these estimates. Nonetheless, in our judgment, the costs involved are minimal. This is particularly the case when they are measured against other costs in the criminal justice system. It has been estimated that the cost of incarcerating an offender can amount to $11,000 per year; a typical police patrol car costs the taxpayers an estimated $5,500; the cost of an additional police officer in a metropolitan jurisdiction can amount to $29,000 per year; and the total amount of money expended annually for law enforcement and crime control is a staggering $14 billion. Few, if any, of these dollars have been devoted to those citizens who are the victims of crime.

We do not suggest to District Attorneys that creating and staffing Victim Witness Assistance Centers will produce startling reductions in crime: we do, however, suggest that the creation of Victim Witness Assistance Programs, staffed by trained and competent personnel, can, in the long run, serve to strengthen our criminal justice system. Crime victims cannot be treated merely as "objects of proof" for the commonwealth or the state, and, if rehabilitation of criminal offenders is a goal to be desired, then it is equally important that we, as prosecutors, pay attention to the "rehabilitation" of crime victims. We can begin this fundamental reform by establishing clean, comfortable and decent surroundings for those of our citizens who must undergo the trauma of trial through no fault of their own. We think that Victim Witness Assistance Programs should enjoy a very high priority in the criminal justice world and that prosecutors have a special responsibility to lead the way in bringing about such a reordering of our priorities.

These and other commission publications were designed to encourage district attorneys and citizens alike to take another look at how the "system" treats not the offenders but the offended. In its first year of operations, the National District Attorneys Association Commission on Victim Witness Assistance distributed approximately 100,000 copies of its various brochures and pamphlets to district attorneys, criminal justice agencies, and citizens.

While this public and professional information program was being conducted, the commission was also conducting several survey research efforts in an attempt to measure the nature and extent of the problems confronting citizens who were crime victims and witnesses.

Research Findings

In order to confirm—or refute—its a priori assumptions regarding typical victim-witness treatment, the commission launched several survey research projects in its field offices. In July 1975, the commission's Alameda County, California, field office published its final survey research report. In an introduction to that report the District Attorney of Alameda County, D. Lowell Jensen, said:

> In our minds, this survey, albeit modest in scope, is essential validation of the otherwise solely intuitive judgment that the victim of crime and the witness to crime are themselves victims of an inadequate, indifferent criminal justice system. The survey has suggested and stimulated several specific responsive programs in this office and other such programs are contemplated. The true significance of the survey ought to be, however, the recognition of the "rights" of victims and witnesses to justice at the hands of the system, and of the duty of prosecutors everywhere to accept the responsibility of leadership in responding to that duty. Hopefully, prosecutors and others who participate in the system will be of the same mind.

The victim of crime and the witness to crime are themselves *victims of an inadequate, indifferent criminal justice system:* the commission's survey research findings corroborate that unfortunate proposition! In part, the Alameda County survey produced the following findings:

- Almost 12% of those surveyed were never even notified that an arrest had been made in their cases.

- Almost 73% of all victims suffering physical injuries received no compensation.

- Almost 61% of those victims who were injured—and who failed to receive compensation—were not even aware of the fact that state compensation is available in California for the victims of crime.

- Because of the proportion of victims who were unaware of state compensation, the District Attorney of Alameda County concluded that, "clearly, police and Deputy District Attorneys have failed to meet their statutory obligation to inform all victims of the availability of state compensation."

- Almost 30% of all victims never got their property back even though the property had been recovered and had been used in court.

- Almost 13% of the victims and witnesses surveyed were never notified to appear for an interview or for a court session.

- About 45% of those surveyed reported that no one explained to them what their court appearance would entail.

- Witnesses waited an average of two hours before taking the stand to testify, and witnesses in sexual assault cases waited an average of seven hours before testifying.

- Almost 27% of all witnesses called to court are not subsequently called upon to give testimony.

- Almost 78% of those surveyed lost pay from their employment due to the court appearance.

- About 95% received no compensation for their court appearance.

- About 42% of those surveyed were never notified of the outcome of the cases in which they were involved.

In New Orleans, the field office conducted, inter alia, a special survey of victims and witnesses whose cases had been refused by the District Attorney's Screening Division. Following are summarized findings regarding that special telephone survey:

- 70% of the respondents knew that their cases had been refused.

- 30% had no idea what action had been taken on their case.

- Only 23% of the persons who knew their case had been refused were informed by the District Attorney.

- 77% of the persons discovered their cases had been refused through conversations "on the street," i.e., the victim, other witnesses, etc.

- 83% of the respondents reported that no explanation was given for the refusal.

- In cases where an explanation was given, it was accepted only 56% of the time.

These findings confirm what most of us already know: that in far too many cases scant attention is paid to the comfort, security, or sensibilities of citizens who have been harmed by crime.

WHAT THE SYSTEM CAN DO FOR CRIME VICTIMS

The National District Attorneys Association Commission on Victim Witness Assistance has had a substantial impact on the way in which crime victims are treated within its eight participating district attorneys' offices. Moreover, the commission has brought the issue to the attention of the association's full membership. But that is nothing more than a very modest beginning. Nothing short of a fundamental reordering of our attitudes can bring about the kind of permanent reform needed within the system.

In the fall of 1975 there were seven bills dealing with crime victim compensation pending before Congress. These bills, like their predecessor state statutes already in effect in 14 states, address only the issue of monetary compensation for crime victims. It would be hard to argue against such compensatory legislation; still, legislatures should not be allowed to think that the mere passage of a "money bill" will suffice. In so many areas of social reform, we have a history of passing a bill appropriating money, and, having done our duty, we forget that reform entails more than monetary awards. Neither police, prosecutors, nor court officials should view victim compensation legislation as a remedy for the defects within our present system of criminal justice. It has not been, and it is not likely to be.

We ought to have victim compensation systems. More importantly, such systems ought to be linked to court-ordered restitution whenever and wherever possible. But compensation—even handsome money compensation—cannot compensate for inadequate, indifferent, and callous treatment which victims suffer at the hands of the state. What can government—and especially local government—do about that?

All criminal justice agencies can, to begin with, provide secure and comfortable physical facilities to accommodate crime victims when those victims are called upon to participate in the criminal justice process. There is no excuse for the fact that victims sit for countless hours in shabby courthouse hallways, that victims are interviewed in drab police station anterooms, or that victims and defendants alike mingle in corridors waiting to talk with an assistant district attorney. Having failed to protect our citizens from the harm of criminal injuries, we can, *at least,* serve their comfort and convenience by providing decent, clean, and safe surroundings where they can be accommodated by a criminal justice system which is, after all, requiring their presence and cooperation.

Next, criminal justice employees must remember that they are public servants and that police departments, prosecutors offices, and courts do not exist to afford them positions of authority, to support their own ambitions, or to enable them to accommodate the needs of other judges, lawyers, or associates: *they are supposed to be agencies of justice which serve the people.* That means, or should mean, that no one's convenience or needs should receive more consideration than those of the victim. Thus, we can institute simple and effective systems to see to it that crime victims and witnesses no longer are kept waiting for interminable periods of time for "appointments" with criminal justice personnel or for "appointments" in court. The long-standing practice of issuing subpoenas for literally hundreds of witnesses—all of whom are asked to appear at the same time—should be brought to a halt. Proper scheduling, the use of "telephone alert programs," and other simple management devices can be utilized to make certain that victims and witnesses are promptly interviewed and are promptly called upon to testify. Moreover, we can see to it that the number of multiple appearances be drastically reduced. Neither prosecutors nor courts should, as a matter of "professional courtesy," grant or accede to delays or continuances simply to serve the convenience of colleagues in the system or opposing counsel.

Next, we can begin to observe the golden rule in our treatment of victims: treat them as we would like to be treated. Victims, after all, are people and have other things to do and other appointments to keep. Prompt and effective scheduling, among other things, could do much to relieve feelings of frustration experienced by many, if not all, who enter the criminal justice system.

In keeping with this philosophy, criminal agencies could, and should, make other provisions for the convenience of victims and witnesses. Parking space should be made available to those who have been called to testify. Short of that, criminal justice agencies should attempt to work out with appropriate public or private transportation authorities an agreement which would provide for free transportation of those who have been lawfully subpoenaed by the state as prosecution witnesses. In this regard, criminal justice agencies should provide appropriate day-care facilities and services for the convenience of those who need supervision for small children and cannot afford the cost of providing such service themselves. Finally, criminal justice agencies can, and should, assume a greater role in "directing" crime victims to appropriate public social service agencies that can offer help to remedy injuries directly or indirectly caused by criminal acts. A social service referral role is appropriate for police and prosecutors alike, and the assumption of such a role would be a clear demonstation that the criminal justice system has a responsibility to help crime victims.

These are but a few concrete suggestions which, though modest, could do much to reverse a long-standing policy of neglect and indifference. They do not require massive federal or state funding, nor do they require substantial increases in personnel. Principally, they require merely ingenuity and commitment.

REFERENCES

FITZPATRICK, T. (1974). Sunday Times, December 10, pp. 1, 4.
Juris Doctor (1974). "Rape: Who's on trial?" 4(December):25.

Chapter 8

THE EFFECTS OF VICTIM CHARACTERISTICS
ON THE DISPOSITION OF VIOLENT CRIMES

K R I S T E N   M.   W I L L I A M S

This chapter is an empirical analysis of the effect of the victim's characteristics on decisions made by the prosecutor, judge, and jury concerning cases against defendants charged with violent crimes in the District of Columbia. Several hypotheses about the expected relationships between certain available victim characteristics and three key decisions made during case processing were tested. The victim is viewed as both a decision maker, in terms of his behavior as a witness, and an influence on the decisions made by criminal justice personnel.

AUTHOR'S NOTE: *This study was supported by Grant No. 74-NI-99-0008-G awarded to the Institute for Law and Social Research by the Law Enforcement Assistance Administration's National Institute of Law Enforcement and Criminal Justice. Points of view stated in the article are those of the author and do not necessarily reflect the official position or policies of the U.S. Department of Justice.*

This study is part of the research program of the Institute for Law and Social Research. The contributions of several of my colleagues at the Institute were invaluable, including the methodological assistance of Kathleen Brosi and Brian Forst, the conceptual and editorial suggestions of C. Madison Brewer, Sidney Brounstein, William Hamilton and Susan Katzenelson, and the efficient manuscript preparation by Katherine Falkner. Appreciation is also due to Richard Cys, Deputy Chief of the Superior Court Division in the U.S. Attorney's Office of the District of Columbia, for his helpful review from a prosecutor's perspective, to Hans Zeisel for his early analytical suggestions, and to William F. McDonald for his constructive suggestions for revision.

BACKGROUND

The literature relevant to the present analysis comes from two sources: studies of (or references to) the effect of the victim on criminal-justice decision making and social-psychological studies of victims.

There have been few studies, empirical or otherwise, of how the victim influences the criminal justice process. Those which have been done suggest that the victim does have some effect on criminal justice decisions. The victimization surveys have shown that the victim has considerable discretion in terms of whether to bring an offense to the attention of the police (Reiss, 1974:184-185; Hindelang and Gottfredson, Chapter 2 in this volume). A few studies have focused on the effect of the victim on the decision of the police to charge. Goldstein (1967) and Reiss (1971) report that the police are more likely to bring charges in an assault case if the victim and offender are strangers and less likely to bring charges if they are related or know each other. Parnas (1967) and Truninger (1971) each discuss the police handling of domestic disputes, citing reasons why the police might not make an arrest if the victim and offender are husband and wife.

Moving to the court process, a follow-back survey of witnesses (Cannavale, 1976) found that the closer the relationship between the victim and the defendant, the more likely a witness would be labeled a "noncooperator" by the prosecutor. McIntyre (1968) also found the victim-offender relationship to be important when studying the outcomes of preliminary hearings in Chicago. If the victim and the offender were "spouses, lovers, neighbors, or friends whose amiable relationships have been temporarily disrupted," the case was more likely to be dismissed (p. 477). In a survey of prosecutors reported in the *Southern California Law Review* (1974:530), the victim was found to be a "vital subjective variable." If the victim had greater prestige, the case would be less likely to be dropped. Miller (1969:173-178) includes a chapter in his book on prosecution concerning the "attitude" of the victim. He points to three situations in which the prosecutor might be reluctant to charge: Negro assaults, cases in which the victim shares some guilt, and statutory rape in which the victim consented.

A couple of studies have examined how the victim's responsibility for the crime affects decisions of the court and prosecutor. Wolfgang (1958:300) found that in cases of victim-precipitated homicide offenders were less likely to be found guilty than in cases where victim-precipitation was not an issue. Kalven and Zeisel (1971) found that the jury and—to a lesser extent—the judge took the "contributory fault" of the victim into account in their deliberations.

The victim's influence on the decisions made by boards of victim compensation has also been studied. Edelhertz and Geis (1974:270) reveal that "where the victim's conduct contributes to his injury, state statutes usually provide that compensation may be denied or proportionally reduced." In addition, "all states and foreign jurisdictions now bar compensation to those in some way related to or living with the offender" (p. 278). This restriction appears to be largely designed to prevent fraud, but is consistent with other findings concerning police and prosecutor decisions.

In addition to the criminal justice literature, there is a growing body of social-psychological literature concerning the subtle and indirect influences that victims may have on the decisions made by laboratory subjects concerning the victim or the victimizer. Most of the literature is related to the "just-world" theory developed by Lerner (1965) and others.[1] Just-world theory posits that people want to believe that there is justice in the world; people are victimized or rewarded because they deserve it, not because of random forces. The original study (Lerner, 1965) showed that laboratory subjects randomly chosen to be paid for performing a task convinced themselves, and others, that they had done a better job than those not paid. Many additional experiments (for example, see Lerner and Simmons, 1966; Chaikin and Darley, 1973; Aderman and Katz, 1974) have confirmed and refined the theory. Walster (1966) found that the more serious an accident, the more likely persons are to assign responsibility to someone. This suggests the possibility that, in more serious crimes, an observer will want to assign responsibility to someone—the victim or the defendant. Stokols and Schopler (1973:206) have found that "careless victims were perceived as significantly more deserving of their misfortune than innocent ones."

Three recent social-psychological studies are particularly relevant to the present analysis, since they involve crime victims. Jones and Aronson (1974) tested the degree to which subjects blamed either the defendant or the victim of rape, depending upon the "respectability" of the victim. Although more respectable victims were blamed more, the defendant was also punished more severely. Landy and Aronson (1974), in simulating sentencing behavior, found that subjects were affected by the attractiveness of the victim. Sigall and Ostrove (1975), in a similar experiment, found that the attractiveness of the defendant caused subjects to give him a shorter sentence, except if his attractiveness had helped him in his crime.

The implications of these social-psychological studies for criminal justice administration are substantial. Laboratory subjects appear to take characteristics of the victim, such as "blameworthiness" or "respectability," into account when they evaluate the punishment to be assigned to an offender. However, to date, these findings have not been tested on decisions made by actual criminal justice administrators. Using both the social-psychological studies and the studies discussed in the first part of this section, a number of hypotheses were developed to be tested on data from criminal justice administration in one jurisdiction.

HYPOTHESES

The general hypothesis to be tested by this research is that final dispositions in criminal cases are affected by the victim of the crime. There are four parts to the analysis. The first three deal with the victim's indirect influence on decision making, and the fourth deals with the victim's direct influence. The first set of hypotheses, derived from just-world theory, tests whether the victim's perceived responsibility for the crime affects the disposition. The second set of hypotheses concerns the effect of the social relationship between the victim and the offender on the disposition. The third part explores the effect of victim employment on decision making, and the fourth part focuses on the extent to which certain types of victims cause case attrition due to their noncooperation with the prosecutor as witnesses.

The dependent variable in each of the four parts of the analysis is whether or not a case brought by the police against a defendant results in conviction. There are three decision points where a case may be dropped which will be analyzed—two decisions made by the prosecutor and one made by the judge or jury at trial:

(1) The prosecutor may decide at screening to "no paper" an arrest brought by the police; i.e., the charges brought by the police are not filed by the prosecutor.

(2) The prosecutor, after "papering" the case, may dismiss it before trial.

(3) The judge or jury may find the defendant not guilty at trial.

In the fourth part of the analysis, only the first two decisions will be analyzed in regard to the victim's behavior as a "complaining witness."

I. Victim Responsibility

The first hypothesis, derived from just-world theory is:

H_1 Victims perceived as sharing more responsibility for a crime are less likely to have their cases result in conviction.

The assumption underlying this hypothesis is that persons evaluating a criminal event want to assign responsibility to someone—the victim or the defendant. The more responsibility that they assign to the victim, the less that they will assign to the defendant. Thus, when the victim appears to be more responsible for the crime, the case will be dropped.

Specific measurable factors which are hypothesized to increase the victim's responsibility for the crime can be related either to the actual crime in question or to the general characteristics of the victim which would make an observer suspect that the crime was partly the victim's own fault. Further specific hypotheses related to the *current crime* are:

H_{1A} Victims identified as having "provoked" the defendant are less likely to have their cases result in conviction.

H_{1B} Victims identified as having participated in the offense are less likely to have their cases result in conviction.

Specific hypotheses related to whether the victim is *generally* a "blameworthy" individual are:

H_{1C} Victims identified as users of heroin or opiates are less likely to have their cases result in conviction.

H_{1D} Victims identified as chronic abusers of alcohol are less likely to have their cases result in conviction.

H_{1E} Victims having an arrest record are less likely to have their cases result in conviction.

If the victim is seen as weak and helpless, he is more likely to be evaluated as "innocent" and less deserving of victimization. In this case, the victim would be seen as sharing *less* responsibility for the offense. The specific hypotheses related to victim "innocence" are:

H_{1F} Victims in poor health are more likely to have their cases result in conviction.

H_{1G} Victims who are very young or very old are more likely to have their cases result in conviction.

H_{1H} Victims who are female are more likely to have their cases result in conviction.

II. The Relationship Between the Victim and the Defendant

Studies of the police decision to charge suggest that in cases of assault, the police are less likely to charge if the victim and the defendant know each other. Expanding upon this finding is the following hypothesis:

H_2 The closer the social relationship between the victim and the defendant, the less likely the case will result in conviction.

III. Victim Employment

Another variable available for analysis which did not seem to fit into just-world theory is whether or not the victim was employed. The direction of the relationship of this variable to case outcome was not hypothesized, but the variable was included in the analysis in an exploratory framework.

IV. The Victim as a Witness

If some victim characteristic mentioned above is found to be related to case attrition, it may be because the prosecutor, judge, or jury is dropping the case due to a negative perception of the victim. Another possibility, however, is that the victim is refusing to cooperate as a witness, and for this reason the case must be dropped. Previous studies (Cannavale, 1976; McDonald, 1973) have shown that witness cooperation can be a significant cause of case attrition. In order to ascertain whether the victim is actually the cause of case attrition for certain types of victims, a separate analysis was conducted of the characteristics of victims which are associated with case dismissal by the prosecutor due to problems of cooperation with the complaining witness.

ANALYSIS

The Empirical Setting

The present analysis utilizes data from a Prosecutor's Management Information System (PROMIS) installed in the U.S. Attorney's Office for the District of Columbia in the division which services the D.C. Superior Court.[2] Although PROMIS was designed to provide daily management assistance to the prosecutor, it has potential as a rich source of data for research purposes (Hamilton and Work, 1973). For each defendant arrested in the District of Columbia, over 170 data fields are routinely collected at the "initial screening" of the case, i.e., when police charges are reviewed by the prosecutor and during case processing. The information includes items on the defendant, the crime, the victim, witnesses, decisions made during the processing of the case, and the reasons for each decision as stated by the prosecutor. All the data about the victim included in the analysis are collected at the initial screening. (For a list of the questions asked about the victim, and the person responsible for recording the information, see Appendix I.)

Four types of violent crime were included in the analysis: criminal homicide, assault, forcible sex offenses and robbery. (For specific offenses included, see Appendix II.) All cases of violent crime against individuals brought to the prosecutor by the police from January 1 to December 31, 1973, were analyzed—a total of 5,042 cases. Since cases against individual defendants—rather than criminal incidents—were the units of analysis throughout this study, some victims may be included more than once.[3] Although more than one type of offense may be committed during a particular criminal episode, cases were classified according to the most serious police charge in a case; e.g., if a victim was raped and subsequently murdered, the case against the offender was counted once—as a criminal homicide.[4]

When examining the effects of victim characteristics, it is more relevant to study felonies, since individual case assignment allows a prosecutor—and a judge to a lesser extent—to be more aware of the victim.[5] The violent crimes studied are almost entirely handled as felonies, except for simple assault and charges of aggravated assault which are reduced to simple assault. Distinctions will be made between felonies and misdemeanors whenever a sufficient number of cases allows a separate analysis.

Dispositions of Violent Crimes in the District of Columbia

This study is focused on three decisions: whether the prosecutor "papers" a case (i.e., files charges when an arrest is made by the police), whether the prosecutor dismisses the case before trial,[6] and whether a case going to trial results in a guilty verdict or finding.[7] These three decisions collectively account for most of the case attrition. The rates of attrition at each decision point varied widely by type of crime.

Table 1 shows "papering" rates for the four types of violent crimes. Murder and manslaughter cases were virtually always "papered," followed closely by

Table 1. "PAPERING" RATES BY TYPE OF VIOLENT CRIME: DISTRICT OF COLUMBIA, 1973

Type of Violent Crime	"Papering" Rate[a]
Criminal homicide:	
Murder	97.5
Manslaughter	95.9
Assault:	
Aggravated	70.3
Simple	62.6
Forcible sex offenses	74.0
Robbery:	
Personal victim	86.5
Business or institutional victim	95.4
TOTAL	76.6

N = 5,042

a. Rate is computed as the percentage of cases brought by the police in which any charge is filed by the prosecutor.

Table 2. FINAL DISPOSITION OF CLOSED "PAPERED" CASES BY TYPE OF VIOLENT CRIME: DISTRICT OF COLUMBIA, 1973

| Type of Violent Crime | Total | | Final Disposition | | | | | | | |
	Number	Percentage	Dismissed by Prosecutor	Dismissed by Judge	Grand Jury Ignoramus	Guilty Plea	Guilty Finding or Verdict	Not Guilty Finding or Verdict	Other
Criminal homicide:									
Murder	148	100.0	17.6%	7.4%	5.4%	50.0%	11.5%	8.1%	0.7%
Manslaughter	41	100.0	41.5	12.2	12.2	17.0	4.9	4.9	—
Assault:									
Aggravated	1,284	100.0	44.3	7.6	2.1	28.3	9.1	7.6	0.9
Simple	403	100.0	45.7	3.7	1.0	22.6	14.6	12.4	—
Forcible sex offenses	278	100.0	44.6	13.7	6.5	23.0	7.2	4.7	0.4
Robbery:									
Personal victim	1,028	100.0	39.6	10.5	2.9	28.5	11.8	5.6	1.1
Business or institutional victim	167	100.0	32.9	3.0	4.8	44.9	10.8	3.6	—
TOTAL	3,349[a]	100.0	41.3	8.4	3.0	28.9	10.6	7.1	0.7

a. Out of 5,042 violent crimes, 1,180 were "no papered," and 513 were still open at the time of analysis, yielding 3,349 closed "papered" cases.

business or institutional robberies. The rate for personal robberies was relatively high, 87%, but significantly less than that for institutional robberies. Forcible sex offenses and assaults were less likely to be "papered," with aggravated assaults (with a weapon) more likely to be "papered" than simple assaults (without a weapon).

Table 2 shows the final dispositions of cases that were "papered" in 1973, excluding open cases.[8] The most common disposition for all cases of violent crime, except murder and business or institutional robbery, was a dismissal by the prosecutor. For murders and business robberies, guilty pleas were most common. When a case results in a disposition of guilty, it is much more likely to be a plea than a finding or verdict of guilty at trial. The proportion of prosecuted cases which go to trial is less than 30% for each of the crime categories. If the case goes to trial, the judge or jury is more likely to find the defendant guilty than not guilty, except for cases in which the most serious charge is manslaughter.

Statistical Methods

For the first three parts of the analysis dealing with the victim's indirect influence on decisions made about a case, the analysis proceeded in three steps. First, bivariate tables were developed showing the relationship between the victim characteristics and the three decisions to be analyzed for the group of violent crimes. Next, breakdowns of these bivariate relationships by specific crimes were assembled if enough cases were available for analysis, in order to look for differences by type of crime. In general, a specific type of crime will not be discussed unless there were differences. Lastly, stepwise multiple regression analysis was used to see if any of the victim characteristics turned out to be important after controlling for some other factors which influence decision making. The bivariate analysis has a descriptive purpose: do cases with certain victim characteristics drop out more frequently at various points in the process? In the discussion of the multivariate analysis, the question to be addressed is aimed at explanation: do any of the victim's characteristics appear to be determinants of case attrition, after controlling for other factors?

The multiple regression analyses were conducted individually for each type of crime and each decision, whenever enough cases were available. (See Appendix III for a table of the regression analyses completed showing the number of cases.) The control variables included in the regression analyses were personal characteristics of the defendant (age, race, sex, employment, health, etc.), characteristics of the defendant's previous arrest history, the seriousness of the crime, characteristics of the judge and prosecutor handling the case at various points in the process, time delays between court events, and the extent and type of evidence available.

There are undoubtedly other variables not currently available which could explain more of the variation in the decisions made by the prosecutor, judge, and jury. Nevertheless, many of the important determinants of the decisions have been controlled. In each analysis, victim variables will be discussed if they were found to be "significant" determinants of the dependent variable in the regression equation at least at the 5% confidence level.

The analysis of the direct influence of the victim on final dispositions through his behavior as a witness was based on two regression analyses. The first had as a dependent variable whether the prosecutor indicated a complaining witness problem as the reason a case was "no papered." The second had as a dependent variable whether the prosecutor indicated a complaining witness problem as the reason he dismissed a case. The independent variables included were the victim characteristics as well as the control variables mentioned above.

FINDINGS

I. Victim Responsibility

Some evidence was found to support the first hypothesis that the more responsibility that could be attributed to the victim, the less likely that the defendant's case would result in conviction. The results varied for each of the eight specific subhypotheses H_{1A} through H_{1H}.

Responsibility for the Current Crime—Provocation or Participation. At the initial screening, when the prosecutor decides whether to file charges, he answers two questions which will be entered into PROMIS and which aim to determine whether there was victim provocation or participation in the offense. These variables represent a screening prosecutor's perception of whether the victim provoked the defendant or participated in the offense, based on what he is able to learn from the police presenting the case and any witnesses he interviews. Hence, the validity and reliability of these data are open to some question.

"Victim provocation" is similar to the concept of "victim precipitation" measured by Amir (1970), Curtis (1974), and Wolfgang (1958). The general concept is that the victim, through his actions prior to the offense, helps to "cause" the criminal event. However, "provocation" is a legal concept, whereas "precipitation" is a behavioral science concept. A social scientist, in analyzing a criminal episode, may see evidence of "victim precipitation," whereas legally "victim provocation" would not be present.

Provocation varies in definition, depending on the crime. Victim provocation is never a sufficient legal basis for dismissal in cases of violent crime. In homicide cases, however, it can be a reason for charge reduction. In murder of the second degree, the government must prove that the defendant killed the victim with "malice," i.e., that the defendant did not injure the deceased in the heat of passion caused by adequate provocation. The heat of passion could include both anger and fear, but mere words of provocation by the victim are not enough, no matter how insulting. The provocation must be sufficient to arouse the "reasonable man." If the prosecution cannot prove that the homicide was not committed in the heat of passion, the defendant can be convicted only of manslaughter.

Another possibility is that in some proportion of the homicide and assault cases in which victim provocation is perceived by the prosecutor, self-defense would later be claimed. Self-defense implies that the victim actually attacked or threatened to attack the defendant first, causing the defendant, as a reasonable man, to be fearful of "severe bodily injury" or death. Provocation is not this extreme. Thus, self-defense would imply provocation, but not vice versa.

Victim participation differs from provocation in that it implies criminal involvement on the part of the victim. This participation may be general, as when a drug dealer is murdered, or specific, as when a robber accidentally murders his accomplice.

A legal concept related to victim participation is consent. In cases of rape, consent of the victim takes away a necessary element of the offense, unless the victim is under 16 and a charge of carnal knowledge or indecent acts is brought. In all other forcible sex cases, the government must prove that the victim did not consent. Consent can also be an issue in assault or robbery. For a case of simple assault, touching could be considered an assault. Thus, many normal instances of one person touching another would be assault, except that normally consent is given or implied. In robbery, consent can also be an issue, if the defendant claims, for example, that the victim gave him the money.

Of all arrests made for homicide, assault, forcible sex offenses, and robbery during 1973, the prosecutor identified 14, 14, 6, and 2% of the cases, respectively, as involving provocation. Participation by the victim in the offense was less common: 9% of the assaults and forcible sex offenses were labeled as victim participation, as well as 7 and 2% of the homicides and robberies.[9]

The bivariate analysis showed that cases identified by the screening prosecutor as involving victim provocation or victim participation were more likely to be dropped at each of the three decision points (Table 3). The differences for the prosecutor's screening decision and his decision to dismiss before trial were statistically significant at the 5% level of confidence. At trial, cases in which provocation or participation was indicated were more likely to result in a verdict or finding of not guilty, but the difference was not statistically significant. The difference in the percentage of cases dropping at each point, according to whether provocation or participation was indicated, was much

Table 3. CASE-PROCESSING DECISIONS IN CASES OF VIOLENT CRIME BY PROSECUTOR'S PERCEPTION OF PROVOCATION OR PARTICIPATION BY THE VICTIM: DISTRICT OF COLUMBIA, 1973

Case Processing Decision	All Cases	Provocation by Victim			Participation by Victim		
		Yes	No	Difference Significant (.05)	Yes	No	Difference Significant (.05)
Percentage of:							
Defendants "no papered" (number of arrests)	23% (5,042)	51% (495)	20% (4,547)	Yes	56% (349)	21% (4,693)	Yes
Cases dismissed by prosecutor (number of cases initially filed at screening)	41% (3,349)	49% (222)	41% (3,127)	Yes	50% (139)	41% (3,210)	Yes
Defendants found not guilty (number of cases tried)	40% (593)	48% (29)	40% (564)	No	45% (22)	40% (571)	No

larger for the screening decision than for either the decision to dismiss the case or the trial decision.

The multiple regression analyses, conducted for each of the three decisions by type of crime, indicates that provocation and/or participation by the victim has an effect on the initial screening decision of the prosecutor, but not on the subsequent decision of the prosecutor to dismiss and not on the trial decision. After controlling for other factors, provocation by the victim appeared to cause aggravated assaults, simple assaults, and forcible sex offenses to be "no-papered," but there was no effect on the screening decision in robbery cases. Victim participation appeared to cause aggravated assaults, forcible sex offenses, and robberies to be "no-papered," but had no effect on simple assaults. Robbery cases involving victim provocation and simple assault cases involving victim participation were more likely to be dropped at screening according to the bivariate analysis, but, after other factors were controlled, these relationships were not significant.

With respect to the prosecutor's decision to dismiss a case and the decision of guilt made at trial, provocation or participation was not significant in any of the analyses, except in the analysis of the decision to dismiss for 430 unindicted felony assaults. Contrary to the expected pattern, victim provocation appeared to cause a case to remain in the system; i.e., not be dismissed by the prosecutor.

The fact that victim provocation and participation had a generally more consistent impact on the initial screening decision of whether to "paper" a case, rather than on later decisions, can possibly be attributed to a number of factors. Since the screening prosecutor both decides to fill out the item on provocation and participation and makes the decision of whether to prosecute, these two decisions are probably made simultaneously, in some instances. In other words, when a prosecutor decides to drop a case, he also may decide to indicate provocation or participation. Since decisions to drop a case at screening are reviewed by a senior prosecutor, there is probably some indication of provocation or participation in the case jacket, but the indication may be "stretched" in some instances and ignored in others. It can at least be said that the screening prosecutor's perception of provocation or participation appears to him to be a legitimate factor in dropping a case.

Because the screening prosecutor indicates provocation or participation, a later prosecutor, in deciding whether to dismiss the case before trial, may have a different perception of the case than the screening prosecutor. This is also true for the judge and jury at trial. Thus, from this research it cannot be concluded that the perception of victim provocation or participation does not influence the decision of a prosecutor to dismiss a case before trial or the decision to find a defendant not guilty at trial. In order to address this question more precisely,

Table 4. CASE-PROCESSING DECISIONS IN CASES OF VIOLENT CRIME BY WHETHER THE VICTIM HAS USED OPIATES OR IS A CHRONIC ALCOHOLIC: DISTRICT OF COLUMBIA, 1973

		Victim Has Used Opiates			Victim Chronic Alcoholic		
Case Processing Decision	All Cases	Yes	No	Difference Significant (.05)	Yes	No	Difference Significant (.05)
Percentage of:							
Defendants "no papered" (number of arrests)	23% (5,042)	46% (56)	23% (4,986)	Yes	49% (144)	23% (4,898)	Yes
Cases dismissed by prosecutor (number of cases initially filed at screening)	41% (3,349)	52% (31)	41% (3,318)	No	61% (66)	41% (3,283)	Yes

the perception of provocation or participation would have to be ascertained for each decision maker.

General "Blameworthiness"—Opiates, Alcohol, and Previous Arrests. Three additional variables hypothesized to increase the victim's responsibility for the crime concerned characteristics which might make an observer conclude that the victim's plight was "his own fault." These variables (use of heroin or opiates, chronic alcohol abuse, and an arrest record), do not involve the current crime, but are characteristics which would make the victim appear to be generally undeserving or blameworthy.

There were very few cases (56) in which the victim's habit of using heroin or opiates was known at the time of screening. By the time of trial, there were only 6 cases, too few to be analyzed. The findings at screening, however, are suggestive of what might be found if a larger sample were analyzed.

The attrition rate for the 56 at the initial screening in which the victim had used heroin or opiates was 46% (Table 4). This was exactly twice the "no-paper" rate for all other cases—a difference which was highly significant. The rate of dismissal by the prosecutor for "papered" cases was also higher for the cases in which the victim had used heroin or opiates, but, with only 31 cases, the difference was not statistically significant.

In the multiple regression analyses of the screening decision, victim use of opiates did not show up as a significant determinant of whether a case was "papered." The only multivariate analysis in which it did appear significant at the 5% level was the decision to dismiss an indicted robbery case. The direction of the relationship was as hypothesized. Some of these robbery cases probably involved the holdup of a drug dealer. Such an individual would be unlikely to generate any sympathy, and the prosecutor might feel that such cases should not be given much attention. When faced with an overcrowded work load, these cases may be the first to be dropped.

Alcohol abuse by the victim was hypothesized to have an effect on decisions in the same direction as the heroin variable. Of the 144 cases of violent crime that involved a victim who was identified as a chronic alcohol abuser, one-half were dropped at screening and another 60% were later dismissed by the prosecutor, leaving only 8 cases which went to trial. Therefore, only the former two decisions will be discussed.

Unlike heroin or opiate use, chronic alcohol abuse was found to be an apparent determinant of case-processing decisions in several of the multiple regression analyses. For aggravated assault, forcible sex offenses, and robbery, victims who were chronic alcohol abusers were more likely to have their cases "no-papered" at screening. The variable did not appear as significant in terms of the decision to dismiss, or at trial, however. One of the prosecutor's criteria in deciding which cases to accept for prosecution is the anticipated behavior of key witnesses. As will be seen in the later section on the contribution of the victim as a witness, alcoholic victims may cause witness problems later in the case. They may not show up, or, if they do show up, their testimony may be garbled. It appears that these cases get screened out very quickly by the prosecutor. Even though such behavior by the prosecutor may be quite rational, it should be noted that there is nothing in the law which states that victimization of chronic alcoholics is an offense of less seriousness than the victimization of any other citizen. Practical considerations, however, may be causing these cases to be dropped.

The arrest record of the victim is a variable which has a legal basis for influencing case-processing decisions. In the District of Columbia, a witness is impeachable if he has a prior conviction. This means that a subset of the victims with arrest records is impeachable.

Of the 5,042 arrests for violent crimes brought by the police in 1973, 548 involved victims with an arrest record known by the police. Although the differences in "papering" and dismissal rates were not as dramatic with the victim's arrest record as with the two previous variables, the differences were significant and in the expected direction (Table 5). The differences at trial were not in the expected direction, but were not significant.

The arrest record was not found to have a significant effect on the screening decision for any violent crimes, after other factors were controlled. For the later decision to dismiss a case, a significant effect was found for forcible sex offenses, but not for homicides, assaults, or robbery. This may be due to the fact that it is very difficult to obtain a conviction in rape cases. Therefore, an additional negative factor—such as an arrest record—might lessen the victim's credibility to the point of case dismissal. Another possible explanation for this finding is that the victim's previous arrests could be for prostitution.

The fact that victims with an arrest record appear not to be discriminated against is particularly interesting, since alcoholic victims do appear to have trouble having their cases accepted for prosecution. The victim's anticipated behavior as a witness probably accounts for the fact that alcohol abuse is more important in leading to case attrition than opiate use or an arrest record.

The "Innocent" Victim—Health, Age, and Sex. Weak or helpless victims can be seen as less responsible for their plight due to their inability to successfully resist attack. Therefore, it is hypothesized that cases with such victims would be less likely to be dropped before conviction, or to result in an acquittal.

Table 5. CASE-PROCESSING DECISIONS IN CASES OF VIOLENT CRIME BY
WHETHER THE VICTIM IS KNOWN TO HAVE AN ARREST RECORD:
DISTRICT OF COLUMBIA, 1973

		Victim Has Arrest Record		
				Difference
				Significant
Case Processing Decision	All Cases	Yes	No	(.05)
Percentage of:				
Defendants "no papered"	23%	28%	23%	Yes
(number of arrests)	(5,042)	(548)	(4,494)	
Cases dismissed by prosecutor	41%	47%	41%	Yes
(number of cases initially filed at screening)	(3,349)	(336)	(3,013)	
Defendants found not guilty	40%	38%	41%	No
(number of cases tried)	(593)	(47)	(546)	

The presence of a physical disability or poor health in the victim, as recorded
by the prosecutor, showed no relationship to case processing decisions. The
decisions to "paper," to dismiss, or to find a defendant not guilty were not
influenced by this variable in either the bivariate or multivariate analyses.

The age of the victim at its extreme values was hypothesized to affect
dispositions. The very young and the very old might be seen as unable to defend
themselves adequately. It was hypothesized that defendants accused of attacking
such victims would be less likely to have their cases dropped, despite the fact
that very young and very old victims may cause problems due to the question of
their competency in testifying as witnesses. The "very young" were defined as
age 12 and below, and the "very old" as age 60 and above. A separate category
was also included for teenagers 13 to 17 years, to determine whether this group
received particular consideration when decisions were made.[10]

The hypothesis that the cases of the young and old victims would be less
likely to be dropped was supported only for the "initial papering" decision
(Table 6). Children 12 years or under and adults over 60 years were the victims
less likely to have their cases rejected at screening, while victims aged 18 to 59
years were more likely to have their cases dropped at this point. A chi-square
test of the table frequencies for "papering" showed them to differ significantly
from what would be expected if age made no difference in whether the case was
dropped, at the 5% level of confidence.

Although the same pattern was found for the decision to dismiss, a chi-square
test of the table frequencies showed them to be insignificantly different from

Table 6. CASE-PROCESSING DECISIONS IN CASES OF VIOLENT CRIME BY AGE OF VICTIM: DISTRICT OF COLUMBIA, 1973

		Age of Victim				
Case Processing Decision	All Cases	Less Than 13 Years	13-17 Years	18-59 Years	60 Years and Over	Unknown
Percentage of:						
Defendants "no papered" (number of arrests)	23% (5,042)	16% (108)	24% (207)	25% (2,570)	17% (180)	23% (1,977)
Cases dismissed by prosecutor (number of cases initially filed at screening)	41% (3,349)	42% (77)	44% (141)	43% (1,684)	39% (122)	40% (1,325)
Defendant found not guilty (number of cases tried)	40% (593)	45% (11)	52% (25)	40% (286)	48% (23)	38% (248)

the frequencies which could be obtained if there were no "real" differences in the dismissal rates for different age groups.

The decision of guilt at trial did not follow the pattern of special consideration for the very young and the very old victims. However, chi-square was not significant for these figures.

In the multivariate analysis of the three decisions of interest by type of crime, there were only four instances in which the age of the victim appeared to have an effect on decision making after other factors were controlled. The direction of these relationships was always as hypothesized.

Victim age appeared to influence both the decision to "paper" and the later decision to dismiss, in cases of forcible sex. For the initial screening decision, cases with victims under the age of 13 were significantly more likely to be "papered." The largest proportion of child victims of violent crimes were found in the forcible sex offenses category. The prosecutor appears to be conscientious about not dropping these cases, despite the fact that testimony may be more difficult to obtain from a child, if the case ever goes to trial. Since the question has also been raised as to whether a child's testimony in a rape case can affect the child's psychological adjustment (Gagnon, 1965; Schultz, 1973), it would be expected that the prosecutor would try to obtain convictions in these cases without going to trial.

For the prosecutor's decision to dismiss cases of forcible sex, however, the opposite pattern was found for victims 13 to 17. Teenage victims were significantly more likely to have their cases dropped. This may be due to the fact that many of these teenage cases are "statutory rapes," involving a consenting victim. In cases of forcible sex, there appears to be a marked difference in the treatment of the case depending upon whether the victim has reached puberty.

The hypothesis that older victims would be seen as defenseless—and that, for this reason, their cases would more likely result in conviction for the defendant—was confirmed for only one type of crime, homicide. Cases in which the homicide victim was 60 or older were less likely to be dismissed by the prosecutor, in the multivariate analysis.

The fourth instance in which victim age had a significant effect on a case-processing decision, after controlling for other factors, was in cases of assault which were prosecuted as felonies, but not indicted. If the victim of the assault was between the ages of 18 and 59 years, the case was more likely to be dismissed. This was consistent with the hypothesis that it is the extreme age ranges that are of more concern to the prosecutor in evaluating a criminal event.

Western culture has traditionally used sex as an indicator of strength or weakness. The male is considered the stronger sex; the female the weaker sex.

Table 7. CASE-PROCESSING DECISIONS IN CASES OF VIOLENT CRIME BY SEX OF VICTIM: DISTRICT OF COLUMBIA, 1973

		Sex of Victim			Difference Significant[a] (.05)
Case Processing Decision	All Cases	Male	Female	Unknown	
Percentage of:					
Defendants "no papered" (number of arrests)	23% (5,042)	21% (2,639)	29% (1,637)	19% (766)	Yes
Cases dismissed by prosecutor (number of cases initially filed at screening)	41% (3,349)	41% (1,737)	45% (1,038)	34% (524)	Yes
Defendants found not guilty (number of cases tried)	40% (593)	40% (326)	45% (170)	31% (97)	No

a. Male compared to female.

Since this analysis of decision making is focusing on the perceptions of the prosecutor, judge, and jury, the traditional view of the differences between the sexes was used. Thus, it was expected that the female victims would be seen as more defenseless and that their accused attacker(s) would more likely be convicted.

The bivariate results were not consistent with the hypothesis. Cases in which the victim was female were more likely to be "no papered" at screening or dismissed before trial or were more likely to end in a finding of "not guilty" if the case was tried (Table 7).[11] The differences were significant for the screening and dismissal decision. At trial, the direction of the relationship was consistent, but not statistically significant.

In understanding these findings, the first question becomes: are the crimes committed against males and females different? According to arrest statistics, females were victimized less frequently than males in cases of murder, manslaughter, aggravated assault, and robbery. They were victimized more frequently only in the case of rape and simple assault, which have high rates of attrition. Another possible contributory factor is that crimes against male victims are generally more serious and involve defendants with more extensive criminal backgrounds. Whether the victim in a crime was male was found to be correlated with defendant and crime seriousness. As a result, in the multivariate analysis, after controlling for these factors, the victim's sex did not appear to influence decision making, with one exception. The sex of the victim was found to be a significant determinant of the decision to dismiss for felony assaults that were not indicted. For these cases, the effect was as originally hypothesized; female victims were less likely to have their cases dismissed by the prosecutor.

II. The Relationship Between the Victim and the Defendant

At the time of screening, the police officer who has made the arrest indicates the social relationship between the primary victim and the defendant. Of the 5,042 arrests during 1973, data on this relationship were available for 3,826 cases. These cases were used to test the hypothesis that the closer the relationship between the victim and the defendant, the more likely the case will not result in conviction.

The possible relationship categories from which the police officer chooses are numerous. Table 8 shows the frequency distribution of arrests made during 1973 according to the relationship between the victim and the defendant. The distribution of relationships varies by type of crime—with homicide, assault, and forcible sex offenses having a larger proportion of closer relationships, and robbery having a larger proportion of crimes between strangers.[12]

Table 9 shows the bivariate relationship between case-processing decisions

Table 8. NUMBER AND PERCENTAGE OF ARRESTS FOR VIOLENT CRIMES
BY RELATIONSHIP BETWEEN THE VICTIM AND DEFENDANT:
DISTRICT OF COLUMBIA, 1973

Relationship Between the Victim and Defendant	Arrests in Which Relationship Known	
	Number	Percentage
Family:		
Child/Parent	38	1.0
Spouse	333	8.7
Other	135	3.5
Friend or Acquaintance:		
Ex-spouse	20	0.5
Cohabiting	79	2.1
Girlfriend or boyfriend	250	6.5
Friend	402	10.5
Neighbor	213	5.6
Employer-employee	33	0.9
Acquaintance	692	18.1
Stranger	1,631	42.6
TOTAL	3,826	100.0

and the victim-defendant relationship. In general, the hypothesis was confirmed that, when the victim and defendant have a closer social relationship, the case is more likely to be dropped before conviction. Of cases in which the victim and defendant were members of the same family, the overall percentage that were dropped at each of the three stages was higher than the average for all relationship categories. Likewise, the percentage of dropped cases in which the victim and defendant were strangers was lower than the average. It is more revealing, however, to examine the more specific relationship categories, such as "spouse" or "friend," within the broader categories of "family" or "friend or acquaintance."

Beginning with the closer relationships, the rate of "no-papered" cases at screening and the rate of dismissal was highest for spouses, compared to any other relationship category. Cases of violent crime between a parent and child, however, were only slightly more likely to be dismissed before trial than other cases. The category "other family" had a rate of dismissal higher than the "child-parent" cases, but lower than the "spouse" cases, for each point in the process. It appears that it is the cases between spouses which contribute most to case dismissal in the "family" category. These cases between spouses are usually assaults.

Another specific relationship category which had a high rate of case dismissal is the group which has some kind of past or present romantic involvement,

Table 9. CASE-PROCESSING DECISIONS IN CASES OF VIOLENT CRIME BY THE
RELATIONSHIP BETWEEN THE VICTIM AND THE DEFENDANT:
DISTRICT OF COLUMBIA, 1973

Relationship Between the Victim and Defendant*	Case-Processing Decisions		
	Defendants "No Papered"	Cases Dismissed by Prosecutor	Defendants Found Not Guilty
Family:			
Child/Parent	26% (38)	36% (25)	
Spouse	45% (333)	62% (169)	50% (28)
Other	·31% (135)	57% (82)	
Friend or Acquaintance:			
Ex-spouse			
Cohabiting	37% (349)	57% (208)	59% (17)
Girlfriend or boyfriend			
Friend	39% (402)	44% (213)	
Neighbor	24% (213)	45% (142)	31% (65)
Employer/Employee	9% (33)	37% (27)	
Acquaintance	21% (692)	43% (479)	44% (87)
Stranger	15% (1,631)	37% (831)	39% (227)
TOTAL	24% (3,826)[a]	43% (2,518)[b]	40% (425)[c]

*Cases where the relationship was unknown were excluded.

a. Number of arrests in which relationship was known.
b. Number of cases initially filed at screening in which relationship was known.
c. Number of cases tried in which relationship was known.

composed of the relationships of "exspouse," "cohabiting person," and
"girlfriend or boyfriend." The rates of attrition for these cases were far above
the average for all cases, for each of the three decision points. Again, these cases
are usually assaults.

At the other end of the relationship categories, crimes between strangers are
less likely to be dropped than other crimes. The percentage of these cases
dropped at screening was only 15%, compared to 24% for all cases. The effect of
the "stranger" relationship between a victim and defendant on the decision to
dismiss by the prosecutor and on the finding of not guilty at trial was less than
the effect on the initial decision to file the case, but in the same direction.

All the relationship categories were included in the multiple regression
analysis as dummy variables. The social relationship between the victim and the
defendant frequently made a difference in decision making after other factors
were controlled.

The relationships found to be important varied by type of crime. At least one
type of social relationship between the victim and the defendant appeared to be

Table 10. CASE-PROCESSING DECISIONS IN CASES OF VIOLENT CRIME BY THE EMPLOYMENT STATUS OF THE VICTIM: DISTRICT OF COLUMBIA, 1973

| | | Employment Status of the Victim | | | |
Case Processing Decisions	All Cases	Employed	Unemployed	Unknown	Difference Significant[a] (.05)
Percentage of:					
Defendants "no papered"	23%	20%	29%	23%	Yes
(number of arrests)	(5,042)	(2,379)	(1,521)	(1,142)	
Cases dismissed by prosecutor	41%	39%	47%	39%	Yes
(number of cases initially filed at screening)	(3,349)	(1,635)	(964)	(750)	
Defendants found not guilty	40%	41%	42%	37%	No
(number of cases tried)	(593)	(329)	(130)	(134)	

a. Employed compared to unemployed.

significant at the 5% level of confidence for each analysis of the screening decision. For aggravated assault, the two relationships found to be significantly associated with cases dropped at screening were "spouse" or "friend." For simple assault, neither of these was significant, but the variable indicating romantic involvement in the past or present was significant. When the victim and defendant were exspouses, cohabiting persons, or girlfriend-boyfriend, cases of simple assault tended not to be filed. Whether the victim and defendant were "friends" (excluding romantic relationships) was the important variable in regard to forcible sex offenses. These cases were less likely to be prosecuted. In robbery cases, romantic involvement between the victim and the defendant or friendship was a significant factor in a case being dropped. One can imagine that consent would be more difficult to disprove when such a relationship exists.

As with the screening decision, the results varied by type of crime for the decision to dismiss a case after screening. For the 189 closed "papered" homicide cases, those in which the victim and defendant were related were more likely to be dismissed—though not when a child or spouse was involved. When they were friends, however, the cases were less likely to be dismissed. The decision to dismiss an assault case was examined for three groups: misdemeanors, unindicted felonies, and indicted felonies. For the latter two more serious groups of crime, no relationship was found to be important. However, for the 971 assaults prosecuted as misdemeanors, three relationships affected dismissal: when the victim and defendant were spouses, when they had a romantic involvement, or when they were related, though, again, not when a child or spouse was involved. The decision to dismiss robberies and forcible sex offenses was not influenced by the relationship between the victim and defendant. It appears that the closer relationships among these cases are eliminated at screening.

III. Victim Employment

The effect of the victim's employment status on decision making could not be predicted from just-world theory. The employment status of the victim was included in the analysis for exploratory purposes, to test whether this characteristic of the victim is considered at all in case-processing decisions.

Of the 5,042 arrests for violent crime, the victim was employed in 47% of the cases and unemployed in 30%, and his or her employment status was unknown in 23% of the cases. All three categories were examined, since it seemed as plausible that unemployment of the victim would influence decision making as employment.

Table 10 shows the relationship between employment status and case processing decisions.[13] Without controlling for other variables, victims who were unemployed were significantly more likely to have their cases dropped by the prosecutor.

Despite this fact, victim employment was not a significant variable in the analysis of case-processing decisions after other factors were controlled, with only one exception. Victim unemployment was found to increase the probability that the prosecutor would dismiss the case for 517 unindicted felony robberies. Due to these results, it appears that cases with employed victims are easier to prosecute due to other characteristics, rather than employment itself.

IV. The Victim as a Witness

The purpose of examining the victim's behavior as a complaining witness was to clarify which cases were being dropped due to the prosecutor's perception of certain characteristics of the victim and which were being dropped due to the victim's own lack of cooperation as a witness. Some victim characteristics, such as age, could have an effect on case attrition, not because the prosecutor was treating such cases differently, but because the victims in such cases were behaving differently as witnesses.

For screening and dismissal decisions, the prosecutor records in PROMIS his reasons for either "no-papering" a case or dismissing it at a later point. Several possible reasons involve problems with the complaining witness.[14]

A confounding factor in using these reasons for analysis, illuminated by a recent study of witness cooperation in the District of Columbia (Cannavale, 1976), is that the victim may be attempting to cooperate, but is misperceived by the prosecutor. For purposes of this analysis, it will be assumed that when the prosecutor indicates a complaining witness problem as the reason for dropping a case, it means that he is having some type of testimony problem with the victim but that it is not necessarily the victim's *intention* to cause problems.

For the decision to "paper" a case at screening and the decision by the prosecutor to dismiss after screening, a multiple regression analysis was constructed in which the dependent variable was whether or not the case was dropped due to a complaining witness problem. The cases studied were (1) 1,180 cases of violent crime "no-papered" at the initial screening and (2) 1,382 cases of violent crimes dismissed by the prosecutor before trial. Each of these two types of dismissals can be seen as due either to complaining witness problems or to other factors.[15]

The results shed further light on some of the findings in the previous sections. The findings discussed in the first three parts of the analysis will each be discussed in relation to the results of the analysis of complaining witness problems.

Victim provocation and victim participation were both found to be important in the prosecutor's decision to "no-paper" a case at screening. As would be expected, neither of the variables appeared to cause cases to be dropped due to the victim's lack of cooperation. In fact, cases which were identified as involving victim participation and which were "no-papered" were significantly less likely to have been dropped due to a complaining witness reason. Victims who participated in the crime were more likely to have their cases dropped, but the reason for the dismissal was not their own unwillingness to cooperate.

Of the three victim variables hypothesized to increase the perception of the victim as generally more blameworthy, and therefore responsible for his plight, only the alcohol variable was significant in predicting a complaining witness problem. "Victim chronic abuser of alcohol" was a factor in the decision to dismiss before trial due to a problem with the complaining witness, but not in the initial decision to "paper" the case. It was at the time of screening, however, that the prosecutor appeared to be taking alcohol abuse by the victim into account, rather than after screening. This suggests that the prosecutor is weighing the victim's alcohol problem in his decision at screening, possibly due to his anticipation of a witness problem later in the case, based on his past experience with such victims.

The victim's sex and age also had an impact upon the probability of complaining witness problems. Females were less likely to be uncooperative witnesses at screening. As discussed in a prior section, males were significantly more likely to have their cases "papered" than females, without controlling for other factors. It can at least be claimed that the reason that male victims are favored is not due to problems with the cooperation of female victims as witnesses.

Victim age was a significant variable in the prosecution of forcible sex cases. The prosecutor was more likely to "paper" forcible sex cases involving a victim under 13 years of age and more likely to dismiss before trial forcible sex cases involving a victim between 13 and 17 years. Related to the latter result is the finding that the variable "victim 13 to 17" was significant in the analysis of complaining witness problems both at screening and later in the case, but in opposite directions. Cases involving victims 13 to 17 years old were significantly less likely to be "no-papered" for a complaining witness reason at screening, but significantly more likely to be dismissed for a complaining witness reason later in the case. It appears that one explanation for teenage cases of forcible sex being dismissed before trial is, at least in part, their behavior as witnesses. Many of these cases may be statutory rape cases in which the victim and defendant know each other. At screening the victim is willing to cooperate, but becomes uncooperative as the case proceeds, perhaps due to an attachment to the defendant.

The relationship between the victim and the defendant appeared to influence the prosecutor's decision to file charges at screening for three categories: friend, spouse, and intimate acquaintance. Predictably, friends and intimate acquaintances were found to be associated with complaining witness problems at screening. Spouses appear to show up initially, but are found to be uncooperative at the later stage of dismissal. As with the teenage and alcoholic victims, a prosecutor may initially refuse to prosecute, anticipating that the victim will later lose interest in cases in which the victim and defendant are married.

Intimate acquaintances who have a past or present romantic involvement not only appear to lose interest in the case at screening but also seem more likely to lose interest later in the case. Friends who survive screening by both cooperating and having their cases prosecuted seem to cooperate at later stages. Victims to whom the defendants are strangers are significantly less likely to be the cause of a witness problem later in a case.

It would appear that, when the victim and defendant have a close social relationship, dispute resolution may be occurring outside the courtroom. At best, one can say that such family cases, and perhaps cases between close friends, are best settled out of the criminal setting. At worst, a pattern of violence between a husband and wife may continue with the beaten spouse unable or unwilling to leave the family setting and, hence, unwilling to continue to testify in a criminal case. If a wife is dependent upon her husband for support, jailing him for simple assault may not seem to her to be the best solution. Initial willingness to prosecute may fade as the case continues. This same problem probably also exists with couples who are cohabiting or have a dependent boyfriend-girlfriend relationship.

SUMMARY AND CONCLUSIONS

The general hypothesis of this study was confirmed: victim characteristics do affect the case-processing decisions made in cases of violent crime. Victim characteristics affect the prosecutor's decisions at screening and later in the case. However, the decision of whether the defendant was guilty or not guilty at trial did not appear to be influenced by the characteristics of the victim. It may be that the actual determinants of the decision of guilty or not guilty are beyond the scope of the available data, hinging instead on specific legal issues. Another possibility is that 593 cases was not enough to see the effects.

In regard to the more specific hypotheses, some were supported and others were not. The first hypothesis that the more responsibility that can be attributed to the victim, the more likely that the case will not result in conviction was partially substantiated. Hypotheses H_{1A} and H_{1B} concerning victim provocation and participation were supported for the screening decision, but not for later decisions. Cases in which the screening prosecutor perceived victim provocation or participation were more likely to be "no-papered." Since these two variables are subjective assessments, unlike victim sex or age, it seems necessary to have a more precise measure of the perceptions of the other decision makers before concluding that victim provocation or participation does not influence their decision making. The three variables hypothesized to increase the victim's "blameworthiness" (opiate use, alcohol abuse, and previous arrests) had effects on decision making in the directions expected according to hypotheses H_{1C}, H_{1D}, and H_{1E}, when found to be significant. Alcohol abuse appeared to have an impact on the initial screening decision for every type of crime except simple assault. The victim's use of opiates and prior arrest record, on the other hand, did not appear to have an effect on the screening decisions. However, unlike victim alcohol abuse, which had no effect on the decision to dismiss, use of opiates appeared to influence the decision of the prosecutor to dismiss indicted robbery cases, while victim arrest record was found to increase the probability that a forcible sex case would be dismissed.

The three hypotheses—H_{1F}, H_{1G}, and H_{1H}—that the victim's "innocence" would less likely cause a case to be dropped was also partially supported. The variables frequently were not significant in influencing decision making, but when they were significant, it was in the expected direction. The indication that the victim had a physical disability or poor health did not have an impact on any decision, whereas victim age and sex had varying impact, depending upon the type of crime. Victims of forcible sex under 13 years were more likely to have their cases "papered" than were other victims. In contrast, victims of forcible sex offenses aged 13 to 17 years were more likely to have their cases dismissed by the prosecutor after they were initially accepted for prosecution at screening. Victims of homicide over 60 years old were less likely to have their cases dismissed before trial. Victim sex was significant only for one type of case—felony assaults that were not indicted. The relationship was as hypothesized; assaults involving female victims were less likely to be dismissed.

The hypothesis that the prosecutor, judge, and jury make decisions based on the concept that the more responsibility that can be attributed to the victim, the less that should be attributed to the defendant, cannot be wholeheartedly accepted based on the results of this study. Almost every relationship between victim characteristics and decision making which was based on this concept and which had a significant effect had the direction which would be expected. However, in many instances, these victim characteristics concerning responsibility had no significant effect. Testing the same hypothesis on new data from other jurisdictions might contribute further evidence.

The second hypothesis of the research was that cases will less likely result in conviction when the social relationship between the victim and the defendant is close. This hypothesis was generally supported. Without considering more specific relationship categories, cases apppeared to be dropped if they involved a family relationship and pursued if the victim and the defendant were strangers. Upon closer analysis, it appears that the critical family relationship in terms of dismissal is that between husband and wife and, to a lesser extent, other family relationships, such as aunt or uncle. If the victim and defendant are spouses, the prosecutor is less likely to "paper" aggravated assault cases and more likely to later dismiss assaults filed as misdemeanors. Homicide cases and misdemeanor assaults were more likely to be dismissed if the victim and defendant were related, but not a husband, wife, or child. It appears from these results that the child-parent relationship does not have the same impact on decision making as the spouse or other family relationship and should be analyzed separately.

In the general relationship category of friend or acquaintance, romantic involvement between the victim and defendant in the past or present appears to have an effect on decision making, as well as any indication of friendship. Cases in which the victim and defendant were exspouses, cohabiting persons, or girlfriend-boyfriend were more likely to be dropped at screening for simple assault and robbery and more likely to be dismissed later for assaults prosecuted as misdemeanors. Whether the victim and defendant were perceived by the police as friends also had an impact on some decisions. Aggravated assault, forcible sex offenses, and robbery were more likely to be dropped at screening if the relationship between the victim and defendant was labeled as friend. The only contradiction to the original hypothesis was the finding that homicide cases were less likely to be dismissed if the victim and defendant were friends.

The third part of the analysis, which explored the effect of the victim's employment status on decision making, found that generally this variable was not considered by the prosecutor, judge, and jury. The one significant finding was that unindicted felony robberies were more likely to be dismissed if the victim was unemployed.

The fourth part of the analysis was an examination of the characteristics of victims which are associated with complaining witness problems. These results modify some of the earlier findings. Some victim characteristics appear to increase the likelihood that the victim will cooperate, such as victim participation, but the prosecutor drops the cases for other reasons. Still other victim characteristics appear to influence a prosecutor's decision to drop the case at screening, perhaps in anticipation of the witness problems which were found to appear later in the case. According to just-world theory, cases with victims who used opiates, abused alcohol, or had arrest records should more likely be dropped. The findings were in the expected directions, when significant, but the results were much more consistent for alcohol abuse than for the other two victim characteristics. It is alcohol abuse which is associated with complaining witness problems later in the case, but not at screening. Anticipation of a witness problem with the alcoholic victim appears to be causing the high attrition rates at screening of cases with such victims. The same mechanism appears to be operating in cases of forcible sex with a teenage victim.

One of the explanations for the dismissal of cases in which the victim and defendant have a close relationship is that the victim reconciles with the defendant or perhaps is fearful of testifying due to a continuing relationship. The findings from the analysis of the characteristics of victims who refuse to cooperate with the prosecution support this interpretation. The relationships leading to victim cooperation problems at screening are "friend" and "intimate acquaintance." Later in the case, intimate acquaintances and spouses are more likely to cause a case to be dismissed, due to a victim testimony problem. It appears that the effect of the social relationship between the victim and the defendant explains, in large part, the victim's decision to refuse to cooperate. There also appears to be an anticipation by the prosecutor at screening of future witness problems when the victim and the defendant are spouses, since these cases are "no-papered" at a high rate, but the victim cooperation difficulties do not appear to surface until later in the case.

This study indicates that the victim is considered in determining the final dispositions in cases of violent crime. Most of the victim's impact occurs before trial. It is the prosecutor who appears to be taking the victim into consideration in his decision not to prosecute or to later dismiss, perhaps in anticipation of how the judge and jury will perceive the victim. The victim affects the prosecution in two ways—in terms of the prosecutor's perception of him and as a witness. Relatively few cases go to trial, and it appears that much of the decision making with the greatest impact occurs before this stage.

APPENDIX

I. ITEMS ON THE VICTIM COLLECTED IN PROMIS

Question and Possible Responses	Person Completing the Form
What are victim's sex and age?	Police officer
Does victim have any physical or health problems?	Police officer
(a) Physical disability or bad health.	
(b) Indication of use of heroin or other opiate, at any time.	
(c) Indication of chronic alcohol abuse.	
Is victim employed?	Police officer
Does victim have an arrest record?	Police officer
What is the relationship of victim to defendant?	Police officer
Spouse (including common law)	
Child	
Other member of family	
Ex-spouse	
Cohabiting person	
Girlfriend or boyfriend	
Friend	
Acquaintance	
Neighbor	
Employer or employee	
Stranger	
Other (specify)	
Was there provocation by victim?	Prosecutor*
Victim participation?	Prosecutor*

*In some instances, it is possible that these items were recorded by the police officer.

II. VIOLENT CRIMES INCLUDED IN THE ANALYSIS

The following table lists the offenses included in each of the broad categories of violent crime analyzed.

Type of Crime	Number of Cases Brought by the Police During 1973
A. Criminal homicide	
First degree murder	122
Second degree murder	78
Manslaughter	49
B. Assault	
Aggravated:	
Assault with a dangerous weapon—gun	640
Assault with a dangerous weapon—knife	768
Assault with a dangerous weapon—other	594
Simple:	
Simple assault*	604
Threats to do bodily harm*	80
C. Forcible sex offenses	
Rape	297
Assault with intent to rape	32
Attempted rape*	7
Sodomy—female victim	21
Sodomy—male victim	21
Carnal knowledge	27
Indecent acts	44
Seduction by teacher	1
D. Robbery	
Personal victim:	
Robbery	1,294
Attempted robbery	45
Assault with intent to rob	101
Business or institutional victim:	
Robbery	204
Attempted robbery	4
Assault with intent to rob	9
TOTAL—All violent crimes	5,042

*Misdemeanors

Some additional explanation of these specific offenses is necessary:

(1) The manslaughter charge included under criminal homicide does not include involuntary manslaughter, such as a traffic death.

(2) Forcible sex offenses include adult female rape, rape of a male victim, and sexual offenses against children. A charge of carnal knowledge is brought when the victim is a female under 16 years, whereas "indecent acts" may involve either a male or a female under 16 years. In either case, consent is not an issue, since a person less than 16 is not felt to be capable of giving an informed consent. Thus, some of these cases may have involved willing victim participation, termed "statutory" rape in some jurisdictions.

(3) The robbery cases may be either robberies of individuals or "holdups" of liquor stores, banks, etc. In the case of a business or institutional robbery, there is usually also a personal victim—for example, a bank teller. It is the characteristics of this personal victim which will be included in the analysis.

III. MULTIPLE REGRESSION ANALYSES

Below is a table showing the multiple regression analyses conducted for each decision point and type of crime. The decision to prosecute was not analyzed separately for homicide, since only 7 out of the 249 cases were dropped at screening. For the decision to dismiss, separate analyses were conducted for assault and robbery, depending upon whether the case was a misdemeanor, unindicted felony, or indicted felony. Since only indicted felonies would receive individual attention by being assigned to a particular prosecutor, it was felt to be important to do separate analyses. Homicide and forcible sex offenses were each handled as a group due to the small number of cases. Since only 593 cases went to trial of the 5,042 cases of violent crime brought by the police, a separate analysis could not be conducted for each type of crime for this decision point.

The Decision and Type of Crime	Number of Cases
Decision to prosecute:	
Aggravated assault	2,002
Simple assault	684
Forcible sex offenses	450
Robbery	1,657
Decision of the prosecutor to dismiss a case:	
Homicide	189
Assault	
Misdemeanors	971
Unindicted felonies	430
Indicted felonies	286
Forcible sex offenses	278
Robbery	
Unindicted felonies	517
Indicted felonies	639
Finding or verdict of the judge or jury at trial:	
All violent crimes	589

NOTES

1. For a review of the development of just-world theory, see McDonald, Chapter 1 in this volume.

2. This division of the court is equivalent to a state court of general jurisdiction.

3. There are two methodological problems with using court cases against one individual defendant, rather than criminal incidents, which may involve several victims and defendants. When there is more than one offender arrested for a crime, the same victim may be included several times in the analysis. If particular types of victims are more likely to be victimized by several offenders, their characteristics will be given added weight. This was not deemed a serious difficulty, since multiple defendants are only common for robbery. Analysis using criminal incidents would have involved many additional methodological difficulties. The other problem with using court cases against one defendant is that information on only one victim was available for each case, although several victims may have been involved in the incident. It was assumed that the person identified as the primary victim would be the one most likely to affect decision making.

4. Seriousness was determined by looking at each charge in the case and choosing the one with the highest maximum sentence. The charges brought by the police were used, rather than those filed by the prosecutor, in an attempt to stay as close to the actual criminal event as possible. For example, the prosecutor may reduce an aggravated assault from a felony to a misdemeanor, not because a weapon was not involved in the offense, but rather due to other evidence problems in the case which will make it difficult to obtain conviction. The disadvantage in using police charges, however, is that the police may overcharge.

5. Felonies and misdemeanors follow a different procedure in the Washington jurisdiction. Misdemeanors and felonies before indictment are handled in an "assembly line" fashion—i.e., responsibility for a case shifts from one prosecutor to another as the case proceeds from screening to trial. Once indicted, a felony case is specially assigned to a judge and prosecutor who handle that case through the final disposition. The individual assignment in felony cases allows more contact with the victim.

6. This is known as nolle prosequi in the case of misdemeanors and unindicted felonies.

7. A separate analysis was not made of jury versus bench trials, since an analysis of 1973 PROMIS data showed this to be an unreliable field.

8. At the time that data from 1973 were assembled for analysis, some cases still remained open, i.e., had not reached a final disposition. The percentage still open ranged from 24% of all "papered" murder cases to 6% of all "papered" simple assaults. When "papered" cases are discussed, the open cases are excluded. If the final disposition of the open cases were known, the distribution of final dispositions might differ from the distribution of the dispositions of the known cases. Further research is under way to clarify this issue.

9. Error is to be expected in this figure in both directions. Some cases in which provocation or participation truly existed will not be labeled as such by the prosecutor; other cases will be included in which there was no provocation or participation by the victim. Since the screening prosecutor fills out these items, they are probably fairly accurate measures of his perception of whether there was victim provocation or participation in the case. The later prosecutor, who may dismiss the case, and the judge and jury may not share this perception.

10. Cases in which the age of the victim was unknown were also analyzed. The percentage of cases dropped at each of the three decision points for cases in which age of the victim was unknown was not significantly different from the percentage dropped for all cases in which age was known. This suggests that the cases in which age was unknown were randomly distributed.

11. Cases in which the sex of the victim was unknown showed a unique pattern. For each decision, cases in which sex of the victim was unknown were significantly less likely to be dropped, compared to cases in which the sex of the victim was known. This raises the question of how the results might be altered if the sex of the victim was available for all cases.

12. In the analysis, "closeness" is not meant to imply psychological closeness, but denotes the social differences implied by the descriptive titles used, such as "spouse," "friend," and the like.

13. Cases in which employment status was unknown were also included in the table. The differences between the percentage of cases dropped at each of the three decision points for cases in which employment status was known was not significantly different from those in which employment status was unknown. This suggests that cases in which employment status was unknown were randomly distributed.

14. If one of the following reasons was given by the prosecutor either at screening or upon dismissal by the prosecutor, it was considered a complaining witness problem: (1) complaining witness signs off, refuses to prosecute, or is reluctant; (2) complaining witness does not show or appears unfit for trial (drunk, etc.); (3) complaining witness is unavailable (sick, out of town); (4) complaining witness cannot be located.

15. The proportion of cases not filed at screening due to a problem with the complaining witness was 52%; the proportion later dismissed due to a complaining witness problem was 40%.

REFERENCES

ADERMAN, D.; BREHM, S.S.; and KATZ, L.B. (1974). "Empathic observation of an innocent victim." Journal of Personality and Social Psychology, 29(3):342-347.

AMIR, M. (1970). "Forcible rape." Pp. 644-653 in M. Wolfgang (ed.), The Sociology of Crime and Delinquency. New York: Wiley.

CANNAVALE, F.J. (1976). "A study of witness cooperation with District of Columbia prosecutors." In W.D. Falcon (ed.), Witness cooperation. Lexington, Mass.: D.C. Heath.

CHAIKIN, A.L., and DARLEY, J.M. (1973). "Victim or perpetrator: Defensive attribution of responsibility and need for order and justice." Journal of Personality and Social Psychology, 25(2):268-275.

CURTIS, L.A. (1974). "Victim precipitation and violent crime." Social Problems, 21(4):594-607.

EDELHERTZ, H., and GEIS, G. (1974). Public compensation to victims of crime. New York: Praeger.

GAGNON, J.A. (1965). "Female child victims of sex offenses." Social Problems, 13(2):176-192.

GOLDSTEIN, H. (1967). "Policy formulation: A proposal for improving police perform-ance." Michigan Law Review, 65(6):1123-1146.

HAMILTON, W.A., and WORK, C.R. (1973). "The prosecutor's role in the urban court system: The case for management consciousness." Journal of Criminal Law and Criminology, 2(June):183-189.

JONES, C., and ARONSON, E. (1974). "Attribution of fault to a rape victim as a function of the respectability of the victim." Journal of Personality and Social Psychology, 26(3):415-419.

KALVEN, H., and ZEISEL, H. (1971). The American jury. Chicago: University of Chicago Press.

LANDY, D., and ARONSON, E. (1974). "The influence of the character of the criminal and his victim on the decisions of simulated jurors." Pp. 195-204 in I. Drapkin and E. Viano (eds.), Victimology. Lexington, Mass.: D.C. Heath.

LERNER, M.J. (1965). "Evaluation of performance as a function of performers' reward and attractiveness." Journal of Personality and Social Psychology, 1(4):355-360.

LERNER, M.J., and SIMMONS, C.H. (1966). "Observer's reaction to the innocent victim: Compassion or rejection." Journal of Personality and Social Psychology, 4(2):203-210.

McDONALD, W.F. (1973). "Prosecutorial discretion at the initial screening: An analysis of case mortality of five serious crimes." Paper presented at the annual meeting of the American Criminological Society, New York.

McINTYRE, D.M. (1968). "A study of judicial dominance of the charging process." Journal of Criminal Law, Criminology and Police Science, 59(4):463-490.

MILLER, F. (1969). Prosecution: The decision to charge a suspect with a crime. Boston: Little, Brown.

PARNAS, R.I. (1967). "The police response to the domestic disturbance." Wisconsin Law Review, (fall):914-960.

REISS, A.J. (1971). The police and the public. New Haven, Conn.: Yale University Press.

——— (1974). "Discretionary justice in the United States." International Journal of Criminology and Penology, 2(2):181-205.

SCHULTZ, L.G. (1973). "The child sex victim: Social, psychological, and legal perspectives." Child Welfare, 52(3):147-155.

SIGALL, H., and OSTROVE, N. (1975). "Beautiful but dangerous: Effects of offender attractiveness and nature of crime on juridic judgment." Journal of Personality and Social Psychology, 31(3):410-414.

Southern California Law Review (1969). "Prosecutorial discretion in the initiation of criminal complaints." 42:519-545.

STOKOLS, D., and SCHOPLER, J. (1973). "Reactions to victims under conditions of situational detachment: The effects of responsibility, severity, and expected future interaction." Journal of Personality and Social Psychology, 25(2):199-209.

TRUNINGER, E. (1971). "Marital violence: The legal solutions." Hastings Law Journal, 23:259-276.

WALSTER, E. (1966). "Assignment of responsibility for an accident." Journal of Personality and Social Psychology, 3(1):73-79.

WOLFGANG, M.E. (1958). Patterns in criminal homicide. Philadelphia: University of Pennsylvania Press.

Chapter 9

THE EFFECTS OF VICTIM CHARACTERISTICS ON JUDICIAL DECISION MAKING

DEBORAH DENNO and
JAMES A. CRAMER

There has been little interest directed toward the victim in criminal justice proceedings. The attention which exists has centered primarily on the failure of the victim to notify the police. Only recently have researchers turned to an examination of the victim in the courtroom. Most of this research, however, has been conducted in laboratory settings using simulated juries and hypothetical cases. A notable exception is the study by Williams (see Chapter 8 in this volume).

The present study focuses on the possible effects of the judge's reaction to victim characteristics as it affects the sentencing decision, in addition to physical and situational characteristics of the victim which may influence the overall judge's reaction. It is suggested that the knowledge in this area is critical for the development and use of a multiple perspective of sentencing through the recording of information relating to both legal and extralegal factors, with particular attention focused on the defendant and victim. Efforts in this direction should result in a more realistic framework within which judicial research in this area might be conducted.

CONCEPTUALIZATION

Numerous investigators have noted the role of extralegal considerations in the judicial process (Anderson, 1962; Kalven and Zeisel, 1966; Smith and Blumberg, 1967; Hogarth, 1971; Hagan, 1974). Additional research has pointed to specific extralegal factors which often affect adjudication and sentencing procedures (Sellin, 1935; Parker, 1965; Nagel, 1969; Kaufman, 1975). Thus traditional legal theory or the "legal factors only" approach to rendering verdicts and sentences, as well as judicial decision making in general, has been called into question (Hogarth, 1971).

Earlier studies of sentencing often focused on the inclusion of extralegal factors by the court which led to discriminatory behavior in sentencing. Sellin (1935) examined dispositions rendered by the court and found discrepancies between different ethnic and racial groups. Gaudet (1949) later found that "sentences are unevenly and capriciously applied and the primary influence upon sentences is the personality of the judge . . . in terms of his social background, education, religion, expressive temperament, and social attitudes." Hood (1972) also found disparities in his study of urban magistrate courts, noting that there existed considerable variation in sentencing procedures and outcomes.

The research cited above, in addition to the position of a growing number of practitioners in the legal realm, suggest that judicial discretion in this area is characterized by a lack of uniformity. Further, the absence of a common sentencing philosophy and the presence of conflicting goals and varying informational resources among judges appear to lead to a problem of disparity in the entire decision-making process. The enormous discretion allotted to judges permits them to express, through legal decision, personal idiosyncrasies or philosophies which are of questionable utility in the judicial process. Such practice often results in an emphasis on judicial style rather than the legal process itself (Anderson, 1962).

In an effort to examine more closely the behavioral factors which appear to be relevant to judicial decision making, researchers have turned increasingly to the social-psychological level of analysis. More specifically, recent investigations suggest that the perception of individual judges may play an important role in the disposition of cases. It is at this point that attention to the nature of extralegal factors as they apply to judges is consistent with the legal realist position in jurisprudence. The realist advocates have primarily concentrated on the concept of judicial discretion, particularly regarding the interpretation of statutes, and on the extension of the logic of social psychological processes in the courtroom.[1]

A factor which has received increasing attention in judicial research has been that of perception by individual judges. Landy and Aronson (1969) have pointed to the effects of the attractiveness of the defendant and the victim in an experiment involving simulated courtroom situations. They suggest that the personal characteristics of these two parties affect jurors' decision making. Sigall and Ostrove (1974) have also posited the view that defendant attractiveness is an influence in judicial decision making.

Although research has demonstrated that differences between types of offenders and victims are influential in sentencing decisions, difficulties have been incurred in determining the degree and direction of this influence. As judges differ in sentencing practices, so do they differ in their mode of information interpretation and in the amounts and types of factors they process. A more cognitively complex judge—i.e., one who employs a greater number of categories of information presented during the trial—would be more likely to make a greater number of distinctions in his perception of the decision-making situation than would a judge who is cognitively simple (Hogarth, 1971). Further, the restricted use of informational sources in forming an impression of the victim is aggravated by pressures for bureaucratic efficiency. Administrative demand for rapid processing of cases forces the judge to respond to signs of "outer effectiveness" in the victim rather than to signs of "inner substance" (Leventhal and Singer, 1973; Mileski, 1971; Warren, 1971). Such reliance upon efficiency tactics may lead judges to systematically select certain categories of offenders, particularly the poor and minorities, for the most severe treatment (Chambliss and Seidman, 1971).

A less-researched but equally salient issue is that of the impact of the victim as he is perceived by the court's participants. Curtis (1974) attests to the importance of victim precipitation in instances of violent crime. He did not, however, examine victim impact on decision making in the court.

In a more directly relevant study, Lerner (1968) found that the victim of deserved suffering runs a greater risk of being condemned by observers; the highest rate of sympathy is extended to those who are perceived as being undeserving of the suffering that they have experienced. In the courtroom, then, the less deserved or compensated that a victim's suffering is, the less probable that the individual will be devalued. Although Lerner found that male and female reactions to suffering are different in the way that impressions are formed, the relative evaluation of the victim tends to be constant.

Regarding judges' perception of the defendant, Bronfenbrenner et al. (1958) identified four characteristics likely to be significant: (1) physical, (2) actional, (3) characteriological, and (4) experiential. The physical characteristics, which include the age, race, sex, and appearance of the individual, significantly affect the types of traits which are attributed to the defendant or victim. Either extreme on the attractiveness scale, for example, may provoke a sympathetic response. In general, the property of an individual's physical constancy as presented in the trial process itself may produce the illusion of behavioral, and therefore dispositional, consistency especially if the trial extends over a period of time (Jones et al., 1972).

Actional characteristics also appear to be of considerable relevance to the decision-making process. Voice inflection, rate of speech, and the naturalness and sincerity of the speaker, in addition to kinesthetic properties, such as posture and body movement, may all serve as behavioral cues (Kalven and Zeisel, 1966).

The characteriological factor involves properties which reflect an individual's impact, or effectiveness, as a social stimulus (Bronfenbrenner et al., 1958). Impact depends on whether the individual is seen, for example, as amusing, overbearing, or insulting in court. Also included in this dimension would be one's reputation or standing in the community.

The experiential category, finally, deals with the individual's demonstration of internal psychological traits, such as thoughts, feelings, and desires.

In an attempt to evaluate the composite effect of factors such as these, Hastorff et al. (1970) have pointed to the difficulties involved. "It is difficult to make any general statement about our ability to perceive emotions accurately. . . . Our perceptions of the other person's feelings are influenced by context, the labelling process, cultural rules for the expression of emotion, etc."

Notwithstanding this caution, the characteristics noted by Bronfenbrenner can be used in conjunction with attribution theory. Overall, this theory is concerned with a person's motivation to understand the cause-and-effect relations that underlie, and provide meaning for, the changing surface of events which an individual encounters daily. It is assumed that there is a need for individuals to have a veridical understanding for relations in terms of a reality orientation to the world, and a need to predict and apply a control orientation (Jones et al., 1972). Thus, a primary motivation of the judge is to stabilize and structure the information received in a trial so that it makes sense in terms of his previous experience.

By using attribution theory as a framework for analysis, it is suggested that an examination of characteristics of the defendant and victim, as interpreted and acted upon by judges and juries, would be fruitful for gaining insight into judicial decision making and, specifically, the sentencing procedure.

For the purpose of clarity and consistency, it is further suggested that these characteristics be separated into two general categories: (1) physical and (2) situational. The former category consists of readily observable traits and qualities such as age, race, sex, appearance, demeanor, and attractiveness. Situational factors, in turn, are divided into three areas: (1) characteristics which apply specifically to the defendant's or the victim's life situation, such as marital status, mental and physical health, and education; (2) those factors related to the situation in which the crime occurred, such as the offense committed and the degree of violence involved; and (3) variables applicable to the defendant's or the victim's immediate situation during the trial and those affecting his future situation, such as compensation plans for the victim or the prosecutor's recommendation for sentencing of the defendant.

METHODS

In order to examine the relationship between the above mentioned factors and sentencing practices, an analysis of victim and defendant characteristics was conducted at the Provincial Court at Old City Hall in Toronto, Canada, in the summer of 1975. The data for the analysis were gathered through (1) direct nonparticipant observation of criminal case proceedings and (2) interviews with four presiding judges of the court and with prosecuting attorneys representing the province.

Data on 161 cases were compiled which provided information on 194 defendants and 63 victims used for the sample. The observation of court cases was carried out without prior arrangement with court officials in an effort to minimize observer bias and impact on court participants. Structured, open-ended interviews of the four presiding judges and the prosecuting attorneys were conducted after all courtroom observation had been completed.

The in-court observation was centered on the sentencing process in relation to both physical and situational factors pertaining to the victim. Specifically, these characteristics included age, ethnicity, appearance, attractiveness, demeanor, marital status, situation of the victim, victim provocation, and offense committed by the defendant.

As a means of assessing the impact of these factors upon judicial decision making, the dependent variables of the judge's reaction to the victim in court and the defendant's sentence were selected for study. The two variables differentiate, as well as determine, the relationship between what is perceived to be the judge's behavior in court and his actual behavior in terms of sentence. It is assumed that, if a judge displays a certain physical reaction toward the victim in court (favorable or unfavorable), such a response will in turn influence or predict the impending sentence for the defendant. A composite reaction to the victim may therefore serve as a mitigating or an aggravating informational resource for the judge in deciding what is felt to be the appropriate sentence for the accused.

In order to rate the judges' reactions to the victims in court, observations of judges were made several weeks prior to data collection so as to become familiar with their individual differences. Ratings were based primarily on the judges' own in-court utterances and facial cues, consistent with Kalven and Zeisel's method of motivational research. Because some judges tend to show their physical reactions more noticeably than others, ratings were made relative to such discrepancies.

The dependent variable of judge's reaction to victim was categorized into favorable, average, and unfavorable ratings. The independent variables selected were operationalized as follows: age consisted of three groups of 1 to 20, 21 to 30, and 31 and over; ethnicity was separated into four groups of white Canadians, white non-English-speaking Canadians (which included mostly Italians, Greeks, and Ukrainians), blacks and Orientals. The victim's appearance was rated on a scale of sympathetic, average, and unsympathetic, which is a composite variable relating to the overall impression that the victim apparently makes on the judge, as evaluated by the authors during in-court observation.

Victim attractiveness is based on a continuum of attractive, average, and unattractive according to whether he or she gave an appealing or unappealing in-court impression. Appeal reflected an individual's overall "looks" and presentation as determined by Bronfenbrenner's category of physical characteristics. In turn, the sequence of upper, middle, and lower demeanor refers to the indicators of social and economic position based on the victim's attire in court. Upper attire is that which shows "respect for the court" and which was closest to that worn by the judge and the prosecuting attorney. For men, it was a coat and tie or similar dress; for women, a dress or a conservatively fashionable outfit. Middle attire was sportswear or some other type of casual, though not sloppy, clothing. Lower demeanor was indicated by work clothes, torn or dirty dress, etc., which led to an overall unkempt demeanor.

The situational factors selected as independent variables were similarly categorized. Marital status was divided into single and married. The situation of the victim was trichotomized into sympathetic, average, and unsympathetic. The latter variable refers to circumstances in the victim's life before or surrounding the commission of the offense which aggravate the seriousness of the final consequences.

The degree of victim precipitation is rated in a four-point scale of very provoked, provoked, not very provoked, and not provoked. The divisions relate to whether or not the victim was indirectly involved in the commission of the offense or the degree to which the defendant was encouraged, enticed, irritated, etc., by the victim into committing offensive action. The variety of offenses introduced into criminal court cases were grouped into six categories: property, assault, weapons, impaired driving, petty sexual (e.g., prostitution, indecent exposure), and "other." The latter category included victimless crimes such as running a gaming house or disturbing the peace. The defendant's sentence was divided into discharge, probation, fine and/or threat of confinement, and actual confinement.

Lastly, Kendall's Tau B, an ordinal measure of association, was used in the analysis.

FINDINGS

Victim Characteristics and Defendant's Sentence

Taken separately, victim characteristics do not appear to affect the defendant's sentence. The physical factors of age, ethnic identity, appearance, and attractiveness yielded correlation coefficients of less than .10. Demeanor (.11) and sex (.13) were only negligibly higher.

Of the situational characteristics measured, victim provocation (.28) and offense committed (.20) were moderately related. Marital status and situation of the victim resulted in near-zero coefficients.

The most significant relation discovered was that between the judge's reaction to the victim and the defendant's sentence (.51). Although this coefficient is interpreted with caution, it appears that the overall impression of the victim operates as an influence in the severity of the sentence rendered. It is plausible to suggest, for instance, that a victim of an assault who shows marks and wounds is likely to be viewed in a more sympathetic fashion than one who suffered no apparent physical harm. Such feelings by the judge could conceivably be carried over into the sentencing decision. Certainly judges and prosecutors could justify the use of such factors when determining sentencing by concluding that the "best" program for the "rehabilitation" of the defendant has been employed. The inclusion of such factors for decision making, however, would rarely, if ever, be admitted.

Table 1. JUDGE'S REACTION TO VICTIM BY DEFENDANT SENTENCE

Judge's Reaction	Defendant Sentence			Row Total	
	Discharge	Probation	Fine or Custody		
Favorable	0	0	4	4	9%
Average	19	7	8	34	72%
Very unfavorable	9	0	0	9	19%
Column total	28 (60%)	7 (15%)	12 (25%)	47	100%

Kendall's Tau B = .51

Table 2. JUDGE'S REACTION TO VICTIM BY VICTIM PROVOCATION

| | Victim Provocation | | | |
Judge's Reaction	Provoked	Not Provoked	Row Total	
Favorable	0	4	4	9%
Average	12	22	34	72%
Very unfavorable	7	2	9	19%
Column total	19 (40%)	28 (60%)	47	100%

Kendall's Tau B = .41

Victim Characteristics and Judge's Reactions

The data presented here suggest that physical characteristics of the victims are not strongly associated with the judges' reaction to victims. While both appearance and demeanor of the victims were only slightly associated with the judges' reaction (.11 and .12 respectively), ethnic identity (.23) and attractiveness (.26) reflected a moderately low association.

Of the situational characteristics analyzed, the offense committed (.01) was not related to the judges' reactions, while both the marital status (.23) and the situation of the victims (.25) resulted in a moderately low correlation. Only the factor of victim provocation appeared to be strongly associated with the dependent variable (.41).

DISCUSSION

These findings suggest that neither the physical nor the situational characteristics of a victim are major influencing factors on a judge's reaction to a victim. These findings do not support the commonplace courthouse belief that such factors are important components in the disposition of criminal cases. It is a mainstay of courthouse folklore that extralegal factors, such as the appearance of the victim or the defendant, have an influence on the decision making of judges and juries. It has been suggested (see McDonald, Chapter 1 in this volume) that defense counsels and prosecutors are certain in their own minds as to what an ideal victim or defendant is. A defense counsel will plead a client guilty in order to avoid letting a judge see a very sympathy-inducing victim. Likewise, prosecutors may drop cases, or at least charges, if the defendant possesses high sympathy-inducement capability.

Interviews with the judges observed in the present study revealed that the appearance of those brought before them in court did have a general effect on how individuals were perceived, although none of the judges would indicate whether or not such a factor specifically influenced their sentencing policy. In response to the question, "How influenced are you by the appearance of the individual?" a variety of answers were given by both judges and prosecuting attorneys.

According to the prosecuting attorneys, appearance did not influence them, though they believed that it did influence judges. One attorney admitted, "It doesn't impress me so much because I realize it's a trick to persuade judges. It's phony for an individual to change his appearance a great deal from day to day. If they don't change their appearance so that they can come to court, it shows they aren't phony, but then again they don't show respect in court." Indeed, one judge admitted that if individuals do not come to court "decently dressed, I tell them to go home and come back dressed properly." Thus, the defendant or victim may be caught in a double bind, charged on one hand by the prosecutor as being phony or not phony, and by the judge as being dressed properly or not.

Dress and general appearance seemed to be the most important considerations mentioned by judges concerning physical factors. One attorney, when asked if he noticed the way people looked in court, offered the following: "Sure you take a good look at people. You use your knowledge of human nature. You look at his face—you know something of his background. . . . People classify by types and you're not very often wrong."

Although mention was not made of specific factors, there was a consensus among judges and attorneys that an individual's in-court appearance was influential in contributing to an overall impression. The statements by both judges and prosecuting attorneys were, for the most part, vague and general. Both groups were reluctant to make any definitive statements regarding the influence of any extralegal factors relating to the victim which would affect their decisions.

Although judges indicated that demeanor and appearance were of significance in their impression of the victim, the correlation between judge's reaction and these variables was negligible (.11 and .12). The relationship between ethnic identity and attractiveness, however, was somewhat higher (.23 and .26).

Thus, an apparent inconsistency between interview responses and the findings emerges. It is unlikely that judges would admit to using ethnicity or attractiveness or other ascribed factors (i.e., those which are assigned to a person regardless of abilities or performance, such as sex and race) in forming their impression of the victim or the defendant for decision making, because using ascribed characteristics is legally unacceptable. An individual obviously cannot be responsible for such attributes. However, the findings show that these characteristics may be of greater importance than is indicated in the interview responses.

On the other hand, judicial officials admit more readily to marking the victim's or defendant's achieved characteristics (i.e., those which may be earned or developed to some extent by the individual, such as education or prestige), since use of such characteristics is more readily justifiable, and interview data support this assumption. It is expected that an individual should be responsible for his or her in-court appearance, and, according to courtroom norms, such factors merit a certain amount of judicial criticism. Thus, the consideration of such characteristics by decision makers is clearly more defensible regardless of what their actual sentencing behavior may be.

SUMMARY

Recent researchers have argued that victim attributes influence the decisions of neutral observers. This line of research obviously has important implications for the administration of criminal justice. For the most part, however, this research has been conducted only in laboratory settings. Until investigations pertaining to victim attributes is carried over to actual courtroom situations, the full implications of this line of reasoning are likely to remain unrealized.

The present study has focused on the role of the victim in judicial decision making. Although the findings were based on a small sample and hence must be regarded as tentative, they point to the necessity of viewing the victim as an important figure in the judicial process. Victim precipitation and the impression projected by the victim appear to be of significance to the judge in the sentencing process.

Methodologically, the necessity of using multiple techniques in data collection is strongly urged. Obtaining data which are sufficient for analysis in the judicial process seem to require the researcher to approach the problem from several vantage points. The use of multiple research strategies, often referred to as "triangulation," offers the investigator the advantage of cross-validating the data obtained from a single source.

In the present research, for example, the data gathered by in-court observation were subject to several limitations, including the classification of perceptions and behaviors of judges. Although the interviews that were conducted provided additional information, certain differences between observed actions and sentencing behavior in court varied with answers to specific questions asked about such behavior.

Such discrepancies have a number of possible sources. It can be suggested that certain kinds of in-court reactions by judges in no way predict what the final decision will be on sentence. Incorporating Kalven's and Zeisel's (1966) techniques of motivational research, it is possible also that judges either are not cognizant of their motives when sentencing the individuals before them or do not relate the motives in court. An understandable alternative is that judges lack candor in providing an explanation for their motives to the interviewer. Obviously, the judge is not supposed to take extralegal factors into consideration; to admit that he does would be contrary to the expectations assumed in his position. Methods for obtaining a "true" response therefore remain problematic.

NOTE

1. Such an analysis includes the advantage of linking together two distinct levels of analysis: (1) judicial discretion and decision making as an institutional arrangement, and (2) actor (judge) oriented processes at the perceptual level.

REFERENCES

ANDERSON, J.W. (1962). "Sentencing: Some social and legal issues." Keynote address to the sixth annual Red Deer Conference. John Howard Society of Alberta.

BRONFENBRENNER, U., HARDING, J., and GALLWEY, M. (1958). "The measurement of skill in social perception." Pp. 29-108 in D.C. McClelland et al. (eds.), Talent and society: New perspectives on the identification of talent. Princeton, N.J.: Van Nostrand.

CHAMBLISS, W.J., and SEIDMAN, R.B. (1971). Law, order and power. Reading, Mass.: Addison-Wesley.

CURTIS, L.A. (1974). "Victim precipitation and violent crime." Social Problems, 21(4):594-607.

GAUDET, F. (1949). "The sentencing behavior of the judge." In V.C. Brandon and S.B. Kutash (eds.), Encyclopedia of criminology. New York: Philosophical Library.

HAGAN, J. (1974). "Extra legal attributes and criminal sentencing: An assessment of a sociological viewpoint." Law and Society, 8:357-383.

HASTORFF, A.H., SCHNEIDER, D.J., and POLEFKE, J. (1970). Person perception. Reading, Mass.: Addison-Wesley.

HOGARTH, J. (1971). "Sentencing as a human process." Toronto: University of Toronto Press.

HOOD, R. (1972). Sentencing the motoring offender: A study of magistrates' views and practices. London: Heinemann.

JONES, E.E., KANOUSE, D.E., KELLEY, H.E., NISBETT, R.E., VALINS, S., and WEINER, B. (1972). Attribution: Perceiving the causes of behavior. Morristown, N.J.: General Learning Corp.

KALVEN, H., and ZEISEL, H. (1966). The American jury. Boston: Little, Brown.

KAUFMAN, I.R. (1975). "The sentencing process and judicial inscrutibility." St. Johns Law Review, 47(winter):215-222.

LANDY, D., and ARONSON, E. (1969). "The influence of the character of the criminal and his victim on the decisions of simulated jurors." Journal of Experimental Social Psychology, 5:141-152.

LERNER, M.J. (1968). "Observers evaluation of a victim: Justice, guilt, and veridical perception." Journal of Personality and Social Psychology, 20(2):127-135.

LEVENTHAL, H., and SINGER, D.L. (1973). "Cognative complexity, impression forma-
tion, and impression change." Journal of Personality and Social Psychology, 25:28-33.
MILESKI, M. (1971). "Courtroom encounters: An observation of a lower criminal court."
Law and Society Review, 5:746-747.
NAGEL, S. (1969). The legal process from a behavioral perspective. Chicago: Dorsey.
PARKER, G.E. (1965). "The education of the sentencing judge." International and
Comparative Law Quarterly, 14(January):206-251.
SIGALL, H., and OSTROVE, N. (1975). "Beautiful but dangerous: Effects of offender
attractiveness and nature of crime on juridic judgement." Journal of Personality and
Social Psychology, 31(3):410-414.
SELLIN, T. (1935). "Race prejudice in the administration of justice." American Journal of
Sociology, 41(September):212-217.
SMITH, A., and BLUMBERG, A. (1967). "The problem of objectivity in judicial decision
making." Social Forces, 46:96-105.
WARREN, D.I. (1971). "Justice in recorder's court: An analysis of misdemeanor cases in
Detroit." Unpublished report prepared for the Equal Justice Council of Detroit.

Chapter 10

THE VICTIM AND CORRECTIONAL THEORY: INTEGRATING VICTIM REPARATION WITH OFFENDER REHABILITATION

STEPHEN SCHAFER

The conventional argument for compensating victims of crime is that since society failed to protect the victim from injury it should, at least, make up for the harm done. This is a noble sentiment but an unnecessarily restrictive and shortsighted one. It calls for helping the victim but it fails to recognize the creative possibilities for integrating victim reparation with offender rehabilitation (Schafer, 1965a, 1965c). The persistent correctional apathy toward the victim's role seems to have been one of the fundamental obstacles in the development of the criminal-victim relationship from its presently neglected position in the criminal justice system. This failure to recognize the rehabilitative potential of victim restitution programs led to the acceptance of victim compensation programs designed only to help the victim. In most countries in the world compensation to victims of crime has been kept in the domain of damages.

In existing correctional systems the usual way of proposing the place of compensation and restitution in criminal law is to attempt to reproduce the experience of civil law. In other words, the purpose is to set up a legal situation where criminal law would merely provide a formalistic recording of a civil law performance. Although this would lead to helping the victim to some reparation of his crime-caused disadvantages, it can result only in the criminological mummification of civil law provisions. However, even this static and minimum understanding seems to meet difficulties, and, as William Tallack said more than three-quarters of a century ago, "the unfortunate victim of criminality is habitually ignored" (Tallack, 1900:10-11).

The failure of criminal justice systems to care for the victim is worldwide. If one looks at the very few victim compensation schemes of different countries, one seeks in vain a country where a victim of crime would enjoy the expectation of full reparation for his harm or injury. In the rare cases where compensation systems exist they either are not fully effective or do not work at all. Where there is no system of compensation, the victim is usually faced with the insufficient remedies of civil procedure and civil execution (Schafer, 1960:101-108). While the punishment of crime is regarded as the concern of the state and thus receives ample official and public support, the crime as a damage to the victim is regarded virtually as a private matter. Therefore little is done—an attitude reflecting a marked absence of public concern. Sutherland and Cressey (1960:278) rightly point out that "under the current system, the state undertakes to protect the public against crime and then, when a loss occurs, takes the entire payment and offers no effective remedy to the victim."

With rare exception, the victim is almost totally excluded from the settlement of the criminal case. This occurs despite the fact that even in the presently practiced retributive penal systems his restitution could be a justified part of the penal consequences. In theory, penal sanctions are applied not only to deter the criminals of the future but, in addition, to help restore law and order and conciliate the disturbed society (Von Hentig, 1948:217). Inasmuch as the individual victim is a part of society, criminal law ought to be used to vindicate his interests as well as those of society as a whole. However, at present, the only satisfaction that the individual victim may possibly get from the administration of criminal justice is the "spiritual satisfaction" of knowing about the sheer punishment inflicted upon the criminal; and studies suggest that he does not get even that. Victims do not learn about the final dispositions of the cases in which they are involved.

It is in any case arguable whether satisfaction to the victim would harmonize with society's present moral and cultural level, if such satisfaction consisted only of social vengeance in some form or other. Police, prosecutors, courts, correctional personnel, and other components of the criminal justice processes view the crime and criminal only in terms of the needs of the society, rather than those of the victim. They do not allow the victim to be a part of the criminal procedure. The question also arises as to whether punishment of the criminal in fact represents a form of symbolic restitution to the victim for his harm or injury. The general experience of victims is that, despite some satisfaction of their demand for vengeance, their lasting pain can hardly be compensated for by mere revenge exacted through punishment. Moreover, the realization of the extent to which his interests are completely subrogated to those of society probably causes the victim to feel wholly dissatisfied after the criminal justice system disposes of the case. In contrast, the criminal, having paid his debt to society, feels he owes no further obligation to the victim or society.

HISTORICAL DEVELOPMENTS

The bridge leading to the emergence of state criminal law had has a strong pillar the system of "composition," which is the last stronghold of private criminal law. The settlement of the amount of composition to be paid by periodic tribal assemblies provides an early example of judicial proceedings. There is more than a germ of truth in the contention that "composition," the medieval ancestor of present-day compensation to victims of crime, was one of the fertilizers of state criminal law. It soon was, however, emasculated by that very law. It was expelled from the penal system and left to the field of civil law. Originally, the monetary satisfaction was owed entirely to the victim or his family and served as a righting of the injury. But, as the central power in a community grew stronger, this financial satisfaction had to be shared with the official state (or overlord or king) for the "trouble in bringing about a reconciliation between the parties" (Oppenheimer, 1913:162-163). This share gradually increased in favor of the government. Finally, as the state fully monopolized the institution of punishment (Starke, 1959:1), the rights of the victim were completely separated from penal law. Thus, composition, as the obligation to pay damages, became divorced from criminal law and entered a special field in civil law. The victim had become the Cinderella of criminal procedure—and continues to remain so (Pfenninger et al., 1946:193).

Criminal law became increasingly concerned with protecting the rights and liberties of defendants. This individualistic orientation of the 18th century radically changed the penal administration of the Middle Ages. But it did not protect the interests of the victims. It maintained the long-standing tradition of avoiding the representation of the victim along with the public prosecution (Von Hentig, 1937:216-217). Even though concern for the victim does not necessarily interfere with penal goals (Waeckerling, 1946:15), the individualistic criminal law proved to be particularistic only on behalf of the defendant. It did not practice individualistic principles in regard to the victim. It excluded him from the criminal process and left him entirely to the hardships of civil procedure.

As the individualistic understanding of crime began to decline at the turn of the last century and the universalistic orientation emerged, the victim continued to be neglected. Moreover, the care for the victim and his involvement in the administration of criminal law grew less and less. By looking at the offender as a social phenomenon, whose criminal behavior originates in the abnormalities of his social existence or in society's attitudes toward him, the defensive function of criminal law began to lean toward the interests of the universe (that is, society), rather than those of the individual. However, criminal law did not perceive the obvious. The interests of society cannot be separated from the interests of the individual. The universalistic approach to the crime problem apparently recognized that the individualistic orientation might have been an enjoyable and intoxicating understanding, but led only to a shrewd confusion of the functioning social forces. The crime problem now began to be appraoched through man's relation to his social environment. Criminal law thus parted even more fully from consideration of the interests of the individual victim. This development is even more sharply seen in the ideology of totalitarian regimes. There the universalistic understanding of crime is extended to an even higher plane. The crime problem is given a sup200universalistic interpretation. Under this theory a social or political idea is given primacy not only over individual interests but also over the conventional group interests of society, thus offering direct protection and care not to individuals and not even to the group, but to the idea itself.

CIVIL AND CRIMINAL LAW

The decline in the penological importance of compensation and restitution to victims of crime gained support from the endeavor to find different bases for penal and civil liability. The multitude of theories which distinguish between civil and criminal responsibility show, generally, two trends. According to the subjective views, penal liability results from the deliberate infringement of law, something with which civil liability cannot be connected, since civil responsibility results from a less deliberate or even accidental opposing of the will of the state. According to the objective views, however, penal wrong follows from some kind of direct injury to the victim, something to which civil illegality cannot be referred, the latter being an indirect injury exclusively dependent on the statement of the victim. Generally speaking, since the disappearance of the period of talionic "composition" the conventional view is that a crime is an offense against the state, while a tort is an offense against individual rights only (Binding, 1916:433-479; Sutherland, 1947:14). This view is even fortified by the universalistic understanding of criminal law. In spite of the clearly developing situation in which criminal law and civil law (probably as a consequence of the dominating role of the universalistic orientations) tend to be more integrated than ever before, speculations about the elusive boundary between criminal and civil wrongs help to prevent the acceptance of restitution to victims of crime as the reparation of a criminal injury. They also support misconception that restitution is only the recovery of an ordinary debt.

RESTITUTION AND CORRECTIONAL THEORY

If the state power sets a norm of conduct, it should not only punish breaches of this norm but also see to it that, where it is transgressed, a resulting injury is repaired. The proposition that compensation to victims of crime deserves a place in the settlement of the criminal case should be evident if only because, without the crime which is being tried, the victim would not have suffered the damage for which he seeks reparation.

Voices raised against the appearance of restitution in the criminal and correctional procedure could be less effective if restitution or compensation was provided with a correctional character and was in this guise to take its place within the scope of the judgment of crime and the correctional consequences. To require the offender to pay money as a punishment is not something new and, in this sense, would not be strange to the administrators of criminal justice; after all, the origin of the present-day fine is the restitution or, better, its ancestor, the "composition." The only difference is that while the main point of composition was the enrichment of the victim and the community, which interposed itself between the wrongdoer and the vengeance of the victim, fines serve as a source of income for the state. If correctional restitution were allowed to be imposed as part of the sentence, then the administrators of criminal justice would not be dealing with civil damages. They would be dealing with what would then be an institution of criminal law. As Margery Fry pointed out: "To the offender's pocket it makes no difference whether what he has to pay is a fine, costs or compensation. But to his understanding of the nature of justice it may make a great deal" (1951:124).

Such considerations have led to the idea of state compensation based on fines. However, compensation plans, in contrast to restitution plans, have little correctional significance. The compensation plan guarantees that the victim gets his reparation, but that is all the plan achieves. It degrades restitution to victims of crime to a position and role outside the scope of the sentencing judgment and the realm of correctional strategies. It does not aid the possible reform of the criminal. Moreover, it may, in a sense, exempt him beforehand by creating a form of no-fault insurance. Whatever wrong he does, the state will right it (Journal of Public Law, 1959).

In terms of a correctional rejuvenation of restitution to victims of crime, the offender should understand that he injured not only the state, and law and order, but also the victim, in fact, primarily the victim. If this is done, then the institution of restitution would not only make good, within limits, the injury or loss of the victim but, at the same time, help in the correction, reform, and rehabilitation of the offender. "What is required is an evaluation in terms of the deterrent and reformative potentialities of the requirements of restitution" (Columbia Law Review, 1939:1187). As Hentig pointed out, "In many cases payment to the injured party will have a stronger inner punishment value than the payment of a sum to the neutral state" (Von Hentig, 1937:217). Compare also Eglash's (1958:6) idea of "creative restitution" and the disciplinary technique of rectification (Aichhorn, 1935). "Correctional restitution," or maybe "punitive restitution" could be a correctional instrument through which the criminal would understand his social responsibility.

OFFENDERS' ATTITUDES

In a study of criminal-victim relationships in violent crimes, Schafer (1965b) examined the attitudes of offenders toward their obligation to try to repair the damage that they had done to their victims. An inmate population of 819 offenders sentenced for criminal homicide, aggravated or other assault, or theft with violence (robbery or burglary) was studied. In none of the 819 cases had restitution or compensation been made by the offender. Data on attitudes toward restitution was obtained from only 88 inmates, 19 of whom were convicted of criminal homicide, 22 of aggravated assault, and 47 of violent theft.

The overwhelming majority of those convicted of criminal homicide wished that they could make some reparation for the wrong they committed. A much smaller proportion (slightly over half) of those sentenced for aggravated assault felt obliged to do something for their victim. The other half believed that their debt was only to the state. Similarly, among those who committed robbery or burglary, only slightly more than half the offenders admitted any obligation to their victims. The rest could not perceive any legal, moral, ethical, or social link with anyone other than the prison staff.

In the course of interviews with prison inmates of criminal homicide cases, many of them near to their execution, one gained the impression that their feeling of wrongfulness, involving both self-devaluation and apprehension and leading to their preparedness for doing anything good for the victim, grew out of fears of the penal consequences. One felt that their proximity to death, to be administered in the name of human justice, made their experience-evaluating and behavior-selecting attitudes incline toward right, rather than toward wrong. Not the punishment as pain, but the realization of the limits of their natural life seemed to relate them to social obligations, among them the reparation of their wrongdoing. This, of course, could not be experienced by those inmates who were not facing death. Many of the latter did not appear to be intropunitive and apparently could not understand, and thus could not accept, their functional responsibility. Their orientation could not comprehend their wrongdoing relative to social relationships, not even to their individual victim. Their understanding of incarceration seemed to be limited to what they viewed as merely a normative wrong, the debt for which had to be paid to the agencies of criminal justice, but to no one else. Their reluctance to accept more than this isolated and narrow attitude was not due to some deviant logic, but to the lack of understanding of the referent factors of their crime.

SOME CAUTIONS

Some hold the view that punitive or correctional restitution should, in certain cases, completely replace punishment. One reason for this is that it would relieve the state of the burden of supporting in penal or correctional institutions those sentenced for certain offenses. Second, such a reduction in the number of inmates would enable individual methods to be used to better advantage on those committed to these institutions. To relieve the crowded state of penal institutions by totally substituting restitution for punishment, however, may lead to evading the problems of crime. While it appears to be reasonable to use correctional restitution as one method of the socialization of criminals, if that were to be the only sentenced consequence available for crime it might weaken the sense of wrongdoing and the societal moral reproach attached to that crime and, besides, might reduce the degree of socioethical reprimand that the wrongdoer should feel. Also, it could lead to social injustice in that while the wealthy, possibly professional, criminal could buy off his liberty, the financially poor, occasional criminal might eventually serve a longer term of punishment for a minor offense. If restitution could be substituted for punishment or in any way make it possible to buy off correctional consequences with money, it might well have a reverse effect of that intended. Deviance requires correction, and a man should not be permitted to buy his way out of his liability to be corrected; not the medieval composition, but the restitution of our times is proposed to be rejuvenated. The extent to which these potentialities are enhanced or diminished when restitution is exacted by private parties gives a warning to avoid replacing punishment or corrections by restitution. The social and correctional value of criminal restitution may be destroyed if individuals were permitted to compromise crimes by making restitution; this, instead of refining the universalistic orientation, would lead us back to the early and primitive supraindividualistic trends of criminal law.

Correctional restitution may be distinguished from civil damages on this very point. While the latter are subject to compromise and are not in every case satisfied by the wrongdoer himself, restitution, like punishment, should always be the subject of judicial consideration in the criminal procedure. Correctional restitution is a part of the personal performance of the wrongdoer and should even then be equally burdensome, reformative, and just for all criminals, irrespective of their means and crimes, whether they be millionaires or laborers, murderers or shoplifters.

The proposal that the offender should compensate by his own work for the damage he has caused has been made more than once. Herbert Spencer (1898:352) suggested that prison work and the prisoner's income should be the means of making restitution, keeping the offender in prison until the damage was repaired. Garofalo (1914:415-419) suggested that where the offender was solvent, his property should be confiscated and restitution made therefrom by order of the court; while if he were insolvent, he should be made a state workman.[1]

Yet another proposal tried to balance the burden of fines and restitution between the rich and poor. According to this proposal, a poor man would pay in days of work, a rich man by an equal number of days' income or salary. If $2.00 represented the value of a day's work, and the poor man were sentenced to pay $2.00, he would be discharged by giving one day's labor to the victim. The rich man, instead of being sentenced to give so many days of labor, would pay an equal number of days' income or salary, and if this represented, say $200 a day, he would have to pay accordingly (Barrows, 1903:52).[2] Also it has been suggested that the "noble way" to care for the victim is to make it possible for the offender to fulfill his obligation by way of the income of his free work (Waeckerling, 1946:130). This noble way may at the same time be reformative or corrective, provided that it be not forgotten that the "punitive" side of restitution is an effective aid in reforming the criminal. If restitution is unconnected with the offender's personal work and can be performed from his property or by others, this would help the victim, but would minimize restitution's reformative-corrective character. On the other hand, if the performance of the restitutive obligation affected the freedom of work of the offender, or even his personal liberty, this would mean the extension of his sentenced punishment.

However, if the offender were at liberty after he had served his punishment, but had to make restitution to his victim through his personal work, restitution would retain its reformative-corrective character and could be regarded not as an extension but a part of the sentence.

There is something very sad in the disparity between our passion for treatment and our inability to effectively employ it. Deterrence, correction, reformation, and other formulas, almost everything but restitution has been tried out, all without measurable success. Restitution to victims of crime is not the total answer to the failure of our correctional system. However, it could make a valuable contribution to the solution. A modified revival of medieval composition and a rejuvenation of civil law compensation, to form a new concept of correctional restitution, would be an effective response of criminal justice to the functional responsibility of the criminal. The universalistic trend of criminal law attempts to lift crime from its isolated individualistic position and to analyze crime and criminals within a broad social perspective. In our modern understanding of the crime problem, all aspects of deviance and social relationships are to be considered and measured. Consequently, a growing interest in the interrelationship and interpersonal reactions between a criminal and his victim may be anticipated; correctional restitution is one of the ways leading to it.

N O T E S

1. This is a somewhat changed presentation of his proposal submitted to the International Prison Congress held in Paris in 1895. There he suggested that instead of going to prison, the offender should work for the state. He should retain for himself only enough wages to keep him from starving and the rest should go into a "caisse d'epargne" for the reparation of the wrong done (Paris Prison Congress, 1895).

2. This proposal is favored by Garofalo and Prins.

R E F E R E N C E S

AICHORN, A. (1935). Wayward youth. New York: Viking.

BARROWS, S.J. (1903). The Sixth International Congress: Report of its proceedings and conclusions. Washington, D.C.

BINDING, K. (1916). Normen (Vol. 1). Berlin.

Columbia Law Review (1939). "Restitution and criminal law, notes and legislation." 39(7):1187.

EGLASH, A. (1958). "Creative restitution: Some suggestions for prison rehabilitation programs." American Journal of Correction, 20(6):20-34.

FRY, M. (1951). Arms of the law. London.

GAROFALO, R. (1914). Criminology. Boston.

Journal of Public Law (1959). "Compensation for victims of criminal violence: A round table." 8(1).

OPPENHEIMER, H. (1913). The rationale of punishment. London.

Paris Prison Congress (1895). Summary report. London.

PFENNINGER, H.F. et al. (1946). Uber Rechte and Pfilchten des Verletzten im deutschen Adhäsionprogress, in Fetschrift. Zurich.

SCHAFER, S. (1960). Compensation and restitution to victims of crime. London.

——— (1965a). "The correctional rejuvenation of restitution to victims of crime." Pp. 159-168 in W.C. Reckless (ed.), Interdisciplinary problems in criminology. Columbus, Ohio.

——— (1965b). "Criminal victim relationships in violent crimes." Unpublished study for U.S. Department of Health, Education and Welfare (MH-07058).

——— (1965c). "Restitution to victims of crime: An old correctional aim modernized." Minnesota Law Review, 50(2).

SPENCER, H. (1898). Essais de morale de science et d'esthetique. Paris.

STARKE, W. (1959). Die Entschadigung des Verletzten nach deutsche Recht unter besonderer Berucksichtigung der Wiedergutmachung nach geltenden Strafrecht. Freiburg.

SUTHERLAND, E.H. (1947). Principles of criminology. New York.

SUTHERLAND, E.H., and CRESSEY, D.R. (1960). Principles of criminology. New York.

TALLACK, W. (1900). Reparation to the injured, and the rights of the victims of crime to compensation. London.

VON HENTIG, H. (1937). Punishment: Its origin, purpose and psychology. London.

——— (1948). The criminal and his victim. New Haven: Yale University Press.

WAECKERLING, C. (1946). Die Sorge für den Verletzten in Strafrecht. Zurich.

Chapter 11

CRIME VICTIMS AND
VICTIM COMPENSATION PROGRAMS

GILBERT GEIS

Who is a crime victim?

The posing of such a question may appear a bit jesuitical. But it should be recalled that one of the minor classics of American criminology is a piece by Paul W. Tappan (1947), a sociologist-lawyer, entitled "Who is the Criminal?" Tappan argued that only persons adjudicated as criminal by the courts reasonably ought to be so regarded. In particular, Tappan was aggrieved (see also Caldwell, 1958) by what he saw as the promiscuous labeling by Sutherland (1940) of violators of administrative codes and similar kinds of regulations as "white-collar criminals."

Recently, criminologists have again taken to the semantic barricades, this time to insist that the designation "criminal" rightly belongs to persons who violate what are seen to be fundamental human rights (Krisberg, 1973a; Schwendinger and Schwendinger, 1970). For such scholars, the acts of "warmongers" (i.e., a number of recent U.S. Presidents) and persons in similar preeminent positions who are deemed (by these criminologists) to have abused their power and trust should constitute the subject matter of research into criminal behavior.

As there is apt to be in such things, there is also a middle position. It suggests that a criminal is a person who has violated a criminal law, regardless of whether he is caught or convicted (Bloch and Geis, 1970). The criminologist again is left

[237]

to judge whether the act at issue did in fact violate the law. The advantage of this middle ground, it is claimed, is that it allows consideration of persons who behaved similarly, without having to take account of the vicissitudes of apprehension and conviction. Individuals who perform acts that are meretricious, evil, and/or vicious, but whose behavior does not violate any criminal law, are said to fall into a category other than the criminal. Such persons are a proper (perhaps even a superior) realm of study for whosoever cares to look at them and their behavior and to try to determine why what they do is not legally proscribed. But they are not criminals.

All three positions stress that, whatever may be the best definition, criminals are of many types. There are some criminal acts, such as murder, which have comparatively few perpetrators, and there are others, such as consumer fraud, petty theft, income tax violations, and minor assaults, which are perpetrated by very large segments of the population (cf. Wallerstein and Wyle, 1947). The word "criminal," therefore, tends to be so ill-fashioned a concept that generalizations about the subject-class that it is supposed to embrace become virtually meaningless.

The same sorts of things may be said about victims of crime. Delineation of crime victims must be tied closely to the satisfactory designation of what constitutes crimes and criminals. If Presidents Kennedy, Johnson, and Nixon were "war criminals," then it becomes a considerable matter to indicate satisfactorily (and, from a social scientific viewpoint, usefully) who the victims of their offenses were. Presumably, they included the Vietnamese population (at least in the north of the country, though perhaps throughout it), the American servicemen, taxpayers in the United States, and all others who bore derivative costs of the Asian conflict.

The amorphous nature of the concept "crime victim" can be noted even when there *is* agreement on who is the "criminal." Part of the problem lies in the fact that generally there are many more victims than there are criminals and that it is the exception (e.g., multiple offender rapes) when there are more offenders than persons offended against. Take, for instance, the criminal offense of short-weighting merchandise (Margolius, 1965). Every person engaged in shopping at some time or other likely will be victimized, given the widespread practice of having intentionally incorrect measuring devices in places such as supermarkets and gasoline stations. Property offenders, such as burglars, prey upon very large numbers of households. Indeed, one of the most intriguing unanswered questions in criminology concerns the true size of the cadre of practicing burglars in the United States. Frank Zimring (1969) has speculated that every burglar ultimately is caught, since very few burglars probably cease the activity after only a few offenses, and that the statistical chances, however small, of being apprehended finally result in their capture. Zimring suspects that a survey of incarcerated burglars, collecting accurate information on all of their criminal offenses, might in the course of a decade account for virtually every nonjuvenile offense in a jurisdiction. Robert Martinson (1976), on the other hand, thinks that offenses such as burglary may, as in the case of other economic ventures, respond directly to market conditions. Thus, when many burglars are incarcerated other persons move into the occupation in order to reconstitute the most efficient cost-benefit ratio. The difficulty here may be, of course, that for burglary the market (i.e., sites to rob) seems almost limitless, so that considerations other than supply and demand may be conditioning the number of burglars at work at any one time. No matter what, though, it is clear that for offenses such as burglary, larceny, and auto theft (the index crimes showing the largest total of offenses) there are relatively few criminals and huge numbers of victims.

Another analytical difficulty inheres in the fact that in most instances criminals *act,* while victims of crime are *acted upon.* While an indictable act may be, as Holmes (1881) noted in his classic analysis of the common law, any voluntary muscular contraction, in most criminal episodes it is a good deal more than this. This makes the criminal act rather easily recognizable and the intent of the actor readily inferable from what he did. The victim, however, as a passive participant, rarely has chosen consciously or voluntarily to undergo the experience that befalls him. Thus, studies of crime victims are pressed to judge things such as the degree of "victim-precipitation" (Virkkunen, 1975; Wolfgang, 1958; Amir, 1971) in order to be able to examine victim behaviors that are somewhat equivalent to acts of offenders. The matter becomes more problematic when there has been no interaction between offender and victim prior to the crime. In such instances, criminologists are left to delineate the processes by which the offenders choose victims, a matter most commonly depicted through portraiture of the demographic characteristics of the victims (Hindelang, 1974; Kalish, 1974). Or else they can attempt to study the reactions of victims to their victimization (Geis, 1975; LeJeune and Alex, 1973). For a social science that places great emphasis on determining causality such efforts are apt to be regarded as peripheral enterprises.

The definitional problems associated with the study of crime victims no doubt reside in large measure in the fact that criminal law has not been particularly concerned with designating a victim in any precise manner, since there is nothing of particular social or legal importance attached to the role. A parallel might be seen in our linguistic designations for grandparents. The United States is one of a few places where no single, commonly employed terms distinguish maternal from paternal grandparents. In some groups, such oldsters are differentiated by a seemingly inexhaustible vocabulary which provides pinpoint information about their social position. In the United States, however, which of several older people are being discussed is a matter of no great importance.

So, too, with crime victims. Note, for instance, that if there are a considerable number of victims, prosecutors will select a few who seem to make the best witnesses. The remainder of the victims are superfluous. Indeed, in most jurisdictions, once the arraignment and preliminary hearing stage has been passed, the contest becomes one between the prosecutor and the offender (via his attorney), and the victim recedes far into the background.

TORT LAW AND CRIMINAL LAW

Tort law provides something of an exception to these generalizations, of course. In tort law, it is necessary to demonstrate that, as a plaintiff, one has been victimized and deserves reparation; a victim, then, in a tortious sense, can operationally be seen as one who is able to collect money or other things of value from another person or entity. Little contemporary study has gone into consideration of why certain victims select the tort route for remedy, while others remain satisfied with using the criminal law. Perhaps the simplest answer is that the criminal law largely is employed against persons with little or no wherewithal: there is no sense in attempting to press to obtain a manslaughter conviction against executives of an airplane manufacturing company for allegedly criminal negligence when there exists the much more attractive possibility of securing a settlement of several hundred thousand dollars in a civil suit (for review of a case in point see Geis and Monahan, 1976). And it is axiomatic of prosecutory tactics that, unless other extremely compelling reasons exist, a case will not proceed to criminal conclusion if the victim is reluctant to pursue the matter.

Edwin H. Sutherland (1924), the dean of American sociological criminology, rather peevishly questioned this distinction between torts and crimes in the first edition of his textbook, written more than fifty years ago. Sutherland noted that, in theory, civil law was said to be concerned with wrongs against the individual for which reparation or restitution was the method of treatment. Criminal law presumably was occupied with wrongs against the public, for which punishment was the decreed response. In the criminal court, the state is in control; in the civil court, parties oppose one another. But Sutherland found such distinctions less than logical (pp. 17-18):

But in recent years this historical differentiation is questioned by many people, first, because it is sociologically unsound to make such an opposition between the individual and the public. If a tort (that is, a violation of civil law) injures an individual, it injures the public to some extent. Some torts do more injury to the public than some crimes. Most crimes and most torts injure some particular individual more than other individuals. But it is not necessary that a particular individual be injured either by a tort or a crime, for there are torts, known as "penal actions," in which any individual whatever who will bring suit may recover damages for injuries done to the community, and there are crimes, such as treason, that need not cause special injury to one individual more than to another. In addition criminal courts in the last generation especially have been using reparation very frequently as one method of dealing with offenders; and civil courts have been assessing exemplary damages in civil actions, which amount to punishment.

Sutherland did not further explicate or even repeat this thesis in later editions of his book. Instead, he emphasized, as I have above, the predilection of some crime victims to have recourse to civil rather than to criminal law. "Prosecutors complain because victims refuse to act as complaining witnesses after restitution has been made," and, thus, "the criminal law acts as a collecting agency for victims of crime," Sutherland (1934:8) noted in the second edition of his book. Sutherland (1934:20) also made an essay toward a definition of the crime victim, noting that since the cost of law enforcement is spread throughout the populace, "in this sense every individual in the state is a victim of crime." More specifically, he observed (1934:20) that anybody who directly loses anything of value might be regarded as a victim of crime. Victims of rape, Sutherland pointed out, frequently lose status in the community, a loss "immensely magnified by the continued publicity given to [the crime] in the newspapers." Sutherland (1934:20) also entered an observation that has not been accorded adequate attention by later students of victimology. "The loss of status may be suffered by persons not ordinarily considered to be victims, as the relatives of the prostitute or of the murderer or embezzler." In this regard, a colleague and I (Geis and Soler, 1971) found a number of women murderers insisting that they had pled guilty rather than go to trial, despite their now-stated belief that they had satisfactory defenses, because they did not wish to expose their relatives to the unfavorable glare of publicity associated with notorious murder trials, especially those involving female defendants.

Finally, Sutherland (1934:20) offered another glimpse into victimology that today remains relatively unexplored. The victim of crime, he noted, may not appreciate his having been victimized until some time has gone by, or he may never understand the link between his situation and what was illegally done to him. For illustrative purposes, Sutherland pointed to the child employed in violation of child-labor laws, who "may never realize the relationship of his childhood labor to his subsequent career."

Authorities on tort law (Seavey et al., 1964:1) grant Sutherland's point that an affinity remains between the criminal law and the law of torts. Their distinction between the two areas is essentially a pragmatic one, rather than a logical differentiation. Largely because of historical circumstances, they observe, some acts are regarded as torts; others are crimes. The matter is summarized by Seavey et al. (1964:1) in the following way:

> In tort actions there remain elements that underlie the law of crimes; thus, sometimes punitive damages are allowed, and sometimes the supposed deterrent effect of compensatory damages influences development of the rule allowing recovery in tort. But another element underlying tort law—and usually more significant than revenge, retribution, appeasement, deterrence, or reform—is the concern with compensation for harm done. The primary function of the law of torts is to determine when loss shall be shifted from one to another, and when it shall be allowed to remain where it has fallen. . . . Fault is the usual basis for liability.

This background material on torts and crimes is important for our purposes for a number of reasons: For one thing, tort law offers something of a prototype for approaching a satisfactory definition of crime victims. For another, state compensation to crime victims—the subject of this chapter—is essentially an attempt to interconnect the areas of crime and tort (cf. Linden, 1969; Covey, 1965) by bringing crime victims formally within the ambit of what essentially is a form of tort law that places the state in the position of the offender, subject to a process that allows public compensation to be awarded to the crime victim. The development of victim compensation programs, particularly with regard to the kinds of persons embraced within the compensation laws and the rationales for inclusion and exclusion of potential claimants, will concern us below.

CRIME VICTIM COMPENSATION: BACKGROUND

Twelve American states (Alaska, California, Delaware, Hawaii, Illinois, Maryland, Massachusetts, Minnesota, New Jersey, New York, North Dakota, and Washington) now provide compensation from public funds for victims of violent crime, using a wide variety of administrative arrangements, philosophical rationales, and eligibility structures. The federal Congress also seems likely to enact legislation shortly that will provide substantial subsidies to states with compensation efforts, a move which undoubtedly will encourage those without programs to undertake them. Rhode Island (General Laws § 12-25-1, 1972), for instance, has enacted a compensation program that is not to become operative until or unless the federal measure is signed into law. The federal Congress (see U.S. Senate, 1972) also is reviewing proposals to allow compensation of up to

$50,000 for victims of crime in the District of Columbia and in other areas under federal jurisdiction.

In Canada, most of the provinces now have crime victim compensation programs, as do a majority of the Australian states. The Canadian efforts differ particularly from most of the American systems by making all crime victims eligible for assistance, rather than only those showing "serious financial hardship" (a term of art found in many of the American laws), and by tying arrangements closely to those of workmen's compensation (see, e.g., Bryan, 1968; Eremko, 1969). The Australian programs are rather placebo-like enterprises, efforts that can be cited as indicative of state concern, while costing very little and helping very few (Chappell, 1972).

New Zealand, which pioneered in this area by inaugurating a victim compensation program in 1963 (Weeks, 1970), has now carried the matter to what might appear to be its logical conclusion by incorporating the crime victim compensation into a comprehensive no-fault insurance program, covering virtually all victims of debilitating events (Szakats, 1973; Palmer, 1973). Great Britain, which in 1964 followed New Zealand into the field, is in the process of providing a statutory foundation for its experimental ex gratia undertaking (Great Britain, 1973:8). The annual cost of the British program is now about $9 million (Great Britain, 1974:5), a figure that needs to be regarded in terms of the widespread free medical services available in Britain and that country's relatively low crime rate when compared to the United States.

There is a very considerable literature regarding crime victim compensation programs (for bibliographies see Geis, 1967:175-177; 1969:1587-1593; Edelhertz and Geis, 1974:294-302). But writings on the subject are almost exclusively confined to detailed and intricate analysis of statutory provisions (the best pieces are Lamborn, 1971, 1973a, 1973b), to philosophical concerns (Atiyah, 1970), to public administration issues (Brooks, 1973a, 1973b), or to reviews of the history and operation of the domestic and foreign programs (Edelhertz and Geis, 1974).

The impact of the crime victim compensation programs upon their clientele, the crime victims, the nature of the populations being served, and the ideological characteristics of the programs have received only fleeting scholarly attention. Yet, there are intriguing policy and social science issues involved in these matters. Most statutes, for instance, include a provision that the victim must have cooperated with the police in order to be eligible for compensation. The public policy rationale for such a rule is obvious. From a sociological viewpoint, it is equally obvious that a person remains a crime victim, and perhaps one in need of state aid, whether or not he chooses to cooperate with the police investigation, for whatever reasons move him to such an attitude. This matter, one of numerous similar kinds of issues involved in victim compensation, highlights the fact that the victims embraced within the laws, like criminals adjudicated by the courts, are but a selected portion of the total behavioral universe.

THE ISSUE OF VICTIM PROVOCATION

One (indeed, the only) exception to the relatively uninflected analyses of crime victim compensation programs is that provided by David Miers (1972) in a paper presented in Toronto before the Third International Conference on Compensation of Victims of Crime. Miers discussed the issue of "provocation" as it bears upon compensation awards. It was this matter which had led to one of the more memorable exchanges during Parliamentary debate (Great Britain, 1964) regarding inauguration of the British program. The Government had proposed that provocation should serve to reduce the amount of compensation or, if the provocation were of sufficient character, that it should call for total rejection of the claim. Speaking against this idea, Lady Barbara Wootton tried to predict its consequences:

I think the end of this story will be that it will be found impossible to determine the measure of fault of the victim. . . . This attempt to assess people's needs after they have suffered serious and possibly permanent injury by the question of whether it is their fault or anybody else's fault is an illogical and uncivilized approach to the subject. [p. 1381]

Nonetheless, the clause remained in the British scheme. Its presence, as Lady Wootton guessed, has been the matter that most disturbs the English board in its deliberations (U.S. Senate, 1972:495). Rather oddly, though, provocation has not been much of a bother to the largest program in the United States, that in New York. There, the board makes little attempt to measure with any precision the extent of provocation and to adjust awards accordingly; instead, it either approves the claim or rejects it altogether (Edelhertz et al., 1973).

Miers' paper (1972) maintained that inclusion of the provision regarding victim provocation was not merely a matter of coincidence. Reviewing the work of the Ontario Criminal Injuries Compensation Board, he concluded that three kinds of victim behavior raised adjudicatory problems for the board: (1) when the victim was an active participant in criminal behavior, (2) when the victim actively participated in "perceived reprehensible" behavior, and (3) when the victim circumstantially participated in criminal behavior.

Gang fighting typified the first kind of situation, and the crime victim invariably was denied reparation, largely on the ground that the aim of the statute was not to subsidize criminal behavior. Miers finds this to be only a partial explanation for the board's rulings. More fundamental, he believes, is the matter of arriving at a proper definition of a "deserving victim." This, Miers feels, is tied to things such as preconceptions and misconceptions, the ability to interpret a sequence of events, and the desire to ascribe blame or distribute responsibility for the injury.

The second group of victims includes individuals engaged in what is seen as "reprehensible" behavior, behavior which most often involves drunkenness or illegal sexual activity. "Certainly," Miers (1972:186) notes, "the Ontario Board takes a dim view of boozing and wenching." In one case—in re *Thrush*—an applicant for compensation had been living in a hotel with a married woman. The woman's husband discovered them and shot and killed his wife and paralyzed the applicant. Ruling on the compensation claim, the Ontario Board observed that "the victim's conduct during the ten days preceding the shooting was completely irresponsible and morally disgraceful." The amount awarded was reduced considerably from what normally would have been given for such injuries.

Prostitutes, drug users, persons with criminal records, and others on the periphery of what is regarded as proper and respectable society constitute the third grouping of victims whose awards are apt to be reduced by the compensation board. In one Ontario case, a man released from jail returned home to find his wife with a lover, and in the ensuing dispute the husband was shot. He received a full award, but only after the board members hotly disputed his "contribution" to his condition. A typical intrusion of moral judgment into the Ontario crime victim compensation decisions appears in a case in which a boy was "exploding" frogs with firecrackers and was told by a man standing nearby to stop. The man then hit the boy in the eye, causing superficial damage. The man was found guilty of assault, but when the boy applied for compensation, his application was rejected on the ground that he had been indulging in reprehensible behavior.

The fact that money awarded under the compensation program represents state funds is what Miers believes intrudes so intense a vein of moral judgment into compensation decisions. Administrators fear censure if they are deemed to have dispensed taxpayer funds to morally unattractive persons.

THE SOCIAL PSYCHOLOGY OF VICTIMIZATION

The work of Miers, singularly different from other investigations of crime victim compensation, is fleshed out by a considerable body of social-psychological literature on responses of victims to various of life's exigencies. Research in victimology, unfortunately, has failed to pay sufficient heed to this corpus of research. Some of the social psychological work, at least from a sociological perspective, suffers from a concentration on minutiae, combined with a tendency toward overexpansive generalization. Nonetheless, sophisticated ideas abound in the psychological journals about diverse aspects of the victimization process, ideas that can be meshed synergistically with information and insights gathered from scrutiny of the work of the crime victim compensation programs.

Ellen Berschied and Elaine Walster (1967), for instance, note that the common response to harming another person takes one of two forms: either justification or compensation. Harm-doers (and compensation board members perhaps serve as surrogates of harm-doers) may minimize the amount of harm, deny responsibility for the harmful act, or convince themselves that the victim was deserving of the suffering. Criminologists will recognize these forms of response as partially equivalent to the "techniques of neutralization" suggested by Gresham Sykes and David Matza (1957) in regard to the behavior of juvenile delinquents.

In their experimental work, Berscheid and Walster investigated the effects of the adequacy of compensation—that is, the amount of compensation given to make up for a perceived wrong. The experimental situation they mounted is susceptible to caricature by criminologists whose subject-victims often are involved in what literally are life-and-death situations. Berscheid and Walster's "victim" was a person who experimentally had been manipulated into failing to win a prize of two books of green stamps in a cooperative game staged among church women. The results of the experiment were generalized to the observation that if persons are able to provide equivalent kinds of compensation they will do so, but if the compensation available to them is either insufficient or extravagant in terms of what the victim has lost, their tendency is to do nothing at all. The authors explain their point with a wry analogy (p. 440):

> Thus, an errant husband may not attempt any compensation at all to a person whom he has "robbed of the best years of her life," but may compensate if the act in question were said to result in harm of a lesser degree, say just enough harm to be compensated for by a new dishwasher.

Equally interesting is the thesis of Melvin Lerner and Carolyn Simmons (1966) that most people, for the sake of their own sanity, cannot afford to believe in a world governed by random reinforcement. Instead, people come to see the world as a just place, one in which individuals get what they deserve. To maintain such views in the face of contradictory evidence, persons often are pressed to take the view that unfortunate people earned or merited their fate. Thus, they denigrate or "blame the victim" (Ryan, 1971). On the other hand, norms of compassion and altruism (Staub, 1972) dictate that the unfortunate should be assisted. Work by Freedman et al. (1967) suggests that the motivation for such assistance, particularly for the wrongdoer, but also for onlookers (Rawlings, 1968), may not be so much the idea of making restitution, but rather that of alleviating guilt.

This incursion into a very small portion of the social-psychological literature relating to victimization may be brought into focus as the basis for a set of working research ideas. They suggest that a crime victim will be either derogated or, if the recourse exists, compensated. If compensation occurs, it will aim to reach equivalence (no more, no less) with the harm done, and it will be motivated largely from feelings of guilt rather than from motives of compassion.

These postulates, and many others generated by social-psychological experimentation in laboratory and naturalistic settings, contain a potpourri of ideas for testing in regard to the operation of crime victim compensation programs. The relationship between the backgrounds and the attitudes of board members and their judgments about particular kinds of cases (for parallel work with appellate court judges see Schubert, 1965) would provide interesting victimology material. Longitudinal studies, showing how constant exposure of compensation board members to stories of human suffering affect them, could also be productive. The police, for instance, are said to become frustrated by their lack of ability to offer surcease to crime victims, particularly those deprived by property offenses (Geis, 1975). Do compensation board members, who are in a position to relieve deprivation by monetary awards, become more or less sympathetic to claimants? Does the compensation process vary from jurisdiction to jurisdiction, and, if so, how can such distinctions be tied, if at all, to board memberships and the social climate? A particular advantage for such kinds of analytical efforts is that crime victim compensation boards render specific judgments on sets of fact situations —yes or no, and how much money. These are readily measurable outcomes, and they generally are a matter of public record.

A careful reading of the eight annual reports issued by the New York Crime Victims Compensation Board, for example, provides some clues concerning the possible impact of servicing crime victims over a long period of time. In its most recent report, the New York board (1975) nags at the police for their treatment of crime victims, a matter that really is well beyond the statutory concern of the compensation program. The reprobation against law enforcement, quite different from the rather technical matters usually addressed in board reports, is worth quoting at some length for both its tone and content (p. 4):

> The Board . . . has attempted to prevail upon police agencies as well as other agencies to treat the victim in a different manner than has been customary over the years. . . . The Board . . . firmly believes that the law enforcement officer should take into consideration the trauma that has been visited upon the victim. . . . He should understand the stress under which the victim is reacting.

It is, therefore, felt that the officer should express his concern and understanding for the victim's feelings; that the victim should be, wherever possible, interviewed alone and not in the presence of strangers or other officers.

It has been noted in some instances that the victims felt that the officers at the precinct station were joking and laughing with each other and that the victim feels not only unimportant but actually deserted and may even get the impression that they are laughing at or about him or the incident. These are serious matters and the Board will continue to bring these matters to the attention of investigating law enforcement agencies.

THE GOOD SAMARITANS

In Great Britain and New Zealand, crime victim compensation programs arose only after sophisticated and thorough review of the needs of crime victims, the legal responsibility of the state, and consideration of the applicability of the social welfare ethos to this particular realm. In the United States, contrariwise, crime compensation programs tended to emerge in the wake of sensational individual cases, which were employed by political figures to produce campaign propaganda (besides, assuredly, some relief for crime victims).

The first American program came into being in California in 1965, but it was a skeleton operation, offering a maximum of $5,000 to persons who could meet what were only slightly relaxed welfare assistance requirements. Applicants who qualified tended to be crime victims who could not meet the residency requirements for welfare aid, or persons who were placed into the compensation program by county officials because its costs were carried by the state rather than by the local jurisdiction (Geis and Zietz, 1966).

The next American crime victim compensation program to appear, that in New York, provided the blueprint for most of the later efforts. It was built, in terms of the emotions behind it, on two interesting cases. The first was the murder of Kitty Genovese in Kew Gardens, a New York City suburb, during the night of March 13-14, 1964. The most shocking aspect of the Genovese slaying was reported to be the fact that the victim had lain wounded in an entryway to an apartment building for about forty minutes, while 38 persons, all of whom had seen her stabbed or heard her cries for help, did nothing—offered no aid, made no calls to the police, or took no other constructive action to save her life. The assailant, who momentarily left the scene, returned and murdered and then raped Ms. Genovese (Rosenthal, 1964).

This crime came to epitomize bystander apathy or "Bad Samaritanism" in the United States, largely because a passing reference to the event during a luncheon between a police official and an editor triggered a series of rather sensational articles in the papers (Seedman, 1974:121), articles that were followed by television shows and other media presentations. The news stories notwithstanding, it remains arguable whether the apathy of the Genovese onlookers resulted from disinterest, scorn, fear, confusion, diffusion of responsibility, or other attitudes or impulses. Except for one notorious malefactor (a man who ultimately called the police from a neighbor's telephone, after hopping across a rooftop because he feared to become personally involved), the Genovese neighbors might well have been filled with compassion but baffled by incomprehension regarding what was truly taking place. Today, a scrutiny of social psychology textbooks (see, e.g., Rubinstein, 1975; Wrightsman, 1972) shows that Ms. Genovese's name is more likely to appear in the index than that of many prominent members of the profession. The ability of a particular criminal incident, well publicized, to become the essence of a general portrait of a society (or, at least, its urban portion) can clearly be traced in regard to the Genovese case.

The second episode was even more directly involved in solidifying support for a crime victim compensation bill. The fatal stabbing of 28-year-old Arthur F. Collins came after he tried to assist several elderly women on a subway car who were being bothered by a drunken man. Collins put the man off the train, but the man dashed back in before the door closed and plunged a knife into Collins' chest while Collins' wife, holding the couple's 16-month-old daughter, looked on helplessly.

What is noteworthy, among other things, about both incidents is that they concerned not the general run of crime victims, but rather persons engaged (or not so engaged, who allegedly should have been) in Good Samaritan behavior. The Collins case, for instance, was an almost stereotypic instance of boomeranging Good Samaritan intentions. Collins' assailant maintained that he could not tolerate the insult of being rudely pushed out of the subway car. The assailant had a record for getting into trouble because of a tendency to become volatile while drinking: Collins had picked the wrong man at the wrong time. Paradoxically, the ensuant New York legislation—as does much crime victim compensation law—ignored Good Samaritans; and Mrs. Collins, whose plight had been the motive force behind the bill, was not able to collect under the state measure. She did, however, receive reparations from New York City under a hastily enacted ordinance that authorized awards for the death or injury of any person other than a police officer caused during an attempt on a public street or in a city-owned transit facility to prevent a crime or to preserve the peace.

A similar Good Samaritan bill, the first in the nation, had been enacted during the 1965 California legislative session as a companion measure to that state's general crime victim compensation program (Culhane, 1965). Unlike the regular compensation provision, the Good Samaritan law allowed recovery not only for medical expenses and/or loss of wages but also for property damage sustained while preventing a crime, apprehending a criminal, or assisting a police officer. In 1969, the Good Samaritan measure was broadened to include citizens who rescued others in immediate danger of injury or death as a result of fire, drowning, or other catastrophe.

Several other states now have only Good Samaritan statutes (e.g., Nevada and Georgia), while a number have incorporated the Good Samaritan provision within their general compensation system (e.g., Hawaii). The Uniform Crime Reparations Act, which so far has been adopted solely by North Dakota, includes Good Samaritans by defining the term "victim" to mean "a person who suffers personal injury or death as a result of a crime, a lawful effort to prevent a crime, or a lawful effort to apprehend a person suspected of committing or attempting to commit a crime" (cf. Rothstein, 1974).

Good Samaritan crime victims, though important to the genesis of compensation efforts, have been accorded comparatively little attention in victimology research and theory, with the exception of the work of two foreign scholars, Leon Sheleff (Shaskolsky) (1970, 1972-1973), a South African, and Janez Pecar (1971, 1972), a Yugoslavian. Sheleff (Shaskolsky) has emphasized that the examination of the psychological and social interplay between the criminal and the victim may overlook third parties who often contributed significantly to the manner in which the criminal act developed. Pecar has stressed the importance of a third party, labeled the "involved bystander," in sometimes prompting the criminal to embark on an offense.

Good Samaritan crime victims probably differ significantly from other crime victims. Preliminary information from an ongoing investigation in California (Huston et al., forthcoming) shows that about 78% of a sample of 40 Samaritans who have collected money under the state compensation law came from either Los Angeles or San Francisco. Extending the geographical scope to the state's two next largest cities—San Diego and Sacramento—embraces 90% of the Samaritan sample. While age comparisons showed the Samaritan victims to be much the same age as other crime victims, the sex distribution was notably different. Hindelang's study (1974:21) found that men are victimized by street crimes about one and a half times more frequently than women. Similarly, Kalish's recent two-city Pilot Survey of Victimization (1974:80-81) found twice as many men as women victimized by personal crime in Dayton (10,800 men compared to 5,510 women) and approximately the same ratio in San Jose (18,880 compared to 9,410). All but one of the Samaritans in the Huston et al. study (forthcoming), however, were men. Things such as greater physical strength, different forms of socialization, and the fact that street criminals themselves are largely male were believed to contribute to this Samaritan sex ratio.

The same study also speculated that there may be something about the behavior of some interveners that leads to their victimization, just as this occurs in other offenses (for illustrations see Maurer, 1955, regarding pickpockets; and Williamson, 1965, regarding mugging victims). One Good Samaritan in the California study sample, for instance, was reported by a friend to have complained about missing out on "all the action" when he heard about robberies in the neighborhood. The same man had served as a volunteer auxiliary officer with a number of police departments. He made his way into the study population when he used his car to block the escape route of three robbers, then chased and knocked one of them down with his flashlight, only to have the offender take a gun out and shoot him through the mouth.

This case and others have led Huston and his colleagues (forthcoming) to enter the following preliminary judgment about the nature of Good Samaritan crime victims:

> Our very tentative impression, after personally interviewing to date only a small number (nine in all) of Samaritans is that they will prove to be quite different than the interveners portrayed in the experimental literature. Our group appears to be made up of risk takers, persons for whom violence, and the potential of violence, is something with which they are on familiar and rather amiable terms. Indeed, we have been struck by the number of Samaritans who derogate others who tried to offer help during the incidents in which they were involved. They seem to see themselves as preeminently qualified to provide assistance, and appear somewhat jealous and put off if others invade the limelight.

Finally, the same study notes that interveners into criminal episodes, unlike interveners into emergencies, often appear to respond out of anger against the criminal rather than compassion for the victim. It cites a newspaper report (*Los Angeles Times,* August 6, 1975) of a motorist who saw a truck driver strike a pedestrian and then drive away. The motorist pursued the hit-and-run offender and forced him onto the side of the highway. He then took out the shotgun he had in his vehicle and held the offender at gunpoint until the police arrived. The woman who had been struck by the truck and left abandoned by both the truck driver and the "Samaritan" died an hour later at the hospital.

Not only the attitude of the intervener toward the victim but also that of the latter toward the former represent areas worth serious study. Gift-bearing Samaritans may fare no better in the minds of their recipients than their Mediterranean neighbors, the Greeks. Elaine Walster and Jane Allyn Piliavin (1972:185) set forth a number of hypotheses on this matter:

Sometimes an innocent victim is helped by others. How should we expect such a victim to react? Society expects him to be grateful. Should we? How a victim feels about his helpers probably depends on whether the helpful act reduces the inequity between the donor and himself or increases it. . . .

A helpful act can be inadequate in at least two ways. The act may alleviate only a minuscule portion of the victim's suffering, or the act may actually increase the discrepancy between the philanthropist's relative outcomes and those of the victim. For example, the rich man who makes a charitable donation as a tax write-off may inflate his own relative incomes more than those of the recipient.

Finally, besides the need to look more closely at Samaritan crime victims, a matter aided by the availability of compensation board records, it appears important to determine whether bystander intervention ought to be encouraged or dissuaded. Vigilantism was a common and unattractive phenomenon in earlier American times; its disappearance perhaps ought not be mourned, and it possibly ought not be resurrected by misdirected attempts to involve citizens in matters they may aggravate rather than alleviate. On the other hand, the parable of the Good Samaritan, so powerful an injunction, talks to the responsibility of each of us for our fellows, a matter which may well lie at the heart of cultures which make a claim to being truly civilized. These issues, debated with sophistication at a conference about a decade ago (Ratcliffe, 1966), remain without empirical investigation for background to value decisions.

THE COMPENSATION PROGRAM CLIENTELE

What further victimological insights, besides those pertaining to Good Samaritans, may be gathered from use of the records of crime victim compensation programs? Only a very few investigations have been based on these original sources. In one, a social work thesis by Sylvia Fogelman (1971), a questionnaire survey was conducted of 49 respondents (out of a total sample of 170 persons) who had collected compensation money in California; the aim was to determine their self-reported need for assistance beyond the fiscal resources provided by the state. The study found the crime victims to be "a truly needy population left on its own to secure help, left unattended and rejected by the very government which it had looked to for protection and consideration" (p. 47). The subjects reported a plethora of emotional and social needs attendant upon their victimization. Thirty-five of the 49 respondents indicated that they wanted "just someone to talk to," someone "to help them sort out their problems and help them get back on their feet" a few months following their victimization. Eleven of the group reported losing friends because of the crime. Thirty of the 49 indicated that they had suffered some form of permanent physical injuries as a result of their victimization.

I have reported elsewhere (Geis, 1975) on interviews with compensated crime victims which were aimed at discovering some of their attitudes toward offenders and toward the criminal justice system. That study noted that two fundamental conditions, seemingly operating at cross-purposes, bear upon the victim of criminal violence when he comes to define his response to his situation. On the one hand, he generally desires revenge. On the other, he often wishes to establish an appearance of mercifulness, to seem to possess an educated understanding of the offender's impulses. A particularly useful catalyst for reconciling these views was said to reside in the concept of "sickness," that is, in the idea that there is something mentally wrong with the offender. Since cure is taken as unlikely, by far the most sensible policy, the victim will suggest, is to eliminate the criminal or at least to isolate him for a very long period of "treatment." Thus, revenge may be had without guilt, and compassion may be indulged without compromising retributive feelings.

The study found a considerable recourse to racism in the statements that the crime victims made to explain what had happened to them and why. At the same time, as case studies gathered in the field so often do, these indicated problems associated with applying generalizations to individual instances. A 66-year-old woman, beaten into unconsciousness and raped in her bedroom, thought that her problem in part was associated with the fact that "the colored race is trying to get that 'black power' going." This fit with our earlier observations. So did her view that there ought to be "whipping posts so that people can see who the criminals are." But then the woman launched into a strong plea for the repeal of laws against prostitution. She said that reversal of such laws would provide additional protection for persons like herself against rape. It was a view, she told us, that she had developed only after her victimization.

Finally, the investigation found that the victims often developed positive feelings toward the police, but that their attitudes toward the court system and its functionaries tended to be very critical. In particular, they were put out by an absence of courtesy and a failure to inform them about the results of the case in which they were involved. Plea-bargaining also was a matter which aroused strong condemnation among the victims we interviewed.

A study of the applicants for compensation in New York (Edelhertz and Geis, 1974:42-44) showed that only 29% of the claimants were women, a figure probably conditioned by the fact that loss of wages cannot be claimed by housewives who are crime victims. The compensation program also seems to benefit older persons more often than their percentage of the total crime victims would indicate, probably because they are better able to demonstrate "serious financial hardship" in accord with the law's requirement. Twenty of the 30 women claimants in 1969, for instance, were beyond the age of 50. The eligibility requirements, knowledge of the statute, willingness to take time to comply with the regulations, and, perhaps, the kinds of injuries suffered by members of different age groups, as well as their general health and resiliency, were all things that might contribute to the age patterning.

I have also gone through perhaps a thousand or more applications filed during recent years with the California State Board of Control by crime victims seeking compensation. These materials provide only bare-bones kind of information, just enough to establish whether the applicant is eligible to submit more detailed data. Even so, they are marked by much of the pathos, horror, humor, matter of factness, and terror that so often are associated with criminal victimization. They tease any investigator interested in pursuing victimological studies into heading for the field to try to determine in a systematic way who these people are, what happened to them, how they are doing now, and numerous other matters of fundamental concern to victimology as a growing field of scientific and social interest.

"I was kidnapped, raped, and severely beaten about the head and body," one of the applications notes. "I had a brain concussion, cuts and abrasions over my body and legs." The applicant lost 35 days of work, her clothing and shoes were ruined, and she had to pay out babysitting expenses. The Kaiser Foundation covered her medical expenses. She would like to get $984.50 from the state. Another rape victim requests property reimbursement (though she will not get it under the provisions of the law) for her Norwegian sweater ($50), underwear ($5), blouse ($7), and slacks ($8), the poignant and prosaic wreckage of the sexual assault. A third claimant, said to have suffered atrial fibrillation from a murder attempt, flatly requests compensation of $50,000, far above the maximum of $5,000 then possible under the statute. Another claimant, having been beaten during a riot in a park, wants $9.95 to reimburse him for the left-handed fielder's glove he lost. Then there is the victim who had her nose bitten off by the wife of the man she was riding with. The wife caught them together, reached into the vehicle, and held her victim's head while she took the bite out of her.

A stab victim includes a surgical report, a sterile, scientific document that flattens out the emotion of the criminal event that served to produce it—"Two thoractomy tubes were then introduced into the stab wounds at the 5th and 7th intercostal spaces at the mid-axillary. Their tips were directed respectively toward the apex and toward the posterior costovertebral gutter"—these are two sentences out of the four page step-by-step account of the operation. The same file includes an item that often finds its way into debates on victim compensation: a $45 bill from an ambulance service. Supporters of compensation programs note that an offender would not be so billed; rather, the state would pay these expenses for him.

There is also the case of the man requesting $90 to compensate him for the loss of three ewes ($30 apiece) killed by dogs belonging to his neighbor. Then there is a brief footnote to history: a request for $419.32 by a young man who suffered a bullet wound in his left thigh on June 5, 1968, as part of the assassination of Robert F. Kennedy. Another claimant notes: "I was shot in both legs while being an innocent bystander." Then there are reports which provide specific details only about the unimportant things, such as the one filed by a victim's attorney: "Two men were have an argument on a public sidewalk at approximately 6:30 P.M. Applicant walked by innocently, and was shot by one of the men." Automobile episodes seem to be notably provocative. Many reports tell of persons stopping to challenge a motorist who had somehow offended them by grazing a fender, making a gesture, speeding by, or by behaving in some other way regarded as untoward. These incidents often seem to result in very severe beatings. There are also in the files a seemingly endless procession of cases of older women hanging onto their purses until a thief pushes them forcefully to the ground to get them to release their hold. Serious hip injuries are common in these instances. Finally, it is notable that many applicants specifically name the offender an uncommon number of times. It is as if somehow they have formed a kind of symbiotic relationship now with *their* criminal and feel compelled to associate themselves with him in the claim application.

CONCLUSION

The foregoing review touches only the tip of a data mine lying buried in the files and archives of state victim compensation programs. It would be interesting to learn, for instance, whether the inclusion of pain and suffering awards increase the ability of victim compensation programs to make the victim whole. How does the inclusion of the necessity to demonstrate "serious financial hardship" in New York, a clause not present in the New Jersey statute, affect the roster of each state's awards? Do persons whose claims are rejected end up more bitter than they had been as a result of their victimization? Indeed, the fundamental issue of whether compensation mediates the harshness of victimization, both financially and psychologically, is a matter that requires thorough exploration.

It also appears worth discovering how offenders feel about crime victim compensation efforts. Galaway and Hudson (1972) have reported on an attempt in Minnesota to mount a program in which the offender and victim come together to work out a mutually satisfactory program of reparation. Will this produce better results than a more impersonal state compensation effort, or will it further aggravate an already disturbing situation? We would also like to know whether crime victims tend to report (or to make up) crime events more often because of compensation programs, and if they are more cooperative with the police. Do the police themselves feel that the compensation programs offer them an opportunity to tell of some tangible assistance that may be available to a victim, and does this make their job more reasonable? The questions that crime victim compensation raises for the general study of victimology and its implications can be expanded at considerable length; the foregoing is but a sampler.

In short, then, this paper suggests that the matter of proper definition of the "crime victim" involves as many, and probably more, complications than have traditionally been associated with the question of who is the criminal. The appearance of programs to compensate crime victims, it has been suggested, offers one definable (though highly selective) group of victims and holds out the possibility of initiating some basic research bearing upon questions of importance to the study of crime victimization.

REFERENCES

AMIR, M. (1971). Patterns of forcible rape. Chicago: University of Chicago Press.

ATIYAH, P. (1970). Accidents, compensation and the law. London: Weidenfeld and Nicolson.

BERSCHEID, E., and WALSTER, E. (1967). "When does a harm-doer compensate a victim?" Journal of Personality and Social Psychology, 6(August):435-441.

BLOCH, H.A., and GEIS, G. (1970). Man, crime, and society (2nd ed.). New York: Random House.

BROOKS, J. (1973a). "Compensating victims of crime: The recommendations of program administrators." Law and Society Review, 7(spring):445-471.

--- (1973b). "Crime compensation programs: An opinion survey of program administrators." Criminology, 11(August):258-274.

BRYAN, G.J. (1968). "Compensation to victims of crime." Alberta Law Review, 6(2):202-210.

CALDWELL, R.C. (1958). "A re-examination of the concept of white-collar crime." Federal Probation, 22(March):30-36.

CHAPPELL, D. (1972). "Providing for victims of crime: Political placebos or progressive programs?" Adelaide Law Review, 4(December):294-306.

COVEY, J.M. (1965). "Alternatives to a compensation plan for victims of physical violence." Dickinson Law Review, 69(summer):391-405.

CULHANE, J.E. (1965). "California enacts legislation to aid victims of criminal violence." Stanford Law Review, 18(November):266-273.

EDELHERTZ, H., and GEIS, G. (1974). Public compensation to victims of crime. New York: Praeger.

EDELHERTZ, H., GEIS, G., CHAPPELL, D., and SUTTON, L.P. (1973). "Public compensation of victims of crime: A survey of the New York experience." Criminal Law Bulletin, 9(January):5-47; 9(March):101-123.

EREMKO, J. (1969). "Compensation of criminal injuries in Saskatchewan." University of Toronto Law Journal, 19(2):263-276.

FOGELMAN, S. (1971). "Compensation to victims of crimes of violence—The forgotten program." Unpublished M.S.W. thesis, University of Southern California.

FREEDMAN, J.L., WALLINGTON, S.A., and BLESS, E. (1967). "Compliance without pressure: The effects of guilt." Journal of Personality and Social Psychology, 7(October):117-124.

GALAWAY, B., and HUDSON, J. (1972). "Restitution and rehabilitation: Some central issues." Crime and Delinquency, 18(October):403-410.

GEIS, G. (1967). "State compensation to victims of violent crime." Pp. 157-177 in President's Commission on Law Enforcement and Administration of Justice (ed.), Task force report: Crime and its impact—An assessment. Washington, D.C.: U.S. Government Printing Office.

——— (1969). "Compensation for victims of violent crimes." Vol. 13, pp. 1559-1597 in National Commission on the Causes and Prevention of Violence. Washington, D.C.: U.S. Government Printing Office.

——— (1975). "Victims of crimes of violence and the criminal justice system." Pp. 61-74 in D. Chappell and J. Monahan (eds.), Violence and criminal justice. Lexington, Mass.: D.C. Heath.

GEIS, G.,sand MONAHAN, J. (1976). "The social ecology of violence." Pp. 342-356 in T. Lickona (ed.), Moral development and behavior. New York: Holt, Rinehart and Winston.

GEIS, G., and SOLER, J. (1971). "Response of female homicide offenders to press coverage of their trials." Journalism Quarterly, 48(autumn):558-560.

GEIS, G., and ZIETZ, D. (1966). "California's program of compensation to crime victims." Legal Aid Briefcase, 25(December):66-69.

Great Britain, Criminal Injuries Compensation Board (1973). Ninth report. London: Her Majesty's Stationery Office.

——— (1974). Tenth report. London: Her Majesty's Stationery Office.

Great Britain, House of Lords, Parliamentary Debates (1964). "Victims of crimes of violence: Amended scheme." 257(May7):1351-1419.

HINDELANG, M.J. (1974). An analysis of victimization survey results from the eight impact cities: Summary report. Albany, N.Y.: Criminal Justice Research Center.

HOLMES, O.W. (1881). The common law. Boston: Little, Brown.

HUSTON, T.E., GEIS, G., GARRETT, T., and WRIGHT, R. (forthcoming). "Good Samaritans as crime victims."

KALISH, C.B. (1974). Crimes and victims: A report on the Dayton-San Jose Pilot Survey of Victimization. Washington, D.C.: U.S. Department of Justice.

KRISBERG, B. (1975). Crime and privilege. Englewood Cliffs, N.J.: Prentice-Hall.

LAMBORN, L.L. (1971). "The methods of governmental compensation of victims of crime." University of Illinois Law Forum, 1971(4):655-681.

——— (1973a). "The propriety of governmental compensation of victims of crime." George Washington Law Review, 41(March):446-470.

––– (1973b). "The scope of programs for governmental compensation of victims of crime." University of Illinois Law Forum, 1:21-87.

LEJEUNE, R., and ALEX, N. (1973). "On being mugged: The event and its aftermath." Urban Life and Culture, 2(October):259-287.

LERNER, M.J., and SIMMONS, C.H. (1966). "Observer's reaction to the 'innocent victim': Compassion or rejection?" Journal of Personality and Social Psychology, 4(August): 203-210.

LINDEN, A. (1969). "Victims of crime and tort law." Journal of the Canadian Bar Association, 12(February):17-33.

MARGOLIUS, S. (1965). Buyer, be wary! New York: Public Affairs Committee.

MARTINSON, R. (1976). Untitled paper, in preparation.

MAURER, D.W. (1955). Whiz mob. New Haven, Conn.: College and University Press.

MIERS, D. (1972). Untitled paper. Pp. 176-191 in Proceedings of the Third International Conference on the Compensation of Victims of Crime. Toronto: Ontario Criminal Injuries Compensation Board.

New York, Crime Victim Compensation Board (1975). Eighth annual report.

PALMER, G.W.R. (1973). "Compensation for personal injury: A requiem for the common law in New Zealand." American Journal of Comparative Law, 21(winter):1-24.

PECAR, J. (1971). "Vpleteni 'opazovalci'–Viktimoloska razclemba." Revija Za Kriminalistiko in Kriminologijo, 22/23:172-184.

––– (1972). "Involved bystanders: Examination of a neglected aspect of criminology." International Journal of Contemporary Society, 9:81-88.

RATCLIFFE, J.M. (ed., 1966). The Good Samaritan and the law. Garden City, N.Y.: Doubleday.

RAWLINGS, E.I. (1968). "Witnessing harm to other: A reassessment of the role of guilt in altruistic behavior." Journal of Personality and Social Psychology, 10(4):377-380.

ROSENTHAL, A.M. (1964). Thirty-eight witnesses. New York: McGraw-Hill.

ROTHSTEIN, P.F. (1974). "How the Uniform Crime Reparation Act works." American Bar Association Journal, 60(December):1531-1535.

RUBINSTEIN, J. (1975). The study of psychology. Guilford, Conn.: Dushkin.

RYAN, W. (1971). Blaming the victim. New York: Random House.

SEAVEY, W.A., KEETON, P., and KEETON, R.E. (1964). Cases and materials on the law of torts. St. Paul, Minn.: West Publishing.

SCHUBERT, G. (1965). The judicial mind. Evanston, Ill.: Northwestern University Press.

SCHWENDINGER, H., and SCHWENDINGER, J. (1970). "Defenders of order or guardians of human rights?" Issues in Criminology, 5(winter):59-69.

SEEDMAN, A.A. (1974). Chief! New York: Arthur Fields.

SHELEFF, L. (SHASKOLSKY) (1970). "The innocent bystander and crime." Federal Probation, 34(March):44-48.

––– (1972-1973). "The innocent bystander: Socio-legal aspects." Pp. 197-209 in S. Shoham (ed.), Israel studies in criminology. Jerusalem: Jerusalem Academic Press.

STAUB, E. (1972). "Instigation to goodness: The role of social norms and interpersonal influence." Journal of Social Issues, 28(3):131-150.

SUTHERLAND, E.H. (1924). Criminology. Philadelphia: Lippincott.

––– (1934). Principles of criminology. Philadelphia: Lippincott.

––– (1940). "White-collar criminality." American Sociological Review, 5(February):1-12.

SYKES, G.M., and MATZA, D. (1957). "Techniques of neutralization: A theory of delinquency." American Sociological Review, 22(December):664-670.

SZAKATS, A. (1973). "Community responsibility for accident injuries: The New Zealand Accident Compensation Act." University of British Columbia Law Review, 8(1):1-33.

TAPPAN, P.W. (1947). "Who is the criminal?" American Sociological Review, 12(February):96-102.

U.S. Senate, Committee of the Judiciary, Subcommittee on Criminal Law and Procedures (1972). Victims of crime (92nd Congress, 1st Session). Washington, D.C.: U.S. Government Printing Office.

VIRKKUNEN, M. (1975). "Victim-precipitated pedophilia offenses." British Journal of Criminology, 15(April):175-180.

WALLERSTEIN, J.S., and WYLE, C.J. (1947). "Our law-abiding law-breakers." Probation, 25(April):107-112.

WALSTER, E., and PILIAVIN, J.A. (1972). "Equity and the innocent bystander." Journal of Social Issues, 28(3):165-189.

WEEKS, K.M. (1970). "The New Zealand criminal injuries compensation scheme." Southern California Law Review, 43(1):106-121.

WILLIAMSON, H. (1965). Hustler! New York: Doubleday.

WOLFGANG, M.E. (1958). Patterns of criminal homicide. Philadelphia: University of Pennsylvania Press.

WRIGHTSMAN, L.S. (1972). Social psychology in the seventies. Monterey, Calif.: Brooks/Cole.

ZIMRING, F. (1969). Personal communication.

Chapter 12

TOWARD A THEORY OF VICTIM-CRIMINAL JUSTICE SYSTEM INTERACTIONS

EDUARD ZIEGENHAGEN

National Crime Panel Survey results indicate that at least half of all crimes committed in major American cities remain unreported (U.S. Department of Justice, 1974a:28).[1] If this is so, how do victims cope with criminal behavior and why do they behave as they do?

Although scholarly interest in victimology has its origins in the late 19th century, the systematic study of the process of criminal victimization has only begun, and only fragmentary information is available for the purpose of formulating responses to these questions. The purpose of this effort is to direct attention to empirical aspects of the victim's response to criminal behavior and to propose a tentative framework for consideration of victim responses.

Defining the Victim Population

Difficulties in defining the population to be studied reside in disagreement among investigators regarding the phenomena of criminal victimization, in terms of the attributes of both the victim and the criminal and their relationship to each other and in terms of the social institutions of the society of which they are a part. Those concerned with social criticism include in their definition of victims persons who are lawbreakers and are punished by a ruling elite. Acts of punishment by the elite are viewed as criminal behavior. Some researchers are interested in explaining why some persons tend to be victims and others are not.

An argument has been advanced that some individuals attract behavior to their detriment because they suffer from mental, physical, or social deficiencies which make them vulnerable to exploitation by others. Other researchers identify criminals simply as those who act contrary to criminal law and are processed by the criminal justice system (Quinney, 1972; Von Hentig, 1948; Tappan, 1970; Sutherland and Cressy, 1966). It is beyond the scope of this effort to explore the full range of definitions of victims, but it is necessary to indicate how victims are to be defined. This effort draws upon empirical studies of victims, and these studies are focused upon describing the attributes of a subset of victims. This subset is composed of persons who perceive behavior to their detriment as contrary to criminal law. In many cases, such judgments were confirmed by criminal justice agencies. The population to be described is composed of victims of crime. Each crime is established by legal proscription of specific acts. Concern with this particular subset of the victim population reflects the predominant interest of most of the researchers in the relationship of victims to the criminal justice system, especially the degree to which victims act in support of legal proceedings against the offender.

Categorizing Individual Responses to Criminal Victimization

Given the predominant interest in criminal justice activities disclosed in most studies of victim behavior, it seems inescapable that one category of individual responses to criminal victimization should include behavior which involves invoking criminal justice agencies. However, these same empirical studies disclose that individual responses to criminal victimization are not confined to utilization of criminal justice agencies; therefore, some effort must be made to develop tentative descriptive categories which encompass what little is known about such responses. These categories reflect speculation about the function of the behavior manifested by the individual victim. The categories include (1) personal retribution, reflecting efforts to secure vengeance individually through punishment of the wrongdoer; (2) loss evasion, achieved through attempts to avoid retaliation by the offender and/or investments of time and effort required by participation in legal proceedings against the offender; and (3) compensation, indicating efforts to restore the victim's enjoyment of benefits lost through criminal action.

Invoking Criminal Justice Agencies as a
Response to Criminal Victimization

One of the several responses open to victims of crime is reporting the incident to the police. This is usually a prerequisite to further involvement with district attorneys, judges, penal and probation officers, and their support personnel.

Criminal justice agencies are dependent on victims of crime and witnesses to such events for further information respecting criminal behavior. Without information about criminal behavior, it is impossible for criminal justice agencies to take action against those who engage in behavior which is proscribed by law. Individual victims may depend on such agencies for protection from criminal behavior and from retaliation, when and if criminals are processed by the agencies. What appears to be a mutually supportive relationship, however, is not substantiated by the volume or quality of interactions among victims of crime and criminal justice agencies. Americans appear to invoke criminal justice agencies in a highly selective manner, reflecting various attributes of the crime, the degree of confidence that victims have in criminal justice agencies, and the attributes of victims themselves.

Reporting Personal Crimes and Property Crimes

A Portland, Oregon, study indicates that the tendency to report crimes involving property appears to be most closely related to the dollar value of the property itself. The higher the dollar value of the property, the more likely the crime is to be reported. The degree to which victims have confidence in the capabilities of the police and the degree to which they identify with the community in which they live become important only in cases of property crimes of lesser dollar value (Schneider, 1975:23). Even then, it is difficult to discover the victims' reasons for reporting high value property crime to the police. Victims may report the crime because they wish to collect the insured value of the property. This behavior was reported by Ennis (1967:41), who disclosed that most victims' decisions to involve the law enforcement apparatus are based upon hopes of monetary recovery from insurance companies for stolen property, especially automobiles. This incentive may not be present for reporting crimes involving property of comparatively lower value, or the incentive may be lessened by lack of confidence in the effectiveness of the police to recover the property.

The severity of personal crimes[2] also appears to be linked to the willingness of victims to report the crime to the police (Schneider, 1975; Ennis, 1967). Yet except in a very provisional sense, it is difficult to rank the seriousness of personal crimes because of victim differences in perception of criminal acts and the consequences of such acts. The seriousness of homicide and felonious assault, rape, and so on cannot be measured by their dollar value. Measurement by severity of punishment, stipulated by the state, reflects the norms of society, not the incentive to report a crime which may be operative for individual victims. Perhaps measurement problems are reflected in Schneider's findings that understanding local issues is a slightly better predictor of the tendency of victims to report personal crimes than a rating of the seriousness of the crime. Additionally, the social context of most personal crimes may increase the salience of confidence in criminal justice agencies to arrest and punish the offender (Schneider, 1975:42). If victims do not expect such tasks to be executed successfully, there would be little reason to involve criminal justice agencies because there would be indirect gains from other organizations, such as recovery of the value of insured property.

If the tendency to report personal crime is related to confidence in criminal justice agencies, as Schneider suggests, the behavior of such organizations may contribute or detract from the incentive to report crime. One approach to assessing the contributions of criminal justice agencies' performances to victims' incentives to report crime is to compare victims' expectations of performance with perceptions of performance.

Victim Expectations and Perceptions of Police Performance

Victims of personal crime in New York City who have reported the incident to the police or have had the incident reported by others most often cite the need for immediate protection from continuing criminal acts and/or emergency medical attention as their first priority needs.[3] Second-order needs, according to the victims, involve arrest of the offender and advice about how to cope with the result of the crime, e.g., how to replace broken door locks, how to avoid the offender's friends, etc. The treatment that victims of personal crime receive often varies from that which they desire. Victims of personal crimes report that the police most often first ask for information about the incident and the identity and location of the offender. Because it is often not clear which person or persons are victims or offenders, this procedure is understandable, yet costly in terms of police-victim relationships. Victims often complain that the sympathy and reassurance due them is withheld, pending information-gathering tasks, or is not provided at all. Arrest of the offender is perceived as being a first-order police priority by victims, but the victims themselves repeatedly stress the need for life saving as a first-priority police function. Victims are most appreciative of life-saving efforts and personal attention when they are forthcoming, and they are most critical when victims feel that they have been withheld or performed inadequately (Ziegenhagen, 1974).

It is not surprising that reports of actual police treatment conform to expectations of police treatment. Those victims who expect to be treated better or worse than, or the same as, others report the police actually treat them in such a manner. Yet there is a small but significant number of victims who are not treated as they expected. Only 7% of the white victims of personal crime expected to be treated less well than others, compared with 15% of the black respondents and 16% of the Hispanic respondents. However, 28% of the white respondents had complaints about police behavior, compared with 27% of the black victims, and 20% of the Hispanic victims (Ziegenhagen, 1974). The percentage of complaints from black and Hispanic victims is more in conformity with expectations they will not be treated as well as others, but the negative reports of white victims indicating lack of satisfaction with police performance are not confined to those persons of minority racial or ethnic identities. It is difficult to determine exactly what such reports mean in terms of actual police behavior. Some white victims may have expected to be treated better than they were, or at least they expected to be treated better than those who were considered to be less deserving of good treatment. Expectations of an absolute level of treatment may exist, and treatment judged by such standards may not be consistent with actual police capabilities to render service (Ziegenhagen, 1974).

If victims' reports of actual police behavior are reasonably reliable, it would appear that low expectations of police performance are well founded. According to a national survey of crime victims (Ennis, 1967:49), the police failed to respond to the report of the crime in 23% of the cases and failed to consider the incident a crime in 25% of the instances in which they were contacted and responded to the call. Finally, only in 20% of the cases did the police actually make an arrest. Given these circumstances, it does not seem shocking or unreasonable that victims would place little confidence in the ability of the police to respond to their needs as victims, even if they define their needs in terms of standard police performance.

Although utilization of the criminal justice system is the socially sanctioned response to victimization in most Western societies, such a response often is seen as inappropriate or actually harmful from the viewpoint of the victim. Ennis (1967) reports only 49% of all crimes surveyed were reported to the police, but there is no indication of whether the victim or other persons made the report. Other survey results suggest that the percentage of crimes reported would be even lower if only victim-reported crimes were considered. About one-third of the victims of personal crimes felt that the action characteristically undertaken by the police would be inappropriate given their needs. For example, contacting the police after receiving a beating from a youth gang was viewed as foolish by some victims of crime, because they doubted that the police would be able to locate or arrest the members of the gang involved in the incident. Even if some gang members were arrested, victims believed that they would be released quickly and that they or other gang members would administer an even more severe beating in retaliation for the arrest. In other cases, the offender was a member of the same family as the victim, and arrest was not seen as a solution to occasional violent behavior directed against the victim (Ziegenhagen, 1974). In crimes against property, some victims believed that the criminal justice system may be of help by recovering stolen items, yet 55% of the victims felt that the police would be ineffective (Ennis, 1967:44). Other victims feared economic losses from cancellation of insurance or higher insurance rates.

Once victims have committed themselves to reporting a crime, severe dissatisfaction is generated if the police fail to maintain contact with the victim in regard to progress on the case. Particular kinds of victim interests stimulate demands for information about police progress or the lack of it. For example, in the case of an attempted homicide, a victim feared a second attempt on his life but was frustrated in his efforts to secure information about the possible arrest and detention of the offender. Without this information, the victim did not know if he or members of his family would be vulnerable to attack by the offender. The victim was forced to make a choice between losing his job if he stayed at home with his family for mutual protection or reporting for work and leaving himself and his family exposed to the likelihood of severe injury or death.

Victim Perceptions of the District Attorney's Office and the Courts

The doubt expressed by victims about the capability of criminal justice agencies other than the police to respond to their needs seems to be reinforced if the performance of the system is considered from the victims' perspective. Those victims who anticipate retribution through the utilization of the criminal justice system have false hopes, as victims report only 42% of those arrested were tried. Dissatisfaction with the criminal justice system is particularly high if the accused were acquitted or, in the victim's opinion, given too lenient a sentence. Yet, those who are satisfied with the sentence express a high degree of satisfaction (Ennis, 1967:49).

The criminal justice organizations cannot perform their function as retributive agents without the participation of the victims and witnesses. Police cannot identify and apprehend offenders if victim-witnesses are not willing to provide testimony necessary at the trial of the accused. Although the cooperation of the victim-witnesses is essential for the state to prosecute criminals, there appear to be few features of the victim-witness role that are satisfactory from the victims' viewpoint. In a survey of victims of personal crime, 62 of the 294 persons had any contact with the district attorney's office or were present at the trial of the accused. Of that group, 18 respondents reported dissatisfaction because the accused was not convicted, and 11 victims expressed dissatisfaction with court practices, especially plea bargaining.

Few victim-witnesses feel that they have had the opportunity to relate the incident fully and in a manner which will elicit a proper response from the police, the district attorney's office, or the judge. Many victims were discouraged by what they saw as a lack of care taken to secure their meaningful participation in court proceedings. In addition to unfamiliar legal terms and procedures characteristic of courts, no representative of the criminal justice system assumes the task of making the situation intelligible to the victim. When court-appointed attorneys and representatives of offender service organizations actively participate in court proceedings, it is not surprising that victims feel isolated and incidental to the situation and become strongly dissatisfied. Most often the victims felt that no concern for them as persons was being shown and that no information was provided about the prosecution of the offender. Judges were most often described as impartial, while about equal numbers of victims perceived the judge's behavior as friendly or hostile. Victims felt that they must confine their remarks exclusively to information which is useful to the state for the purposes of the identification, arrest, and trial of the offender. Attempts to seek information about how to restore the victims' position to something approximating that before the crime is generally believed to be of no concern to criminal justice organizations.

Individual victims reported that attempts to obtain or submit information regarding their interests and opinions apart from apprehension and prosecution of the offender, or attempts to utilize channels other than those provided for such purposes, have met with strong objections from police, district attorneys, judges, and defense attorneys. The objections are based upon claims that such behavior is irrelevant to the tasks of the criminal justice organizations and/or actually hinders their performance. Criminal justice concerns, it was contended, should remain under the control of criminal justice professionals.

Generally, the police are under no obligation to provide information about the progress of an investigation of a crime to the individual victim, and courts are not obligated to provide information about the result of the trial of the accused. Judges, except in some cases in which policemen are victims, do not solicit information from victims; they claim that such efforts would jeopardize their neutrality. Victims' opinions are not solicited by the district attorney in plea bargaining with the defense attorney; the argument is that the victim might want a stronger penalty than was acceptable to the offender's attorney and might demand a trial when the state's evidence against the accused was insufficient. Individual victims tend to feel that they are outsiders and that officers of the criminal justice system are not interested in matters of substantial concern to victims. It is not surprising that follow-up interviews with 47 New York City victims of personal crimes disclosed a striking decline of satisfaction with the prosecutor's office and judges after victims had been exposed to these criminal justice personnel (Ziegenhagen, 1974). Some victims stated that their interaction with these organizations served as a lesson not to become involved again.

Personal Vengeance as a Response to Criminal Victimization

Personal vengeance refers to the victim's efforts or the efforts of his agents to punish those who are believed to have harmed the victim. Generally such acts are contrary to law; and, by involvement, the victim is subject to punishment himself. Personal vengeance provides no anticipated returns for the victim other than whatever satisfaction can be gained from acts of revenge. Such acts are designed to reduce whatever benefits are enjoyed by the perpetrator without necessarily restoring the victim's enjoyment of such benefits. Personal vengeance may be attempted when the wrongdoer's action entails harm to the victim that cannot be rectified (e.g., permanent physical harm) or when there is little confidence that criminal justice agencies are willing or able to extract vengeance.

Very little research has dealt directly with personal vengeance due to the reluctance of individuals involved to provide information which implicates them in criminal acts, yet interpretation of fragmentary information suggests that personal vengeance is present in a substantial percentage of homicides known to the police. Wolfgang (1957) found that in 62% of his sample of homicide cases, the persons killed had a criminal history of victimizing others. Apparently the necessary precautions were not taken to make others accept their tormentor's behavior or to make the behavior of others ineffective. The death of such persons is a logical consequence of a series of interactions previously established, although in these cases the victim and the offender exchange roles. Even then, Wolfgang reports that the persons killed had been engaged in criminal behavior similar to that of the persons who initiated unprovoked violence. Whether vengeance was foremost in the mind of the persons who have killed or injured their tormentors is not known, but it is clear that their behavior was in response to behavior generally considered to one's detriment and that such interaction had a long history of repetition.

De Porte and Parkhurst (1935) published their study of victim-offender relationships over forty years ago, noting that in homicide cases the victims and offenders are generally of the same racial or ethnic group, reside in areas geographically contiguous, and have had previous personal dealings with each other—much as have been reported in recent studies (Ennis, 1967). Physical proximity contributes to the availability of the wrongdoer as a target for personal retribution only among lower-income groups, since theft of property or money is likely to be executed by lower-income persons unknown to the high-income victim (Ennis, 1967). Not only do higher-income groups reside in areas physically apart from lower-income groups, but contact with lower-income groups is limited by such environmental features as transportation. Private transportation in automobiles for upper-income persons, rather than public transportation via bus or subway, reduces personal vulnerability but increases the probability of personal larceny (e.g., automobile theft).

Loss Evasion as a Response to Criminal Victimization

Loss-evasion responses to criminal victimization are designed to prevent further costs to the victim with anticipation that whatever benefits were enjoyed previously cannot be restored. The victim attempts to avoid further losses, such as from retaliation by the offender or from extended results of the offender's initial behavior or, more indirectly, from payment of medical bills or loss of time from work. Loss evasion may take the form of actual relocation in another physical or social setting in an effort to avoid the disruptive features of the offender's behavior. Possibly 37% of the victims of personal crimes reported to the police utilize loss-evasion behavior (Ziegenhagen, 1974). Loss evasion appears to be a default response, resulting from low expectations that any other response will redress the wrongs endured and high expectations of suffering further deprivations. Therefore, loss-evasion behavior is based upon the assumption that it is best to minimize losses when no gains are appropriate or to minimize losses when there is low expectancy that gains will be forthcoming. In such cases, victims may fear indirect losses from participation in proceedings against wrongdoers in the criminal justice organizations or from retaliation by the offender. Losses can accrue from a variety of sources, especially vindictive action by the accused or his friends. According to National Crime Panel reports (U.S. Department of Justice, 1974a:5), 2% of all victims do not notify the police because they fear further harm from the offender. The data do not disclose the percentage of persons who are intimidated by offenders in accord with the type of crime committed. Intimidation may account for a far greater percentage of persons who fail to report the incident when the crime involves personal violence. Victims are accessible to intimidation from husbands, boyfriends, and youth gangs simply because of physical proximity and inability to restrain the behavior of others. Sympathetic and powerful cohorts may not exist to protect the victim, and the police may be uninterested or ineffective. The same factors which make victims vulnerable to crime also make victims vulnerable to intimidation and force them to cut their losses by adopting evasive responses.

Some practices of criminal justice organizations actually increase the victim's vulnerability. For example, information provided the police includes the victim's name and address, which is accessible to the general public and may be published in newspapers. It is not surprising that large city law enforcement agencies have difficulty in locating victim-witnesses for participation in legal proceedings when victims have already taken evasive measures such as giving false names and addresses to the police. The likelihood of effective intimidation and possible harm is enhanced by the inability or unwillingness of the police to provide for protection of individual victims. The police tend to provide protection of victim-witnesses only in cases which have high visibility, such as those involving socially prominent persons, sensational crimes receiving great public media coverage, and organized crime.

Evasion of the possible vengeance of perpetrators of crime can be combined with evasion of the scrutiny of criminal justice organizations themselves. Because it is difficult to differentiate victim from criminal in some instances, the victim may fear the current differentiation will not persist under close examination or that previous criminal activity engaged in by the victim will be disclosed. Many victims have had previous experience as offenders and are not enthusiastic about involvement with the courts or police. A study of victims of aggravated assault by Johnson et al. (1973:73) disclosed that 75% of the male victims had a police record, 34% had several jail sentences, and 19% had prison records. The crimes most frequently engaged in were assault and burglary. The assault charges appear to have been made during sessions of drunkenness and fighting. For some victims, there may be good reason for the police to question the circumstances in which the criminal act takes place.

Participation in proceedings against the offender are also costly in terms of lost time from work and the uncertain time delay before the victim-witness is called to testify. Also medical costs, costs for replacement of property stolen or damaged, higher insurance rates, and possibly attorney's fees may contribute to the belief that the best way to avoid such unsolicited costs is not to initiate responses which entail involvement with criminal justice organizations. Even in cases where the crime is a serious one and the victim's desire for justice could be expected to be very strong, it appears that some victims choose evasion tactics rather than risk recrimination by the offender or incur the costs of participation in the criminal justice system. Of 47 victims of personal crime participating in a follow-up interview, 11 changed their residence in order to avoid intimidation by the offender or his friends and/or to escape the claims of the criminal justice system or creditors (Ziegenhagen, 1974).

Loss-evasion responses may have strong appeal for the victim because of their apparent availability. Evasion such as change of residence or job and, in some cases, change of documentary identity appears to be more within the immediate control of the victim than criminal justice proceedings against the offender. Change of residence is more easily accomplished and appears to have greater protective potential than reliance on the criminal justice system to identify, apprehend, try, convict, sentence, and imprison the offender. Individual attempts to identify and punish the perpetrator may involve even more danger to the victim and with not substantively greater probability for success. The degree to which victims successfully achieve personal vengeance is unknown, but, if the victim could easily reverse roles with the perpetrator, it is not likely that he would have been victimized initially. Therefore, loss evasion may be comparatively more attractive than personal vengeance.

Because of limits on the victim's ability to control the environment which resulted in victimization initially, it may not be possible to become less vulnerable to intimidation by the offender or escape indirect costs through loss-evasion responses. For example, lower-income victims were more likely to become victims of violence initially and are more likely to be victimized again due to their interaction with other persons of low income who are more likely to employ violence. A change of residence or job most likely will not entail a change in the behavior of those with whom they are most likely to interact. This apparent solution to victimization applies only to a particular event, while the long-run problem persists. Additionally, persons appear to vary greatly in their ability to utilize loss evasion. Members of families and older persons are less mobile and more vulnerable than young unmarried persons and therefore may not be able to relocate even though incentive to do so is substantial. Evasion is at best an admission of helplessness and borders on quiescence. Very little is known about this response to criminal victimization, since its objective is to make oneself inaccessible. Perhaps most important is that it is characterized by increasing mistrust of persons in general and public institutions in particular and concurrently contributes to the decline of the criminal justice agency's credibility and effectiveness.

COMPENSATION AS A RESPONSE TO CRIMINAL VICTIMIZATION

Compensation involves behavior concerned with minimizing or balancing whatever losses the victim may have suffered by giving him benefits to equal such losses. It entails the utilization of the services of other organizations for the purposes of reconstituting the victim's enjoyment of benefits in a manner which reflects the situation before the acts of the perpetrator occurred. Objects and real property can be restored or replaced, or their value can be transferred to the victim through monetary awards. Personal injury and death involve conditions which are not restorable or not easily restored.

In socialist nations compensation is an integral part of general social insurance programs which compensate victims of crime in a manner which is similar to compensation of other citizens who are injured or killed as a result of industrial accidents, automobile accidents, etc. In Western European nations and the United States, control of social conditions tends to be less centralized, and a multiplicity of institutions are involved in victim compensation.

Private insurance programs, based upon the contributions of individual policyholders, provide opportunities for compensation of crime victims for proven general, personal, and material losses. Additionally, opportunities exist to secure damages from offenders by civil proceedings in court systems. Civil proceedings are sometimes used by victims in combination with prosecution of the accused by the state. The threat of severe penalties by the state can be used as an inducement to pay damages to the victims. In return for payment of damages, the victim refuses to testify against the offender, and in many instances criminal proceedings against the offender are terminated. This technique to secure redress for individual victims was considered a corruption of the criminal justice system and denounced by members of the legal community, especially district attorneys. Apparently it was believed that compensation for individual victims is of lesser social value than punishment of offenders for behavior considered detrimental to society in general (Sutherland, 1947:14). Although the actual number of instances in which this technique was utilized or attempted is unknown, it is unlikely that a very large percentage of victims was able to secure compensation, considering that the offender was unknown to the victim in two-thirds of all violent crimes (U.S. Department of Justice, 1974b:2-3), and a far greater fraction of those involved in crimes against property are likely to remain unknown. Arrests are made in only 20% of police-confirmed crimes, and of course only 49% of all crimes are reported to the police (Ennis, 1967:49). Additionally, the number of criminals having attachable assets is generally very small, and it is likely that few victims are capable of paying the costs to initiate civil proceedings.

The largest and most comprehensive existing social service system from which persons can draw compensation serves all persons who have sustained personal or property losses, including victims of crime. Both federal and state programs provide services and monetary awards for physical rehabilitation, hospitalization, medical care for dependent children, work retraining, etc. For the most part such services are provided for low-income persons or persons of limited earning capacities. Victims of crime receive no preferential treatment in the type of service rendered or in processing claims to service. Additionally, victims of crime must conform to whatever eligibility criteria has been established by the organizations in question. Only a small percentage of the total number of victims who have reported crimes to the police ever become involved in services from such organizations due to the lack of recognition by such organizations that victims of crime are eligible for service (Ziegenhagen, 1974).

A survey of victims of personal crimes in New York City disclosed that approximately 18% of the victims interviewed sought aid from a variety of social service organizations, including the New York State Crime Victims Compensation Board, Social Services, the Veterans Administration, the public assistance agency, the workman's compensation agency, and various private charities and church groups. Of the total number of victims surveyed, 11% received aid in some form. Generally, low-income persons who have had previous experience with such organizations are those most likely to seek services relevant to needs arising from victimization and are most likely to secure aid. Many of those receiving aid were already clients of organizations which were providing aid to satisfy previous existing needs not related to criminal victimization.

Crime victim compensation programs in America provide a more focused response to claims for compensation arising from criminal victimization. Almost all of the existing programs are characterized by strict eligibility requirements, relatively few awards in proportion to the number of claims, and an almost infinitesimal clientele given the number of victims of crime. All programs are limited to monetary compensation for needs arising from violent crimes, but additional requirements greatly reduce the number of persons eligible for compensation.

The requirement that there be no personal relationship between the offender and the victim disqualifies large numbers of persons who are victims of violent crimes. Since at least 30 to 40% of all violent crimes involve members of the same family, it is difficult to understand the rationale for such a provision, if serving the needs of victims is the actual objective of the program. In such cases, under the existing New York statute, persons are excluded from receiving funds for unreimbursed medical expenses and for loss of earnings, although such persons have made sustained efforts to be contributing members of society.

All crime victim compensation programs in the United States contain provisions which exclude claimants from compensation who are believed to have precipitated the crime. As mentioned earlier, there is reason to believe that about 62% of homicides are precipitated by the victim, although the degree to which victims have provoked other violent crimes is not well documented. Exactly what behavior or circumstances constitutes provocation is also unclear. Several of Von Hentig's (1948) victim categories include persons whose actions precipitate others to commit crimes against them, including tormentors, blackmailers, swindlers, etc. Such persons engage in behavior which, in itself, is unlawful and evokes an unlawful response. Others, however, become victims because of physical or mental deficiency, which allows criminal acts to be taken against them. Among this group would be persons who are addicted to drugs or alcohol. Von Hentig (1948) found that 67% of the male homicide victims in his studies were alcoholics. Wolfgang (1957) found that 48% of both victims and criminals had been drinking. Johnson et al. (1973) found that 34% of the assault victims in their study had histories of alcoholism. In a sense, addiction and use of alcohol and drugs may contribute to the unlawful behavior of others; therefore, such persons are not technically innocent victims. Schafer's (1968) view is that the victim's first responsibility is to do nothing which would contribute to the likelihood of victimization, and apparently this viewpoint is incorporated into many of the victim compensation programs. What appears to be overlooked, however, is that the use of drugs and alcohol, as well as the use of violence for exploitation or retribution, is characteristic of those social groups which victim compensation programs are supposed to serve. Use of drugs and alcohol can be conceived of as intrapunitive means to control social conditions, while violence is an extrapunitive manifestation of efforts to gain control of social conditions.

Most crime victim compensation programs require that the crime be reported to the police within a reasonable time after its occurrence. There is a tendency to make compensation contingent upon the degree to which victims accept and support the law enforcement organization's definition of the incident and treatment of the offender. If the police do not interpret the incident as a crime, there can be no compensation; and if the victim favors remedies other than arrest and possible imprisonment of the offender, the crime is not likely to be reported. Such circumstances are not difficult to imagine, since the police do not verify that a crime has been committed in 25% of the cases in which incidents have been reported (Ennis, 1967:49). Furthermore, the prospect of compensation for physical injuries resulting from the crime are not likely to outweigh the prospects for sustaining further injuries if retaliation is threatened by the offender. Edelhertz and Geis (1974:261) conclude that "there is no evidence, only speculation, that victims will be motivated to cooperate with criminal justice agencies because their compensation may be at stake."

Perhaps the most disconcerting aspect of existing victim compensation programs is that many of the social conditions that contribute to individual vulnerability to the unlawful acts of others also tend to prevent victims from gaining an award from compensation programs. Von Hentig claims that one group of victims is vulnerable because of its lack of knowledge of its rights and duties within a particular culture (e.g., non-English-speaking immigrants). Others are incapable of learning or executing such rights and responsibilities due to physical or mental deficiency. Yet almost all the victim compensation programs require elaborate documentation of claims, and the responsibility for such documentation is placed upon the victim or the victim's survivors. For example, in New York State, the Crime Victims Compensation Board disallows at least

50% of the claims made because of inadequate or incomplete information respecting the claimant's description of the incident, his relationship to the offender, his financial status, the status of his claims for compensation from other public and private organizations, his record of expenses arising from the incident, or, in the case of the beneficiary of a deceased victim, a death certificate and records of the death benefits received or pending.

It is difficult to avoid the conclusion that compensation for victims of crime is administered in a manner which ignores the attributes of the population that is to receive service. Features of programs appear to have been incorporated to exclude sizable portions of the victim population in the interest of maintaining low costs to the state. Such a response has the effect of supporting victim behavior which is basically quiescent or involves victims in personal forms of retribution.

A FRAMEWORK FOR THE ANALYSIS OF VICTIM BEHAVIOR

Why some responses to criminal victimization are selected by victims rather than others and why certain responses persist while others do not will be an area of continuing investigation by social scientists for many years. As in the case of all other areas of the social sciences, data of varying validity and reliability abound, but schemes for their organization and assessment most often are provisional and incomplete. The theoretical scheme offered here is not an exception, although it may establish a line of inquiry which can be pursued beneficially.

In the preceding description of victim behavior, emphasis is placed on the goal directedness of efforts to cope with criminal victimization. Goal-directed activities are intended to manipulate the conditions with which the victim is confronted as a result of criminal behavior. The responses chosen are most likely a function of both the victim's past experience and the various options present or absent in the environment with which the victim must deal. For example, previous satisfactory or unsatisfactory dealings with the police constitute part of the individual's memory of relevant events which contribute to or detract from the tendency to invoke the criminal justice system as a response to criminal victimization. However, no matter how satisfying past experiences were, if the police do not respond to reports of the crime, positive inclinations contribute little to the tendency to invoke the criminal justice system. Birch and Veroff (1966:5-10) suggest that motive, incentive, expectancy, and availability constitute the sources of tendencies to select one response or activity rather than another.

Motive refers to what Birch and Veroff (1966:8) call modifiers of incentives.

Motives reflect the individual's previous experience with consequences of actions of a general class. For example, theft of insured property through criminal action may stimulate incentive to report the crime to the police and to contact the insurance company to recover the loss sustained. A victim who previously has had many unsatisfactory responses from bureaucratic organizations, such as the police and insurance companies, may decide to accept the loss. Others who have had satisfactory dealings with bureaucracies would be more likely to report the theft of property to the police and the insurance companies.

Incentive is concerned with the way in which consequences of behavior add to the strength of the tendency to become involved in particular activities. Consequences or outcomes have varying incentive values for human beings, and each has a valance, i.e., a degree of attraction or repulsion for whatever activities are in question. According to Birch and Veroff (1966:7) "if an organism consistently approaches or consistently escapes certain consequences when free to do so, those consequences are said to have incentive value." The hapless assault-and-robbery victim may expect that, if he reports the crime, the police and the criminal justice system will act effectively in the apprehension and conviction of the perpetrator. Yet the victim also may know that investigation of the crime could disclose information that he had been involved in criminal activities himself at one time. In this case, incentive to report the crime would be mixed.

Expectancy is the tendency to believe that selection of particular responses will actually achieve certain goals. The hypothetical victim of assault and robbery may not contact the police to report the crime because he believes that the police will not respond to his call or consider the incident a crime or be able to apprehend the perpetrator. Expectancy varies substantially in strength, depending upon the relative success that the individual has had utilizing various means to attain objectives in the past. Repeated failure of the criminal justice system to respond to the victim's expectations contributes to the eventual selection of other responses to victimization. If the police fail to respond to the victim's report of an incident, or if the police decide that the incident is not a crime, or if the perpetrator remains unidentified or is not apprehended, it is clear that other responses must be pursued in accord with the strength of the incentive generated. The inability or unwillingness of law enforcement agencies to respond to a victim's reports of crime may impose limits on an individual's range of responses, and the victim's memory of such failures may determine the level of his expectancy that criminal justice agencies will act effectively. Where there are past experiences regarding a particular mode of action, responses of this variety are more likely to be applied to the present situation. For example, if the police recover an assault-and-robbery victim's property and return it to him promptly, and if the perpetrator is apprehended, tried, and convicted, the victim is more likely in the future to invoke the criminal justice system as a means of recovering property and attaining retribution.

An individual's past history or memory with respect to availability can also suggest objectives or goals, as well as means to obtain goals. For example, an assault-and-robbery victim may recall the persistent theme of personal revenge as it is portrayed in popular literature and electronic media. Recovery of stolen goods may decline as an objective, compared to what is believed to be the high degree of personal satisfaction resulting from administering punishment to the wrongdoer without the interference of the cumbersome and possibly ineffectual criminal justice bureaucracy.

These basic concepts drawn from motivation theory can be employed to construct a paradigm of victim response, such as that represented in Figure 1. The value of the paradigm is that it suggests the interrelated nature of responses to criminal victimization, the sources of criminal victimization, and the sources of psychological effects which contribute to particular responses.[4]

Incentive and its modifier motive must be adequate for the victim before the sequence of tendencies is initiated. If incentive to act is inadequate or if its strength is severely reduced by motive, the victim becomes quiescent. Quiescence refers to the tendency not to engage in extrapunitive measures (i.e., those which result in action against others). It may involve acceptance of the losses or harm sustained or intrapunitive measures, such as withdrawal or suicide. Failure of any element of any response category contributes to lessening the probability that the response will be attempted again, although incentive to act remains high. For example, initially, the victim's incentive may be adequate and his expectation may be high that his objectives can be obtained through utilization of criminal justice services, but if the suspect is not arrested even though the incident is judged a crime by the police, the victim is apt henceforth to have lower expectations that criminal justice transactions will contribute to his desired objectives. The attainment of an objective or the failure to attain an objective has a cumulative effect on the probability that the responses will or will not be initiated again. The failure of all responses or the exclusion of those responses in which expectancy is inadequate also contribute to the probability of quiescence. Concurrently, failure to attain an objective, so long as incentive is high, contributes to the expectancy that some other response is appropriate. For example, unsuccessful utilization of criminal justice organizations contributes to expectations that such behavior is not instrumental to securing the victim's objectives and will increase the expectation that other transactions are appropriate.

The linkages between psychological concepts and elements of victim behavior

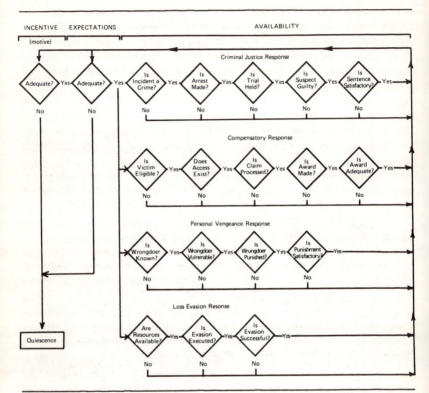

Figure 1. RESPONSES TO CRIMINAL VICTIMIZATION

represented in Figure 1 suggest directions for future development of knowledge about the process aspects of criminal victimization. Although it is known that victims, criminals, criminal justice professionals, and various other members of society interact and that such interaction has consequences for the immediate individual as well as society, very little attention has been given this area of investigation. Major survey efforts to collect data about victims of crime focus on the social characteristics of victims who report or do not report crimes to the police rather than on the process by which such decisions are made. Without a concept of the process of criminal victimization or appropriate data, it is particularly difficult to provide a well-designed response to whatever areas of victim behavior are considered problematic. For example, survey results indicate that lower-income black victims are less likely to report minor property crimes to the police compared to high-income white victims. Such results fail to indicate what aspect of victim behavior is open to change, what options are attractive to victims, and what consequences such options will have for others. Special-purpose data-gathering techniques in combination with new conceptions of the process of criminal victimization will be required in order to provide guidelines for program development and increased knowledge about the phenomena of criminal victimization.

NOTES

1. According to surveys of the victim population of Chicago, Detroit, Los Angeles, New York, and Philadelphia, only 37% of all personal crimes are reported to the police, but as greater personal injury is sustained, the tendency to report the crime increases. Robbery of commercial establishments and auto theft are more likely to be reported than other kinds of crimes. For a report of victim behavior in smaller cities and rural areas, see Richardson et al. (1972).

2. Personal crimes are those in which the victim is in face-to-face confrontation with the offender. The distinction between personal crimes and property crimes is significant in that personal crimes involve the threat of physical danger or actual injury to the victim.

3. The results reported are from initial and follow-up interviews with 294 victims of violent crime residing in New York City. Early investigation of sample attributes indicate similarities to those located in similar victim populations, but given self selection effects dictated by constraints on the mode of contact with respondents and the reluctance of particular subsets to be interviewed, a healthy skepticism about representativeness ought to prevail. The data were collected by the Crime Victim's Consultation Project funded by a grant from the Law Enforcement Assistance Administration and administered by Albert Einstein College of Medicine of Yeshiva University.

4. The paradigm and the theoretical discussion provide for instrumental, not consumatory behavior, as it is represented by Birch and Veroff. Although some of the specific acts described may include the attainment of the objective itself (consumatory behavior), as well as means by which the objective is being sought (instrumental behavior), this distinction does not seem to be crucial to the early stages of the development of the framework used here.

REFERENCES

BIRCH, D., and VEROFF, J. (1966). Motivation: A study of action. Belmont, Calif.: Brooks Cole.

De PORTE, J.V., and PARKHURST, E. (1935). "Homicide in New York State: A statistical study of the victims and criminals in 37 counties in 1921-1930." Human Biology, 7:47-73.

EDELHERTZ, H., and GEIS, G. (1974). Public compensation to victims of crime. New York: Praeger.

ENNIS, P.H. (1967). Criminal victimization in the United States: A report of a national survey. In President's Commission on Law Enforcement and the Administration of Justice (ed.), Field Surveys II. Washington, D.C.: U.S. Government Printing Office.

GANS, H. (1962). The urban villagers. Glencoe, Ill.: Free Press.

JOHNSON, J.H., KERPER, H.B., HAYES, D.D., and KILLINGER, G.G. (1973). The recidivist victim: A descriptive study. Criminal Justice Monograph 4, no. 1.

QUINNEY, R. (1972). "Who is the victim?" Criminology, 10(3):314-323.

RICHARDSON, R.J., WILLIAMS, O., DENYER, T., McGAUGHEY, S., and WALKER, D. (1972). Prospectives on the legal justice system: Public attitudes and criminal victimization. Chapel Hill: University of North Carolina Press.

SCHAFER, S. (1968). The victim and his criminal. New York: Random House.

SCHNEIDER, L. (1975). "The Portland evaluation studies: Use of victimization surveys for evaluation and planning." Unpublished paper prepared for delivery at the 1975 LEAA Victimization Survey Seminar, Washington, D.C., June 24.

SUTHERLAND, E.H. (1947). Principles of criminology (4th ed.). Philadelphia: Lippincott.

SUTHERLAND, E.H., and CRESSY, D. (1966). Principles of Criminology (7th ed.). Philadelphia: Lippincott.

TAPPAN, P.W. (1970). "Who is the criminal?" In M. Wolfgang, L. Savitz, and N. Johnson (eds.), Sociology of crime and delinquency (2nd ed.). New York: John Wiley.

U.S. Department of Justice (1974a). Crime in the nation's five largest cities. Washington, D.C.: National Criminal Justice Information and Statistics Service.

——— (1974b). Criminal victimization in the United States. Washington, D.C.: National Criminal Justice Information and Statistics Service.

VON HENTIG, H. (1948). The criminal and his victim. New Haven, Conn.: Yale University Press.

WOLFGANG, M. (1957). "Victim precipitated criminal homicide." Journal of Criminal Law, Criminology and Police Science, 48(1):1-11.

WOLFGANG, M., and FERRACUTI, F. (1967). The subculture of violence. London: Tavestock.

ZIEGENHAGEN, E. (1974). "Victims of violent crime in New York City: An exploratory survey of perceived needs." Unpublished report to the Crime Victim's Consultation Project.

ABOUT THE AUTHORS

JANIE M. BURCART received her bachelor's degree from the University of Surrey, England, and her master's degree from the University of New Mexico. She is presently on leave from the Ph.D. program in sociology at the University of Oregon, while working with Anne Schneider at Oregon Research Institute.

THEODORE M. BECKER, a partner in the Chicago law firm of Becker and Tenenbaum, is engaged in a practice specializing in criminal and civil litigation at both the federal and state levels. He has published numerous articles in the area of law and social science.

JAMES A. CRAMER is currently a senior research sociologist at the Institute of Criminal Law and Procedure, Georgetown University Law Center. He received his Ph.D. from the University of Tennessee, Knoxville. He has taught at the University of Tennessee, Virginia Commonwealth University, and the University of Maryland, European Division.

SAMUEL DASH is Professor of Law and Director of the Institute of Criminal Law and Procedure, Georgetown University Law Center. He gained nationwide popular attention during the Watergate hearings as Chief Counsel for the U.S. Senate Select Committee on Presidential Campaign Activities (the "Senate Watergate Committee").

DEBORAH DENNO is a junior research criminologist at the Institute of Criminal Law and Procedure, Georgetown University. In 1975 she received a Master of Criminology from the University of Toronto.

WILLIAM DOERNER is an instructor in the Department of Sociology and Anthropology and a Research Associate at the Center of Criminal Justice and Social Policy, Marquette University. He is completing his Ph.D. in sociology at the University of Tennessee.

FREDRIC L. DuBOW is an Assistant Professor of Sociology, a researcher at the Center for Urban Affairs, and Associate Director of the Law and Social Science Program at Northwestern University. In 1973 he received his Ph.D. from the University of California, Berkeley. He has also been on the Faculty of Law, University of Dar es Salaam, Tanzania.

GILBERT GEIS is a Professor in the Program in Social Ecology, University of California, Irvine. He previously taught at California State University, Los Angeles, and at the University of Oklahoma. He served as a consultant to the President's Commission on Law Enforcement and Administration of Justice, and the National Commission on the Causes and Prevention of Violence.

MICHAEL GOTTFREDSON is currently a doctoral candidate in criminal justice at the State University of New York at Albany and a research analyst for the Criminal Justice Research Center in Latham, New York.

MICHAEL J. HINDELANG is Associate Professor at the School of Criminal Justice, State University of New York at Albany. He is currently directing a research project that is analyzing results from the National Crime Panel victimization survey data.

MARY KNUDTEN is Assistant Professor of Sociology and Co-director of the Marquette University Victim/Witness project. She is also the Director of the sociology department's Program in Human Communities. She received her Ph.D. from the University of Chicago.

RICHARD D. KNUDTEN is Professor of Sociology and Director of the Center for Criminal Justice and Social Policy, Marquette University. He is also director of the Marquette

University Victim/Witness study. He received his Ph.D. in Sociology from Case Western Reserve and was chairman of the Department of Sociology at Valparaiso University.

RICHARD P. LYNCH is the Director of the National District Attorneys Association's Washington, D.C., offices. He holds A.B., M.A., and J.D. degrees from the University of Michigan. He served on the President's Commission on Crime in the District of Columbia, in the Office of Law Enforcement Assistance, and in the Select Committee on Crime of the U.S. House of Representatives.

WILLIAM F. McDONALD is Research Director of the Institute of Criminal Law and Procedure and Associate Professor of Sociology at Georgetown University, where he has also been an Adjunct Professor of Law. He received a D.Crim. in 1970 from the University of California, Berkeley.

DAL MANESS, Jr., is a graduate student in sociology at the University of South Carolina.

ANTHONY MEADE is Assistant Professor of Sociology and Co-director of Marquette University's Victim/Witness project. He also serves as Director of the sociology department's Program in Criminology and Criminal Justice. In 1970 he received his Ph.D. in sociology from the University of Tennessee. He has also taught at Emory University.

STEPHAN SCHAFER is Professor of Sociology and Criminology at Northeastern University. He was educated at the University of Budapest and taught Criminology there until 1951. He also taught in England before coming to the United States in 1951. In this country he has taught at Florida State University and Ohio University.

ANNE L. SCHNEIDER received her Ph.D. from Indiana University and joined the political science faculty at Yale University. She became a research scientist at the Oregon Research Institute in 1973.

A. EMERSON SMITH is Assistant Professor of Sociology at the University of South Carolina and Director of Sociology Research Associates. He received his Ph.D. in sociology from Emory University in 1971.

KRISTEN M. WILLIAMS is a research associate with the Institute for Law and Social Research in Washington, D.C. She previously was employed by the U.S. Department of Health, Education, and Welfare. She received her bachelor's and master's degrees in psychology from Stanford University and the University of Pennsylvania respectively.

L.A. WILSON II is a Ph.D. candidate in political science at the University of Oregon. He began work in criminal justice as a research assistant at the Oregon Research Institute in 1974. He is also a research assistant at the Center for Educational Policy and Management at the University of Oregon.

EDUARD ZIEGENHAGEN is an Associate Professor of Political Science and a Research Associate of the Center for Comparative Political Research at the State University of New York at Binghamton. He served on the Crime Victims Consultation Project, New York City, and on the President's Commission on the Causes and Prevention of Violence.

AUTHOR INDEX

SUBJECT INDEX

CRIMINAL JUSTICE AND THE VICTIM

This

INTERNATIONAL EDITORIAL ADVISORY BOARD

LaMar T. Empey, *Sociology, University of Southern California*
Herbert Jacob, *Political Science, Northwestern University*
Norval Morris, *University of Chicago Law School*
Stuart S. Nagel, *Policy Studies Organization,*
University of Illinois at Urbana-Champaign
Frank J. Remington, *University of Wisconsin Law School*
James F. Short, *Social Research Center, Washington State University*
Jerome H. Skolnick, *Center for the Study of Law and Society,*
University of California, Berkeley
Nigel Walker, *Institute of Criminology, Cambridge University*
James Q. Wilson, *Government, Harvard University*
Marvin E. Wolfgang, *Center for Studies in Criminology and Criminal Law,*
University of Pennsylvania

Books in this series:

I. The Rights of the Accused in Law and Action
STUART S. NAGEL, Editor

II. Drugs and the Criminal Justice System
JAMES A. INCIARDI and CARL D. CHAMBERS, Editors

III. The Potential for Reform of Criminal Justice
HERBERT JACOB, Editor

IV. The Jury System in America: A Critical Overview
RITA JAMES SIMON, Editor

V. The Juvenile Justice System
MALCOLM W. KLEIN, Editor

VI. Criminal Justice and the Victim
WILLIAM F. McDONALD, Editor

Volume VI. Sage Criminal Justice System Annuals

CRIMINAL JUSTICE
AND THE
VICTIM

WILLIAM F. McDONALD, *Editor*

SAGE Publications *Beverly Hills* · *London*

Copyright © 1976 by Sage Publications, Inc.

All rights reserved. No part of this book may be reproduced or utilized in any form or by any means, electronic or mechanical, including photocopying, recording, or by any information storage and retrieval system, without permission in writing from the publisher.

For information address:

SAGE PUBLICATIONS, INC.
275 South Beverly Drive
Beverly Hills, California 90212

SAGE PUBLICATIONS LTD
28 Banner Street
London EC1Y 8QE, England

Printed in the United States of America

International Standard Book No. 0-8039-0508-4 (cloth)
International Standard Book No. 0-8039-0509-2 (paper)

Library of Congress Catalog Card No. 75-42754

SECOND PRINTING

PLYMOUTH POLYTECHNIC
LIBRARY

Accn. No.	140181-5
Class. No.	345.05 CRI
Contl. No.	0803905084

WITHDRAWN
FROM
UNIVERSITY OF PLYMOUTH
LIBRARY SERVICES

SEVEN DAY LOAN

This book is to be returned on
or before the date stamped below

- 9 JUN 2003

1 8 NOV 2003

2nd Dec '03

25 April

UNIVERSITY OF PLYMOUTH

PLYMOUTH LIBRARY

Tel: (01752) 232323

This book is subject to recall if required by another reader

Books may be renewed by phone

CHARGES WILL BE MADE FOR OVERDUE BOOKS